I Am a Me

I Am a Metis

THE STORY OF GERRY ST. GERMAIN

Peter O'Neil

HARBOUR PUBLISHING

Harbour Publishing Co. Ltd.
P.O. Box 219, Madeira Park, BC, VON 2HO
www.harbourpublishing.com

Edited by Silas White
Indexed by Sarah Corsie
Dustjacket design by Anna Comfort-O'Keeffe
Dustjacket image by Wayne Leidenfrost, *Vancouver Sun*
Text design by Mary White
Printed and bound in Canada

  Canadä

Harbour Publishing acknowledges the support of the Canada Council for the Arts, which last year invested $153 million to bring the arts to Canadians throughout the country. We also gratefully acknowledge financial support from the Government of Canada through the Canada Book Fund and from the Province of British Columbia through the BC Arts Council and the Book Publishing Tax Credit.

Library and Archives Canada Cataloguing in Publication

O'Neil, Peter Michael, author
    I am a Metis : the story of Gerry St. Germain / Peter O'Neil.

Includes index.
Issued in print and electronic formats.
ISBN 978-1-55017-784-8 (hardback).—ISBN 978-1-55017-785-5 (html)

    1. St. Germain, Gerry. 2. Legislators—Canada—Biography. 3. Canada.
Parliament. House of Commons—Biography. 4. Canada. Parliament.
Senate—Biography. 5. Métis—Biography. 6. Métis—Politics and government.
I. Title.

FC631.S25O54 2016   971.064'7   C2016-905792-5
                                                     C2016-905793-3

Contents

Introduction   7

1   A Son of St. François Xavier   19
2   From St. Boniface to the Downtown Eastside   34
3   From Business to Politics   48
4   Caucus Discipline, from Opposition to Government   66
5   Chief Executive Officer   81
6   The Boss Wants to See You   98
7   Election and Defeat   110
8   Trouble in Paradise   124
9   The Campbell Collapse   143
10   The Aftermath   158
11   Unite the Right   170
12   The Senate and First Nations   191
13   If Mistakes Were Made   208
Epilogue   222

Acknowledgments   233
Index   236

Introduction

Gerry St. Germain has always taken delight in describing himself as a simple chicken farmer who fell off the turnip truck when he arrived in Ottawa as an aspiring Member of Parliament in mid-1983. It's hardly an accurate portrayal of his intelligence, ambition and almost reflexive ability to assume leadership roles during his career as a pilot, police officer, union leader, businessman and politician. Yet this portrayal has always served a couple of purposes. First, it helped temper expectations that he knew he would easily exceed. Second, it was a satisfying jab at big-city "suits" whose dismissive attitudes toward people like him—some would use the "chicken farmer" label as a smear—helped fuel his drive to succeed.

But at least in terms of appearances you couldn't fault those in the nation's capital who made snap judgments that this was not a man to be taken seriously. Even former Tory operative Bob Ransford, a fellow British Columbian who would go on to become St. Germain's aide, Ottawa roommate and lifelong close friend, initially dismissed him as a country bumpkin. The two men were introduced on a brutally humid mid-June afternoon in 1983 when St. Germain showed up at a garden party at the Ottawa residence of BC Tory MP Tom Siddon. It was the day after Brian Mulroney's spectacular leadership win over Joe Clark. Despite several hangovers—St. Germain was one of the few with a clear head, as he'd quit drinking years before—the mood was euphoric. There was a wave of optimism within the party, which had gone through decades of rancour and defeatism. Its flawed leaders and their troops, often appearing more comfortable sniping at each other than at opponents, were consistently unable through most of the twentieth century to challenge the almost mystical dominance of the Liberals, Canada's so-called "natural governing party."

But the flawlessly bilingual Mulroney looked like a winner. Here was someone who was viewed as having the potential to retain the Progressive Conservative Party of Canada's strongholds in Ontario, the West and Atlantic Canada, while finally ending a century of abysmal results in Quebec. One of the most optimistic among the PCs gathered that afternoon was St. Germain. With a ramrod posture honed from his early years in the Royal Canadian Air Force and with a self-made millionaire's robust confidence, he had no trouble asserting his presence. The former street cop was, and remains, a masterful storyteller. But on that celebratory day in 1983 it wasn't just St. Germain's personality that stood out. The aficionado for everything Western—culture, history and especially fashion—was wearing a Stetson and a steel-blue, Western-cut suit. Going from one group of Tories to the next, he told them he planned to seek the party nomination and win the upcoming by-election in the NDP stronghold riding of Mission–Port Moody in the Lower Mainland of BC.

Canada's capital city is a harshly judgmental town. Parliament Hill during the Mulroney era was dominated by big-city lobbyists, lawyers and professional political operatives. The party's elites, from patricians to young up-and-comers, strutted around Ottawa showing off their expensive urban tastes—and it began at the top. When Mulroney travelled in rural Canada, he referred to the trips derisively as his "boonies tours." He was also a name-dropper of the rich and powerful. This was a man who didn't keep secret the fact that he owned a mansion

Gerry St. Germain poses on Parliament Hill in this mid-1980s photo to be published in his "householder," the pamphlet MPs distribute to constituents. St. Germain was deeply hurt in 1988 when voters, upset far more with Mulroney and the federal government's policies than with him, didn't re-elect him. GSG PERSONAL COLLECTION

in Montreal's tony enclave of Westmount, complete with a closet famously filled with Gucci shoes. At his side was the glamorous Mila Mulroney, a multilingual native of Serbia known for her spectacularly extravagant shopping sprees.

The Tories could always boast of a powerful western Canadian wing, with powerbrokers like Don Mazankowski in Alberta, Bill McKnight in Saskatchewan, Jake Epp in Manitoba and Pat Carney in BC. But many of the western rank-and-file were viewed by eastern Canadian urbanites as, shall we say, rather unsophisticated. Some of the Tory MPs, to the amusement of their political opponents and the majority in the parliamentary press gallery, remained obsessed with issues like the Liberal imposition of the metric system and mandatory French on cereal boxes. One, Dan McKenzie, was known for taunting a homosexual MP in the House of Commons and publicly ridiculing the prospects of black majority rule in South Africa. So it was quickly assumed that St. Germain was a stone-ager. As they washed down their burgers with cold beer, Ransford took Siddon aside and whispered to the former university professor, "Who is this cowboy? And who does this hick think he is? He doesn't have a chance of winning."

Ransford, at first blush, wasn't far off the mark. St. Germain had a few things in common with the hard-core right-wingers who were at that time hoping, fruitlessly as it turned out, that Mulroney would move Canada sharply to the right. For starters the self-made millionaire was a true fiscal conservative sickened by spending waste, huge deficits and the bloated bureaucracy under Pierre Elliott Trudeau's governments starting in 1968. St. Germain also favoured capital punishment and was a devout Roman Catholic who throughout his life opposed abortion. The framed photographs on his office walls at the end of his political career—proudly featuring him meeting Ronald Reagan and George W. Bush—said everything about his hawkish foreign policy views. And despite his brash nature he was a maladroit public speaker who would never be the kind of slick glad-hander who would win over the press gallery with nifty one-liners and titillating gossip.

It was easy to predict in Siddon's backyard that even if he managed to win the by-election, St. Germain would have a permanent spot among the marginal figures who have always lurked on the edges of Canada's conservative parties. The snooty political, business and intellectual elites of Toronto, Montreal and Ottawa, who whether Liberal or Conservative have run the country since Confederation, would surely never find a place at the front of the room for someone like St. Germain.

Fast-forward almost three decades to the afternoon of October 30, 2012, St. Germain's last day of his career in Parliament. He entered the Senate chamber for the final time to hear fellow parliamentarians pay homage to his work. St. Germain didn't just defy skeptics like Ransford by winning the party nomination and then the seat he'd targeted in suburban Vancouver. Here was a man who was able to take full advantage of the tools he had, as a bilingual British Columbia MP with a relentless work ethic and disarming interpersonal skills. He became only the second Metis to be named to the federal cabinet in Canadian history. And he managed over his career to become a key behind-the-scenes supporter of the only two Conservative leaders since the mid-twentieth century to win majority governments, Brian Mulroney and Stephen Harper. When that phase in his life ended in 2006, after learning Harper wasn't going to name him to his first cabinet, St. Germain would emerge as a champion in Parliament for Canada's First Nations people.

There was no mistaking him as he entered. Complementing his tailored traditional business suit were some Western touches: high-end cowboy boots and an Apache bolo tie featuring a turquoise-stone centrepiece encased in silver, with a matching bracelet. In a few moments he would be described as "larger than life" by James Cowan, the Liberal leader in the Senate, as Cowan led off a string of senators delivering tributes. While he was accused by some of thinking too highly of himself, those who knew St. Germain well realized he was humble and at times insecure—no doubt due to his roots as the son of a poor Metis trapper and part-time labourer who grew up in an area just outside Winnipeg with a long history of linguistic and racial

divisions. He had mixed feelings that afternoon. He felt proud and
excited to be lavished with attention as his family looked on. But he
also felt some frustration that, as he hit the mandatory age-seventy-five
retirement date, he wouldn't be able to continue his work in advancing
aboriginal issues.

As he looked around the Senate that day he felt a sense of awe,
breathing in the grandeur of his surroundings for one last time. One
of Canada's architectural masterpieces, it is truly something to behold,
standing in elegant contrast to the public's utter contempt for the place
and those who inhabit it. The upper chamber was designed to be a
legislative body providing "sober second thought" in reviewing legislation that has already been passed in the House of Commons. It also
conducts its own studies on major issues like health care and the state
of Canada's national security apparatus. But many ordinary Canadians
tend to view it as they would a grimy Las Vegas bordello, a characterization that has held pretty well since Confederation.

The Senate is a $100-million-a-year institution populated by
just over one hundred unelected Canadians, most of them political patronage appointees earning six-figure salaries while seeming
to do next to nothing. And when Canadians do notice the so-called
Red Chamber, it's almost always for malodorous reasons. A group of
Reform MPs in the 1990s hired a mariachi band to perform in front
of the chamber entrance to highlight the scandal of a Liberal senator
living full-time in Mexico. In the 2015 federal election campaign
NDP leader Tom Mulcair, dripping contempt over the wave of scandalous allegations that had hit the institution starting in late 2012,
said of senators, "They do nothing of use for this country." Better, he
proposed, to turn this historic structure into a daycare.

Yet on this day, anyone observing the events would have seen
the Senate at its best. First-time visitors that afternoon would have
immediately experienced the visual shock of the Red Chamber's
royal burgundy carpeting, upholstery and draperies, which stand
in majestic contrast to the depressingly bland pale green carpets in
the nearby House of Commons. Many visitors would also be struck

by an immediate sense of history. The current chamber, completed in 1922 after a devastating fire gutted the entire Centre Block of the main Parliament buildings six years earlier, is a structural tribute to Canada's heritage. As St. Germain took his seat that afternoon, his front-bench vantage point put him just a few metres to the right of two grand mahogany thrones that were purchased by the Canadian government in 1878 at a cost of $329 for the pair. The larger one is reserved for Canada's monarch, and the smaller one for the monarch's consort. Typically, though, it's the Governor General and Governor General's spouse who take those seats. Above the thrones is an imposing marble bust of Queen Victoria, meant to represent Canada's sovereign at the time of Confederation in 1867 looking protectively over—though it seems like she's glaring disapprovingly at—her subjects.

At one point before the tribute speeches St. Germain's eyes wandered to his favourite of the massive oil paintings gracing the walls of the chamber, four behind the government benches and four behind opposition benches. The eight First World War commemorative paintings, located just below the chamber's stained glass windows, were donated by Max Aitken. Also known as Lord Beaverbrook, the New Brunswick business tycoon became an influential politician in London during both the First and Second World Wars. The painting that always caught St. Germain's eye was a natural attraction for a man who had adored horses since childhood: British artist Algernon Talmage's *A Mobile Veterinary Unit in France*. Talmage, exempted from war service due to a childhood injury, illustrated Canadian members of that unit bringing wounded horses along a barren road cutting through a bleak, treeless landscape from the front lines during the bloody 1917 Battle of Cambrai in northern France. "I sometimes looked at those paintings on the wall from the Great War, and I'd sit there and think 'How did I get here?'" St. Germain later recalled.

Just to his left, and laid before the two thrones on the Senate clerk's table, was the 1.6-metre-long ceremonial mace. Made of gold and brass, it is described by the Senate as the symbol of "royal authority, parliamentary privilege, and the authority of the Senate and the Speaker." No laws can be passed in Canada without the mace in the chamber. Visitors in the gallery that day, including four generations of the St. Germain family, could have allowed their eyes to wander toward ceiling panels featuring thin sheets of gold woven together to depict symbols of the founding European peoples of Canada: the English lion, the French fleur-de-lis, the Irish harp, the Welsh dragon and the Scottish thistle, juxtaposed with Canadian maple leaves.

St. Germain's colleagues on government and opposition benches rose in succession to sing his praises. One of his closest friends and allies during his Senate career, Saskatchewan Conservative David Tkachuk, looked up to the public gallery at his colleague's beaming wife Margaret and their children, grandchildren and great-grandson Tanner, and said, "To his family here today, know that we all love him and respect him. We respect your father, grandfather and great-grandfather. Gerry, we have been well-served." Nancy Greene Raine, the Olympic gold medal-winning skier whom Harper named as a Conservative senator in 2009, later joined in to call her fellow British Columbian an influential mentor.

The Senate also heard words of praise from Conservatives such as government leader Marjory LeBreton, who had a difficult relationship with St. Germain but still delivered a generous speech acknowledging his years of public service. She recognized his role as a senior negotiator in the historic 2003 merger of the Progressive Conservatives and the Canadian Alliance, ending more than a decade of bitterness and division within Canada's small-c conservative movement. Her praise was particularly striking, given that she led the attacks when in 2000 he became the first Progressive Conservative caucus member to jump to the rival Canadian Alliance. "Long before many others—including me, I might add—came to the same realization, he saw the need for a strong, united Conservative Party in Canada and worked for years to make it a reality." LeBreton also praised his work as chairman of the Standing Senate Committee on Aboriginal Peoples in producing strong reports in areas like land claims, safe drinking water, economic development and education.

It was the reaction of opposition MPs, however, that revealed how St. Germain touched people regardless of their views or backgrounds. Liberal Roméo Dallaire, the Canadian general famous for his role during the 1994 Rwanda genocide, praised St. Germain for his non-partisan approach to legislative work, and spoke in particular of the retiring senator's pride in his ethnic roots. "Honourable senators, it is essential to note that Senator St. Germain never denied his franco-phone past—quite the opposite in fact—and is proud to be a Metis. Gerry, French may not be your first language or the first language of your community, but it remained important to you. Those of us who live in Quebec are very proud to see you keep that spirit alive."

The contributions of two women on the Liberal side were particu-larly moving. Lillian Dyck, a left-leaning feminist university professor and member of Saskatchewan's Gordon First Nation, was appointed by Liberal prime minister Paul Martin in 2005. Describing herself as "very shy" when she arrived in the Senate, Dyck lavished praise on the gregarious St. Germain for his openness and warmth in welcoming her to the Committee on Aboriginal Peoples, which he chaired from 2006 until his retirement in 2012. She shared a touching anecdote from earlier that morning when St. Germain chaired his final meeting of the committee. "Gerry said, 'I love you all,' and I said, 'Gerry, I cannot believe that I am saying this: I love you, too, and you are a Conservative.' I never thought I would say that to a Conservative."

Then came Mobina Jaffer, the first Muslim appointed to Canada's Senate and an outspoken advocate for the rights of women and girls in Canada and around the world. A Liberal appointee, she came to Canada with her family in the 1970s after fleeing dictator Idi Amin's terrorizing regime in Uganda. Her father, the late Sherali Bandali Jaffer, decided shortly after their arrival he wanted to be a chicken farmer. He went to the BC Chicken Marketing Board, which handed out quotas for poultry and egg producers in BC's Lower Mainland:

Senator Jaffer: Senator St. Germain was the chair of the board. The farmers in the area did not want my father to be one of them.

My father was different. My father was sitting outside the room when the decision was to be made. My dad was sure he would not succeed in obtaining the quotas. Little did my father know that a complete stranger was fighting for my father's rights. Senator St. Germain, who did not know my father or his circumstances, stood up for my dad. Senator St. Germain would not accept the prejudices of the farmers. My father obtained the licence . . . because of our colleague Senator St. Germain.

Honourable senators: Hear, hear!

Senator Jaffer: Honourable senators, this is who our friend is. He stands up for all of us regardless of race, religion or creed—even people he does not know. Gerry treats all people equally. He opens the door of opportunity for all. Senator St. Germain, thank you for your service, friendship, example and commitment to all Canadians. We will miss you. Gerry, I will miss you.

The main event, of course, was St. Germain's speech. While these farewell sessions are typically described in the official Senate schedule as self-indulgent "tributes," and therefore not to be taken too seriously, St. Germain had Senate officials bill it as an "inquiry" into the "Current State of First Nations Self-Government." In doing so he sent a subtle but clear message to his party leader and prime minister, Stephen Harper, that not enough was being done to improve the lives of Canada's most marginalized members of society. Although he knew it had no chance of ever being passed and becoming law, given his government's position on aboriginal rights, St. Germain tabled the latest version of a piece of legislation he'd worked on for years. He and his staff had spent months drafting the bill, with the help of a number of First Nations leaders including Jody Wilson-Raybould, at the time BC regional chief of the Assembly of First Nations.

St. Germain's bill was a legislative blueprint intended to let bands, at their discretion, govern themselves outside the paternalistic Indian Act. Without the self-government option, St. Germain has long argued, aboriginal Canadians will remain in a soul-crippling state of dependency, never breaking from successive generations of poverty, abuse, and dismal educational and health outcomes. He urged the government in that speech to follow the advice of his committee, which had travelled the country over several years and done reports on the most pressing issues facing indigenous communities. While some of his committee's recommendations were adopted by the Harper government, the Tories had not gone nearly as far as St. Germain would have liked. Pointing to the generations of misery and Third World conditions on Canadian reserves, he implored, "Honourable senators, if we continue to do what we have always done, we are certain to get what we have always gotten."

Then he switched to his own life, thanking his wife Margaret for her support and role in raising their three children while he was usually thousands of kilometres from home during his twenty-nine years in politics. He caused an awkward silence in a chamber filled with Stephen Harper appointees by expressing his deep admiration for Mulroney, lauding him as "Canada's greatest prime minister" for his achievements in areas such as the 1988 Canada–US Free Trade Agreement and end of apartheid in South Africa. St. Germain also spent an inordinate amount of time praising and in many cases singling out by name not only his own staff but Senate employees, including the security guards and messengers who are barely visible to most politicians rushing from meeting to meeting. "I know that I could not have accomplished what I set out to do without the support staff of Parliament. Far too often, I feel that their work is not recognized as it should be."

Then he paused, took a deep breath and shifted to his roots. In a few words he tried to explain how someone of such a humble background would end up excelling in every endeavour he took on, whether it was flying a fighter jet, facing down a hardened criminal, pulling off complex business deals, bringing divergent political groups together or trying to help deeply damaged First Nations communities rebuild their shattered lives. "I am," he said as he begun to tell that story, with his head bowing slightly and voice cracking with emotion, "a Metis."

1

∞

A Son of St. François Xavier

St. Germain's proud affirmation in the Senate chamber of a heritage that once brought him shame provides some clues to explain how he managed to overcome his modest beginnings. For starters, the giant chip he carried on his shoulder while growing up with a sense of inferiority and deprivation, in a Manitoba society with a long history of bigotry against its First Nations, Metis and francophone minorities, became a powerful motivator. St. Germain's familial and regional roots were also assets that fuelled his early rise in politics. Being a bilingual Manitoba-born British Columbian was lucrative political currency in the Progressive Conservative Party in the early 1980s, as new leader Brian Mulroney tried to exorcise his party's anti-French reputation, which dated back to the hanging of Metis leader Louis Riel in 1885.

St. Germain was born in a hamlet known as "Petit Canada" in the St. François Xavier parish along the banks of the Assiniboine River, about thirty kilometres east of Winnipeg. St. François Xavier was once known as Grantown, named after Cuthbert Grant, considered the first and most important Metis leader prior to the emergence of Louis Riel. Later in his life, St. Germain would become engrossed in the history and intricate nuances of his culture. But his lingering shame and relentless ambition would for decades trump these and other interests. St. Germain was barely aware of Riel as a child, and had never heard of Grant until the 1990s, when a genealogist St. Germain hired determined that he was one of Grant's many descendants.

The origin of the Metis dates back to the 1730s, when European settlers, in particular the French, started trading with aboriginal Canadians at the Forks—the area near the confluence of the Red and Assiniboine Rivers in what is now Winnipeg. It's a bountiful patch of land that had been a gathering place for various First Nations dating back six thousand years. "French was the first European language to be spoken on the southern plains of what is now Canada," Frances Russell wrote in her 2003 book *The Canadian Crucible: Manitoba's Role in Canada's Great Divide.* "Indeed, it predates English by almost one hundred years." French language and culture penetrated the region due to "the very different nature of the fur trades practised by those two great empires."

Frenchmen became much more intimately involved in the fur trade than the British traders, marrying the daughters of important First Nations leaders in partnerships referred to as à *la façon du pays* ("according to the custom of the country"). This practice was meant to facilitate the trade of animal furs that were drawing an attractive price in Europe. Those who married aboriginal women starting in the latter part of the eighteenth century left a progeny over the next century "that formed a distinct culture blending European and aboriginal customers," according to Russell. But any idealistic notion that the Metis might somehow integrate seamlessly into the dominant society started to erode under the weight of British colonial expansion, which included the arrival of more and more European women to the region by the mid-1850s. Thanks to that development, as well as prejudices of the time, these marriages of convenience didn't always have much durability.

Attitudes toward the Metis had also been influenced by the arrival of Anglican missionaries at the Red River Colony in 1819–20. The newcomers brought with them the accepted prejudices of that era. "Scholars of the time believed that humankind had evolved into the hierarchy called the Great Chain of Being that placed Europeans on top and Aboriginals on the bottom," University of Manitoba historian Denise Fuchs wrote in the 2002–2003 autumn/winter edition of the journal *Manitoba History*. "Mixed races placed lower than Aboriginals because it was believed they inherited the vices of both races." The Metis were looked down upon because they resisted the aggressive push by the leaders of the British settlers, and especially their Anglican church, to become land-owning farmers rather than semi-nomadic hunters, trappers and traders.

Those wondering if there's anything in his DNA that resulted in St. Germain's impressive career evolution might take note of Cuthbert Grant's career trajectory. The son of a Scotsman and a Cree woman, Grant was born in Fort de la Rivière Tremblante, Saskatchewan, in 1793. Grant, among a smaller sub-section of Metis born of English-speaking trapper fathers and aboriginal women, is believed to have been fluent in English, French and Michif, the French-Cree language of North America's Metis people. Thanks to his father's relative prosperity, he was educated in Montreal. Like his father, Grant started out working for the North West Company, a company founded in 1779 by a group of Montreal-based Scottish merchants who worked closely with members of the French fur trade.

The Nor'Westers had a longstanding rivalry in the fur trade with the London-based Hudson's Bay Company, and that feud worsened after the arrival in 1812 of English- and Gaelic-speaking settlers under the leadership of Thomas Douglas to establish the Red River Settlement. The colony was named Assiniboia and encompassed 300,000 square kilometres of land purchased by Douglas from the HBC. The Nor'Westers started looking for ways to resist, and saw a natural ally in their midst: their partners in the fur trade, the Metis. Grant was among a number of Metis clerks working at NWC outposts. The Nor'Westers eventually appointed several of them to become "captains of the Metis" to lead the opposition to the HBC-sponsored settlers arriving under the authority of Miles Macdonell, who in 1811 was named by Lord Selkirk as the first governor of Assiniboia.

Grant quickly rose up the ladder. He was eventually tapped to lead a police force, and was designated "Captain-General of all the Half-Breeds." His armed group was involved in a number of skirmishes that culminated in one of the most famous events in Metis history: the Battle of Seven Oaks on June 19, 1816. Grant's forces, which included some English and French Canadians as well as Metis and First Nations irregulars, outnumbered the HBC men by a three-to-one margin, and killed twenty-one of them. It wasn't a fair fight, as only one of Grant's forces was killed in the encounter, which was a brutal display of the superior skills of Metis and First Nations warriors who honed their skills on the plains.

It was a short-lived victory because the better-managed HBC soon regained the upper hand in the region. Grant became a wanted man, finally giving himself up in 1817. He was charged in Montreal with murder, theft and arson. Grant skipped bail and headed back west to Qu'Appelle, about fifty kilometres east of Regina in what is now Saskatchewan, to work as a Nor'Wester clerk, and eventually the charges were quietly shelved. When the NWC and the HBC merged in 1821 Grant wasn't brought into the new firm due to his role in the destruction of the Red River Settlement in 1816.

In 1824 there was a new strategy. Governor George Simpson decided Grant would be of more use leading the Metis in the region to take up farming near what is now Winnipeg. The fear was that left to their own devices, the Metis might get involved in illegal fur trading with the Americans, to HBC's detriment. Simpson also concluded that a Metis settlement near the Forks could act as a buffer for the Red River Colony against the hostile Sioux Nation. There was also fear on Simpson's part that the growing Metis population, prevented from leading their buffalo hunt–based lifestyles, could develop a criminal element possessing "the savage ferocity of the Indian with all the cunning and knowledge of the White." Simpson later wrote to a colleague that this plan could rid the Red River Colony of the "greatest evil" (the Metis), adding that Grant could be "useful" to the colony but "requires good management, being an Indian in nature."

Grant, who fathered children with three previous women, including a young Sioux, finally married and settled down during this period with Marie-Marguerite McGillis, a Metis who had nine children with him. Given thirty-four hectares of land and an annual stipend of two hundred pounds by the HBC, Grant was followed to the new settlement by roughly one hundred Metis families. In addition to farming, the community specialized in building boats and producing the famous Red River Carts (a dam and mill project was a flop, however, due to Grant's inadequacies as a hydraulic engineer). He continued to lead his people on buffalo hunts in order to collect meat and fat to make pemmican, hauling with them "Grant's Cannon," a gift from the HBC as protection against possible Sioux ambushes. Grant's land was in an area on the Assiniboine known as White Horse Plain, about twenty-two kilometres west of the Red River.

Grant remained a prominent figure in subsequent years, and was even invited to be a member of the ruling Council of the Assiniboia in 1839. He died in July 1854 due to an illness that gripped him after a fall from his horse. A dozen years after his death, a member of one of the community's best-known families, Moise Breland, married one of Grant's granddaughter's, Philomene Page, at the Roman Catholic church in what was by then known as St. François Xavier. This union brought nine children into the world, including Virginie Breland. In 1894, around the time of an epic battle over French language rights in Manitoba that bitterly divided the country, Virginie married Jean-Baptiste St. Germain, Gerry St. Germain's grandfather. Their son and Gerry's father, Michel St. Germain, was born in the western end of the parish at Pigeon Lake, in 1905.

Michel Alexander St. Germain and Mary-Kathleen James were married on December 29, 1936, at St. Mary's, a cathedral built in 1881 that served English-speaking Roman Catholics in and around Winnipeg. On November 6 of the following year William Joseph Gerald St. Germain was born at St. Boniface Hospital in the French-speaking part of Winnipeg on the east side of the Red River. After arriving back in Petit Canada he was fed and placed in a cradle for the night. "And in the morning—now this is what I've been told—when they came to get me I was covered in snow because there was a snowstorm that night, with a strong wind, and there were cracks in the cabin walls and my bed covers were covered in snow," St. Germain recounted. Two younger sisters followed into the family: Jeanette, born in the spring of 1939, and Christine, born on Christmas day in 1942. The family moved around frequently, which St. Germain attributes to his mother's compulsiveness associated with depression. But they always lived in or around the parish of St. François Xavier, a tiny community thirty-one kilometres east of Winnipeg along the Assiniboine River.

His father struggled to make ends meet, supplementing his hunting and trapping by working in construction or as a bouncer in a local bar. Although his bride was eighteen, Michel was thirty-one when Gerry was born, a fairly advanced age at which to be starting a family. Michel St. Germain had thick dark hair and handsome features that often led to comparisons to a Hollywood heartthrob of that era, Tyrone Power. He was a quiet man who loved to hunt and trap, owning the skills of Metis ancestors famous for their accurate shooting during the spring and autumn buffalo hunts. "He was a good hunter and he could shoot. Deadly. I remember we went up a riverbank one day and a great big buck jumped up in front of us, and I don't know how, but before that buck had moved ten feet, he had him down," his son recalled.

Gerry St. Germain's father Michel was a quiet man but was a skilled hunter with movie star looks. In this photograph, taken in the mid-1920s, he leans against his father's house on the south banks of the Assiniboine River, just west of Pigeon Lake in the parish of St. François Xavier, Manitoba. He is flanked by his sister Laura, laughing, his young niece Rita, and to his left his cousin Maria St. Germain. GSG PERSONAL COLLECTION

Despite their age difference Kathleen, the daughter of a

French immigrant and an English father, was the dominant—and occasionally domineering—force in the family. St. Germain always appreciated his mother for pushing him to succeed at school. His father's main contribution to the discussion over his son's future was to tell him there was no future in the life of a hunter, trapper and seasonal worker. St. Germain adored his father and wished he had stood up to his wife more often. "If the meek truly inherit the earth my father would be one of the biggest land-owners." It has been speculated among those close to St. Germain that this family dynamic played a role in his struggle in future years in dealing with powerful female politicians like Kim Campbell and Pat Carney.

Gerry St. Germain was the first child and only son of Michel St. Germain and Mary-Kathleen James, shown here in this December 29, 1936 photo after their wedding at St. Mary's Cathedral in Winnipeg. Michel and Kathleen worked tirelessly to provide for their family, and Gerry St. Germain especially cherished hunting trips with his father. GSG PERSONAL COLLECTION

St. Germain remembers living in a two-room house at Lido Plage, a hamlet within St. François Xavier that had no running water and was heated by a wood stove. "We used to have to pick roots for the fire, and we used to have to walk for water. We'd have a barrel, and we'd pull this trailer and go and get water." There were two bedrooms, one for the parents and another for the three kids—with a hanging sheet separating St. Germain from his sisters. He used to fetch milk every day from a nearby farm, and in the summer the milk was kept cool in a hole dug in the backyard under the shade of a plum tree. Sometimes it was a struggle for his parents to put enough food on the table. He remembers one evening during a particularly frigid winter at the kitchen table with his sisters and parents. He was about ten, and noticed his parents were simply sitting at the table with their hands folded while the children gobbled down their dinners. "Why aren't you eating?" their son asked. "Not hungry."

St. Germain, who could barely sit still even in retirement, was a hyperactive boy and admits he was difficult for his parents and especially his mother to handle. "I was a holy terror," he recalls, citing one incident around age four when he wandered off and almost drowned in a creek. "That's when my mother used to tie me up. They used to have to put coveralls on me and they tied me up outside the front door. One day I somehow got out, took the coveralls off, took the rope off and headed for town bare naked. And I ended up at a grocery store asking for ice cream." With a toddler at home and expecting a third child, St. Germain's mother shipped her "holy terror" off to live temporarily with his maternal grandparents in nearby Pigeon Lake.

It turned out to be a blessing because at home, St. Germain's bilingual parents spoke only English, but his grandmother, who married an English-speaking immigrant who was the product of the Barnardo Home for Orphans in London, was born in France. She was determined to help her grandson become bilingual and drilled him daily on pronunciation, using a book called *Li La Lu*. They did drills to ensure he developed an accent, as well, which would give him a start for further learning during the summers he later spent with his uncle, Henry St. Germain, in Saint-Eustache, Manitoba. "My two cousins were about to go make their First Communion. We were walking down the road to the church, and they said, 'Gerry might as well just do it with us. But he doesn't speak French that well.' 'Ah,' my uncle said, 'we'll teach him.' So I took my First Communion, all my prayers, in the French church there. I really learned my French there."

A lone wolf, he would regularly sneak out the window when he was living with his parents and sisters, often to go off wandering in the woods. "I once went hunting alone one morning. I kind of got lost and didn't get home until eleven p.m. Oh, boy, was my mother ever mad." As he got older he got into regular fights during recess at school with a classmate named Gerry DesLaurier. DesLaurier's family was also Metis but considered a little "up the ladder" in terms of wealth and social status. "I remember him and me going at it with a vengeance. Once we were in a fight and the teacher tried to break us apart and she got hit about three times before she could break us up."

On another occasion he was playing hockey with a group of boys, including his best friend Garnet Stevenson, when his tenacity saved the day. "We were skating on the Assiniboine, and there was open water further from the shore and we were playing hockey and skating all over the place," St. Germain recalled. "We started skating by the open water and seeing who could go closest. What happened was that I was right behind him and he went right into the water." At that point the other kids playing hockey immediately fled the area, fearing they would be in deep trouble. "The current took him downriver so I skated

Gerry and his sisters attended the one-room Todd School in Petit Canada, a tiny Metis hamlet on the outskirts of Winnipeg. Among the standing row is one of St. Germain's two sisters, Jeanette, second from left in the checked shirt. St. Germain is fifth from the left. To his right is Gerry DesLaurier, whom St. Germain would regularly scrap with, and to his left his best friend Garnet Stevenson, whose life St. Germain saved while the two were playing outdoor hockey. Just below and to St. Germain's left, wearing a white shirt and suspenders, is his other sister Christine, who died of cancer in 1983. On the far right is their teacher, Gervaise Catellier, who took some errant punches trying to break up a St. Germain–DesLaurier scrap. GSG PERSONAL COLLECTION

to the other end and he bobbed up at an opening right where I was. I was laying on the ice with my hockey stick, so the ice wouldn't break, and I picked him up." The two boys lost touch as adults, as Stevenson took on a string of hard-labour jobs in Winnipeg. In 2000 Stevenson was visiting a relative on the west coast and decided to track down St. Germain, walking up to the door of the house on St. Germain's vast ranch in South Surrey, BC. "He showed up in brown suit and running shoes, but he was happy. He said, 'Gerry I've come to thank you for saving my life. Do you remember?' I remembered but I never really thought of it until his visit."

St. Germain also didn't think much of schooling and would regularly skip classes at the one-room schoolhouse he attended with his sisters. He much preferred hanging out in the local pool hall. But in grade ten his teacher at St. François Xavier High School, Sister Jeanne Monchamp, became the first outside the family to recognize his potential. "She saw my aptitude for math and took a great interest in me. I wasn't a model child. I would walk by people studying and I would be going to play pool. I was doing okay in school but she would say to me that I could do better than okay. She started keeping me after school to do my homework there. She took pride in me." Later, as an aspiring Royal Canadian Air Force pilot, he aced a series of math exams that allowed him to fast-track toward his officers' commission. He told that story to Sister Monchamp when he visited her, as a member of the Senate, at a St. Boniface nursing home. "She said, 'I can't believe you made it.'" As St. Germain recalls, "I remember that she often told me, 'Gerry, if you excel at math, you will excel in life.' She was right. The tools I learned there enabled me to achieve my goals." Sister Monchamp also encouraged him to go to a Jesuit school, St. Paul's College in Winnipeg, for grade eleven. He moved to the provincial capital and stayed with his maternal aunt Dorothy and her husband Lucien Robidoux, who owned a grocery store in the Winnipeg community of St. Vital.

While St. Germain took pride in his math skills, which were key to his later success in business, he learned not to feel any sense of superiority over poor aboriginal Canadians who didn't manage to overcome difficult circumstances as he did. "I could learn so well, and you earn respect for that," he recalled. "But that really is unfair. Just because you can't learn doesn't mean you're not a human being." St. Germain's empathy for those less fortunate is often based on memories of his father. Michel St. Germain, despite his movie-star looks and a strong work ethic, was usually too shy to even ask for a job let alone start his own business.

Gerry's trajectory wasn't always headed upward—far from it. Despite getting into the elite St. Paul's College thanks to Monchamp's advice and the financial aid of his aunt and uncle, St. Germain got sick and was in the infirmary for three weeks, causing him to miss his grade eleven exams. Rather than repeat a year he impulsively—and unwisely, he admits now—quit the Jesuit school at age fifteen. He seized on an opportunity to use his math skills to take a job as a clerk at the downtown Winnipeg branch of the Bank of Toronto (which later became the TD Bank following a merger). The appeal was purely financial, because no one as hyperactive as him could survive in a retail bank setting, and he didn't stay long. He had dreams to chase, and one was rooted in a thrilling childhood memory of seeing a plane land on the pasture near Uncle Henry's farm in Saint-Eustache. He was determined to join the Royal Canadian Air Force the moment he hit the mandatory minimum age of seventeen.

While biding his time St. Germain travelled to BC with his father, who was looking for work. They first headed to Timothy Lake in BC's Cariboo Country in the south-central part of the province. While both found jobs at a local sawmill, the younger St. Germain soon left to hitchhike to the Lower Mainland. He took a job in Burnaby as a shift manager at Harvey's, which at the time advertised its famous nineteen-cent burgers. Every evening he'd be out with co-workers trying to boost their paltry pay by playing poker. His manager saw trouble and told him to leave, saying, "Gerry, I'd like to you stay but you're hanging around with a bad crowd." St. Germain felt more and more lost. "I sensed that I needed something. I needed discipline."

Upon reaching his seventeenth birthday in the autumn of 1954, he headed to an RCAF recruiting office in Vancouver. He was told he needed to return to Winnipeg to find the proper paperwork, including his birth certificate, and apply there. So he hopped on a bus for home and made a beeline for the local RCAF recruiting station.

It didn't start well. St. Germain was handed an aptitude test, took his time to answer the first question perfectly—and then felt the supervisor's hand tapping his shoulder to tell him he had to hand it in. He had no idea there was a time limit. "It's okay," the supervisor said, showing pity on his apparently dim-witted recruit. "We need guys for general duties anyway." So he was sent to basic training in St. Jean, Quebec, on the assumption he'd ultimately be assigned to jobs like washing trucks and sweeping floors. "Then I go to Quebec and they give me a similar test and the next thing I know I'm in front of two sergeants and an officer."

"Do you ever lose your mind, or have memory blackouts?" they asked him.

"No."

"Well you only answered a single question in Winnipeg, and here you've answered every question correctly." His superiors even brought in a psychiatrist as they tried to figure out how the young man could perform so erratically. Finally they asked, "What trade did you apply for in Winnipeg?"

"They gave me general duties, but I wanted to be an aircraft controller."

"Nope, you're going to CFB Clinton." So after basic training he was shipped off to Canadian Forces Base Clinton, in a town about two hundred kilometres east of Toronto and just a short drive from the shores of Lake Huron. Clinton is known for its top-secret radar training station for Canadian, British, American and other Allied servicemen during the Second World War, a service it maintained during the Cold War. The station was looking for young men with sharp math skills, vetting recruits through a standard math test with a high failure rate. A professor would then tutor about twenty aspiring

Aspiring Royal Canadian Air Force fighter pilot Gerry St. Germain stands fifth from left in the top row in front of a Harvard training aircraft, in Moose Jaw, Saskatchewan. Shortly after this 1958 photo, and just prior to obtaining his wings and becoming an officer-pilot, he impetuously quit the RCAF when a senior officer snidely suggested he would easily be promoted because of his French Canadian-sounding surname. GSG PERSONAL COLLECTION

radar telecommunications technicians in university-level math and physics. Classes went eight hours a day, six days a week, plus home-work in the evenings, for a month. "He was the most phenomenal instructor I ever met," St. Germain said.

St. Germain ended up completing that program with the highest mark in the class, and was shipped off in late 1957 to Portage La Prairie, eighty-five kilometres east of Winnipeg, to work on communications and electronics equipment on the Lockheed T-33 jet aircraft, used for training. One day he was in a hangar dealing with a radio issue on a bitter-cold prairie winter day. "It was thirty or forty below and they'd roll the airplanes into the hangar and inside the cockpit you'd lean in and you'd check the radio and the various things and I'm not sure what happened but I must have had some kind of virus." He passed out and was discovered lying on the wing of an aircraft by a colleague. "They told me later, 'We didn't know what the hell was wrong with you.' I was out all one day and that night they brought the priest in to give me the last rites. And the next morning I woke up and it was like nothing had ever happened to me."

After he fumbled an assignment that involved mechanical aptitude—he explained to his superiors that he might be sharp in math but was inept at fixing things—it was decided that he might be a klutz with a wrench but clearly with through-the-roof math scores he was bright enough to be sent for officer and pilot training. He was dispatched to London, Ontario, to take an exam intended to determine if he was officer/fighter pilot material. It was an exam scheduled to last for forty-five minutes, but he was done in well under half that time. When the officer took the exam away, he asked "Aren't you going to check it?" St. Germain lifted up his hands and said with a shrug, "They're either all right or all wrong."

He ended up excelling in the program, and was sent to another small and remote Ontario town called Centralia, thirty-eight kilometres north of Clinton, for an officer training program that included physical conditioning and instruction in writing, public speaking and firing a revolver. There was also more math and science, along with basic

St. Germain in front of the de Havilland Canada DHC-1 Chipmunk while training to become a Royal Canadian Air Force pilot in Centralia, Ontario, in the late 1950s. GSG PERSONAL COLLECTION

flight training on the de Havilland Canada DHC-1 Chipmunk, a single-engine trainer aircraft with twin seats for the pilot and the instructor. The early training flights weren't always easy, and at one point he "ground looped," which happens when a pilot loses control upon landing with one wing rising and the other hitting the ground, causing the plane to spin violently.

But he graduated and after completing pilot training on Harvards in Moose Jaw, Saskatchewan, in 1958 he went to RCAF Station Gimli for advanced pilot training, the final step to becoming an officer-pilot. However, he had a meeting with a senior officer during which the willful and proud St. Germain kissed his career goodbye in a matter of seconds. There was resentment at the time among English-speakers in the Canadian military that francophones were getting an unfair advantage, leading the officer to say, "St. Germain—with a name like that you don't have to perform, you're going to get a permanent commission anyway. You're French."

"Well, sir, if that's what it takes to get ahead then I'm out."

"And I quit!" St. Germain recalled. "I resented that. I felt that there was subtle discrimination in my life. Why should somebody gain recognition because of a language or because of an ethnicity?" But he soon realized it was one of the worst blunders of his young life, alongside his decision to drop out of high school. "I shouldn't have let my stupid little mentality take over the situation. But that's how I made decisions," he said. "That's when I realized I really made a mistake, and I wasn't going to make any more."

2

∞

From St. Boniface to the Downtown Eastside

After impetuously leaving the RCAF in a huff in 1959 without getting his wings, St. Germain decided to pursue one of his other childhood dreams. He walked into the RCMP station in Winnipeg and expressed interest in a career as a pilot and officer with the Mounties. The interest was reciprocated but there was a catch: after training in Regina a rookie pilot would most likely have to begin his career in the far north. "That didn't get me too excited." So he headed across the Provencher Bridge connecting downtown Winnipeg with Manitoba's largest francophone community to see if the St. Boniface Police Force was interested. While the officer at reception was dismissive, St. Germain caught the attention of the chief, who invited him in for a chat.

"He asked me if I spoke French and started speaking to me in French. Then he saw how I was standing so upright and asked, 'Are you a military man?'" The answer resulted in St. Germain being promptly dispatched to the fire station to rendezvous with a doctor, who administered a single physical test—running up and down the stairs three times. He was sent back to the police station with a satis-factory medical report. "When I got there I had my badge and gun waiting for me. He says, 'You will start whenever you can but if you've got a suit, put it on and you can work with the detectives today.'"

St. Germain had some bizarre, amusing and at times downright harrowing experiences during his four years in St. Boniface and, after a two-year hiatus as a salesman, a one-year stint with the Vancouver Police Department in the city's infamous Downtown Eastside. One of St. Germain's highly valued skills was his ability to write clear, concise reports in English—not something his francophone colleagues could always pull off. He recalled one tale involving an officer named Touchette, who was doing the paperwork after booking a suspect and following station procedure to file away the accused's spectacles. (Like neckties and belts, it's standard procedure to remove anything that could be used by an incarcerated person to harm themselves or someone else.) His report said, "I removed the man's testicles and put them in an envelope and put them in the Sergeant's drawers."

On another occasion while on patrol, he and a colleague named Al Smith responded to a complaint about goings-on behind the St. Boniface Hospital, where St. Germain was born, and noticed an extended First Nations family in and around a parked car. They were in town to visit a sick family member, and there were children playing around the car and several elders milling about. There were a number of chickens inside the car, and a few attached by a thin rope to the back bumper. After they approached in their police car and observed the scene, a bemused St. Germain said, "You got this one, Al?" St. Germain, often nicknamed "Cochise" (after the famous Apache warrior) or "Red Man" by his colleagues, was assured by Smith, "Yeah, I'll take care of your relatives."

"And he goes over and asks them, 'Why do you have chickens?'

"They say, 'We gotta eat.'

"Al asks why they don't just kill them and they reply, 'Stupid white man. They'll rot in the sun, you dumb bastard!'

"I'll never forget the look on Smith's face."

St. Germain fired his weapon very few times during his time as a policeman. The first was during a power blackout, which led to rowdiness and vandalism on the streets, with a few parked cars set on fire. He and his partner at the time, a tough Korean War veteran, were parked in an area where a group of inebriated men congregated and started rocking the squad car back and forth. "So I take my revolver, get out of the car, and tell the guys to get away from the car. I told them, 'I've got six shots, six of you go down. You're not going to turn this car over with us in it and set it on fire.' I fired one shot above their heads to let them know I was serious. And they broke up."

His best bit of police work involved a window peeper who was becoming a major concern among community residents. In a bid to finally nab him the police chief assigned a group of policemen in plain clothes to roam through St. Boniface's dark streets and back alleys to try to find the culprit. A few days earlier St. Germain and his partner had a call to go to a woman's house following a break-in. The woman who answered the door had blood dripping from her head. "So I ask if we could come into the house. I could see that she was in shock. Evidently there had been a man in there who had raped her and left. Her little boy was sleeping in another room. So we took her to the hospital and left, and that was it. She couldn't give us any information or anything."

A few nights later, when the plainclothes officers were out in an area where the peeper had been reported, St. Germain saw a suspicious-looking man in a resident's backyard. "I chased him for three or four blocks, tackled him, cuffed him and brought him in. I had a hunch that this guy was into more than window-peeping. So I told my boss that I'd like to investigate this further, and he said he wouldn't pay me overtime. So I said I would work for free, but if the guy confessed then I would have time off. So I was there till 8:30 in the morning and he finally confessed to the whole thing—the rape of that woman and the peeping. And that was a good piece of police work. These are the guys you want to get off the street."

One thing St. Germain hated was handing out traffic tickets, and he almost never did. "I don't think that should be a policeman's job, because we're supposed to get along with the public and that just creates bad feelings." He recalled one night in St. Boniface when he and his partner responded to a report that a young boy was choking. They rushed the boy to the hospital, he survived, and nothing more was thought about it until a week later: "I didn't pull many people over, and I pulled this guy over. He said, 'Haven't you got anything better to do?'

"I said, 'I do, but this happens to be part of it.' I looked at him and said, 'Where do I know you from?'

"'I don't know.'

"'You're the father of the kid I took to the hospital five days ago.'

"'So, you're a hero?'

"I said, 'Give me your driver's licence and registration,' and told him he was an asshole. But you know, other than that, I would have let him go! That really shook my faith in humanity."

Hollywood films suggest that police forces in past eras were riven with corruption. There were certainly incidents of police misconduct in Vancouver in the 1960s, but St. Germain saw little of that. "Having been a policeman, I look back at it and 99 percent of the policemen I worked with were honest. There were some guys that did dumb things. There was one time a guy in St. Boniface took a package of cigarettes out of a store after a break-in. I said to him, 'Put them back or I'll arrest you.' To me, if you've got the trust of the people, you shouldn't be stealing from them. But the majority of the police are dead honest."

After leaving the St. Boniface Police Force and relocating to Port Coquitlam, BC, St. Germain spent one year working on the Downtown Eastside with the Vancouver Police Force. He quit after realizing the negative effects of such emotionally demanding work. VANCOUVER POLICE DEPARTMENT

Once, while presenting evidence in a case before the courts, a judge asked him to confirm a particular fact that was crucial in determining whether the accused was guilty or innocent. "The judge asked me a question, and I said, 'I don't know, sir.'

"And he said, 'Well, I might have to let this man off.'

"'Well,' I said, 'it's better you let him off 'cause if I knew for sure, I would tell you.'

"And you know, the guy walked. The judge said, 'Well, I'll have to let him go.'

"And I said, 'Your Honour, you're the judge.'"

The next time he was in the witness box, next to the same judge, he was being cross-examined by defence lawyer Harry Walsh. A legend in Manitoba legal circles until his death in 2011 at age ninety-seven, Walsh was credited for playing a lead role in bringing legal aid to the province. He was also instrumental in convincing the federal Parliament in 1976 to abolish the death penalty. Walsh had enormous courtroom skills, and was capable of leaving a witness stuttering and incoherent on the stand. On this day he was questioning St. Germain's evidence on an impaired driving case.

"And Harry Walsh says to me, 'Officer, I don't believe you.'

"And I said to the judge, 'Well, Your Honour, this is the truth.'

"The judge leans forward and says, 'Mr. Walsh, let me tell you— this is Officer St. Germain. I believe him. He has presented in my court before, and when I ask him a question and he's not sure of the answer, he says so. He doesn't lie. He's not lying now. Carry on.'"

The accused was convicted. "These are the things that make good policemen—always tell the truth," St. Germain reflected.

St. Germain's leadership skills and respect of his peers were evident from the start. One such instance occurred at a Brotherhood of St. Boniface Policemen union meeting seven months after he joined the force. Members were trying to figure out how to get wage parity with their Winnipeg counterparts, but no one wanted to stick his neck out. One of the veterans suggested that young St. Germain put his name forward to be union president. "A lot of the guys were apprehensive about the idea of actually challenging the system. Some guy asked if I would run. I put my name in and was voted in as president, and I took up negotiations." That caused friction with the police chief, but led to a raise for him and his colleagues—though the city wouldn't agree to parity due to concern it would also result in city-wide raises for firefighters and other employees. He also fought successfully for seniority rights on behalf of his membership, even though it didn't sit well with his conservative values. "I believed that you should recognize people for their accomplishments and abilities, not just their seniority."

One of the men he worked with on the police force was Ed Jamault. They became friends and when Ed and his fiancée Alice were about to wed in 1961, he asked St. Germain to be his best man. One of the members of Alice's wedding party was a young woman named Margaret Schilke, who worked as a hairdresser and like St. Germain had grown up relatively poor. Her father worked in construction and she was one of five children. "Alice wanted me to meet Gerry because we were both going to be in the wedding party. I didn't really want to meet him but I had to, and I said to her, 'Leave me alone with him and I'll never talk to you again,'" Margaret St. Germain recounted in a 2016 interview. The four went to the local cinema, and after the movie Gerry drove Ed to the police station for an overnight shift and then drove Alice to her apartment with Margaret in tow. There was an awkward silence after Alice got out of the car, said goodnight and went inside. "And I sat in the car with Gerry, and Alice was peeking through the window to make sure everything was all right," Margaret St. Germain recalled. "Gerry said, 'Do you want to go for a coffee?' and I said, 'Okay!' So we took off, and I just felt very comfortable with him. I thought he was very nice. He was very polite and I wasn't scared of him."

By the time of the wedding they were a couple. St. Germain gave a speech that left guests "pretty impressed," according to Jamault. But if Gerry and Margaret were serious about getting hitched, they faced a problem—St. Germain was a Metis Catholic and Margaret's family were Protestants. "My dad was against Catholics and Indians. He always used to say 'the goddamned Indians.'" But in a pattern that would continue throughout his life, St. Germain's charm won the day. "My father liked Gerry right off the bat. I remember saying, 'Dad, I'm going to get married and he's a Catholic and he's got Indian in him.' And he never said anything. He just put his arm on my shoulder and gave me a little hug." The men remained close until Margaret's father died. "The last time I saw my dad we were leaving on the elevator. My dad was in an old folks' home and we could hear him saying, 'I love you, Gerry, I love you, Gerry.' And I remember thinking, 'What about me, Dad?' That was our last memory of him.'"

To this day St. Germain says his decision to marry Margaret was the smartest move he's ever made, as she supported his obsessive work ethic and ambition while raising three children mostly by herself. She also cracked down on him with blunt talk when he went into what he calls his "spoiled brat" mode. His lifestyle wasn't always easy for Margaret, who gave birth to Michele in the summer of 1962, Suzanne in early 1964 and their only son Jay in February 1966. While St. Germain worked a five-day-on, five-day-off shift, he and some of his police pals would do odd jobs during their time off on the local golf course in exchange for free golf, leading to some boozing weekend golf trips. St. Germain, who was fully immersed in the drinking culture in the RCAF, didn't realize the extent of his drinking once he left the military. "I came home one day and Michele was running around in the yard. I said 'Where's her shoes?'

"Margaret said, 'She hasn't got any.'

"'Why don't you buy her some?'

"And she looked at me and said, 'You spent all the money that was in the bank on your last golfing trip.'

"'That's interesting. Maybe I'm going to stop drinking.'

"And she said, 'Whatever you think.' And I had my next drink twenty years later."

Ed Jamault said it was clear from day one that St. Germain was a natural leader. "He made it known when things weren't correct with the department. He would let superiors know about it." When St.

Germain left the force in 1964 to join 3M as a salesman—selling tape, ribbon and other products in the Manitoba region—Jamault wasn't surprised. "You could just tell standing with him for a few minutes that he was a man who had a vision in life. He was looking at all opportunities and it was just a matter of staying positive." To get the job at 3M he had to beat out dozens of other applicants. It came down to the ex-cop and a highly experienced salesman who represented the Rothmans cigarette company in Manitoba. St. Germain remembers 3M's regional manager at the time, a man named Jack Coghill, telling him the reason he had been chosen: "I believe I can train you better." That approach still makes complete sense to St. Germain. "A good salesman is not necessarily someone trained as a salesman. You could come off the back of a garbage wagon. If you've got attributes like good eye-to-eye contact, you're pleasant, you can laugh and you can laugh at yourself, that's what takes. He took a chance on me and I panned out really well."

While he enjoyed the challenge of sales, Manitoba winters were another thing entirely. One day when he was driving from Winnipeg to Portage La Prairie in the dead of winter in 1965—"it was about sixty below [Fahrenheit] with wind chill"—the car just stopped running. He got out and while cowering against the brutal prairie wind managed to wave someone down. "If somebody hadn't stopped I think I would have frozen to death." He vowed while rubbing his hands together inside the good Samaritan's toasty car that this would be his last winter in Manitoba. St. Germain asked his 3M boss to transfer him to Vancouver, where there were openings. He was denied, so started looking for other career opportunities. Having obtained his commercial pilot's licence after leaving the RCAF, he travelled with Margaret to Los Angeles to interview for a job with American Airlines. Margaret thought it was too far away and refused to move to LA. The next stop was Vancouver and an interview with the city's police chief. "And he said, 'Yes, we need you.'"

Being a policeman in a typical Canadian city is one thing. Being a beat cop and working undercover in Vancouver's Downtown Eastside is something else entirely. But that situation was what St. Germain walked into when he decided to swap the financial advantage of being 3M's top Winnipeg salesman to work in Vancouver's temperate climate, with stunning mountain views and ocean vistas. And so began an even more fascinating policing experience starting in the autumn of 1966, working the 100 block of East Hastings. The street was once the heart of downtown Vancouver, but was also populated by loggers and fishermen who would work seasonally, then crowd into the many cheap hotels. "Beginning in the late 1950s, a number of developments led to a decrease of ten thousand fewer visitors per day in the Downtown Eastside and the gradual marginalization of this community," wrote city planner Jodi Newnham in a 2005 essay. "The streetcars stopped running in the area; the main library moved to a location outside the Downtown Eastside; and in the late 1960s, the City began building a new centre for Downtown Vancouver."

Crime, prostitution and drugs were already prevalent on these streets when St. Germain joined the force in 1966. His first assignment in Vancouver was an inherently dangerous one, but had nothing to do with busting pimps and drug dealers. As a fresh face not known to many on the force, he was asked to dig up information on two officers who were holdovers from an era of rampant corruption, which had culminated in a 1955 inquiry into bribe-taking among top police officials, including chief Walter Mulligan. "The day I start one of them shoots himself in the Cobalt Hotel, and two weeks later the other guy quit." St. Germain started showing up on the street in a suit playing the role of a "rounder," or professional gambler, frequenting bars and illegal gambling dens to try to get in touch with the criminal element.

He was also put on the morality squad before later working on bootleggers and drug dealers in the Downtown Eastside. Despite his morality squad role, he said he never busted prostitutes. "I considered prostitution a necessary evil in society." He told prostitutes on his beat, "'Look, if you step out of line, I'll book you. But I want you to keep me apprised of what's going on on the street. If you keep me informed, I can't give you a licence to operate, but we'll work together to keep the streets safe for you and for everybody else.' And that's basically how I operated." The approach proved successful one day when he arrived at the police station for a weekend shift and his sergeant said, "There's a murder on 100 block. Down on your street."

"Who got killed?" St. Germain asked.

"Some derelict in a rooming house. Homicide has been working on this thing ever since you left four days ago. Do you think you can solve it?"

"Well, I'll check with some of my people." So St. Germain and his partner headed down to the 100 block and started asking the sex workers if they knew anything. All professed ignorance until he eventually talked to one named Bonnie: "Bonnie, we got a murder down here."

"Oh, yeah, those dumb cops are running around in circles."

"You know who did it?"

"Yeah."

"Really? Well, what do you need?"

"Number one, if I get arrested I want a break."

"If I'm on the beat I can guarantee that." The second request was a little tougher to pull off in the mid-1960s: $500. "That's too much, I'll give you $100."

They ended up at $200.

"It's Moose MacKay," she said, directing St. Germain to one of the street's many seedy hotels.

"I walked in and he was sitting there with one other guy and I asked him if he was Moose MacKay and he says yes. I said, 'Would you mind standing up?' And he was about six-foot-four! I said, 'Mr. MacKay, I have to arrest you on the charge of murder.' He replied, 'Officer I didn't mean to kill him.' I told him not to say anything more and gave him the caution and rights."

St. Germain marched MacKay to the paddy wagon and called the sergeant, Gordon Dalton. "'Gordy, I've got him here. The murderer. But I need two hundred bucks.' He says, '$200?' And I said, 'If you don't I'm turning him loose. You're not going to screw me up with my information!' They tried to find out who told me but I wouldn't say. I gave Bonnie $200 and she was happy."

On another occasion he showed up at the police station at 312 Main Street and noticed out of the corner of his eye a sketch on the bulletin board of a man wanted for murder in Edmonton. Not thinking too much about it, he decided to head out again on his own. For no apparent reason Sergeant Dalton shouted out, "Be careful out there alone!" But St. Germain wasn't worried. "There was a law on the street: if you didn't hassle people, you were 99-percent safe. You can do your job down there as long as you don't antagonize people. You'd be surprised the level of respect you get." So St. Germain headed to the corner of Main and East Hastings. "And I sort of looked over to my right and there's this guy who was shuffling along the sidewalk next to a bank." Something seemed odd about the man, so St. Germain started to follow him while trying to avoid being detected. "There was a guy who was drinking across the street and I grabbed him and said, 'You're under arrest!' and the guy nearly shit himself." St. Germain must have watched more than a few James Cagney–era gangster films, because he said he added for good measure, "And no funny stuff!" He pushed the drunk ahead of him and started walking toward the suspect.

"He started to move and I said 'Stop!' I let the drunk go, took my gun out and said again, 'Stop!' And I had no idea why I was picking this guy up. He had no ID on him, and I had a hell of a time trying to figure it out. This was before the Charter of Rights and Freedoms—we didn't abuse people's rights but we were able to do things." He walked him into the back door of the police station. One of the corporals said, "You can't hold this guy!"

"We'll hold him," St. Germain responded.

"For what?"

"He has no fixed address and what have you . . . we can hold him for a few hours." St. Germain was walking out of the station with his partner when it dawned on him. "The sketch! We went back inside and grabbed the sketch from the bulletin board in the sergeant's office. And it was him."

The most riveting St. Germain yarn involved a francophone pimp from Montreal who had been roughing up sex workers under his control. St. Germain had warned him in normal unaccented English about his treatment of the women, though he was leery of being too aggressive because he feared it would cause more brutality. One evening St. Germain and his partner Harold walked into an East Hastings hotel. "And we're standing at the bar talking to the bartender, and this guy is at a table with six or seven guys, and they're all Frenchmen. And this guy says in French, 'You see the biggest of the two guys there? I'm going to kill that bastard.' So I never said anything. I pretended I didn't understand, and sort of looked out and smiled. But he just kept it up. He carried on and called me everything under the sun in French.

"So I took my .38 revolver out and put it in front of me so they couldn't see it. I thought the bartender's eyes were going to pop out, so I said, 'Don't panic.'

"'Harold, you cover these guys and if one of them moves, shoot him.'

"He says, 'Are you crazy?'

"I said, 'Cover 'em!' So I walked up to this guy and I put the .38 to his head and said, 'Stand up.' Then I said to him in French, 'Tu veux me tuer? Cris, je vais t'arranger.'—'you're going to kill me, jerk? Well, I'm going to deal with you.' The guy literally pissed himself right there."

St. Germain ordered the pimp at gunpoint into a back alley behind the hotel, had him lie on his back, crouched over him and stuck his revolver in the man's mouth. "I said, 'You're going to kill me? Anybody that wants to kill me . . . This is the street I work on. But I'll tell you what. You're leaving this street right now. You're getting one chance. If you don't leave, or if you come back, I'll shoot you.' Well, I've never seen terror like I saw in his eyes that night."

St. Germain said he actually suspected the pimp may have been serious about carrying out his threat. A Vancouver policeman had recently been badly beaten with a baseball bat and the crime was unsolved. "And I think it was him that did it, but I didn't know. So I called a cruiser car and I said, 'This guy's leaving town, he's going down Hastings Street. Can you follow him? If he stops, arrest him.' And they followed him right down to the Vancouver–Burnaby boundary to the Trans-Canada Highway." The man was never seen again. After dispatching the pimp out of Vancouver he went back into the bar and approached the table where the pimp's pals remained, telling them in French, "You found that funny? You guys get out of town too.' And they did."

If that sounds like something out of Hollywood, it's no coincidence. St. Germain was always a huge fan of Western films and cowboy culture. Many years later his house would be filled with expensive art reflecting aboriginal and Western culture, and the ringtone for his mobile phone would be the soundtrack from the Clint Eastwood film *The Good, the Bad and the Ugly*. But St. Germain said he wasn't living out a fantasy. As he did with so many decisions in his life, he just made the calculation that he had no other options. "I thought, 'I'm certainly not going to allow anybody on my street who says they're going to kill me. To book him, what are you going to book him on?' So I figured it was the best way to deal with it." But would he have actually gunned the man down if he came back? "No," said a chuckling St. Germain. "I couldn't kill anybody. But I wanted him to believe that I could."

However, the confrontation with the francophone pimp was one of the events that contributed to his decision to hand in his badge and gun a year to the day after he joined the force. It was a decision Margaret supported. "When I was on the 100 block I got so bad that Margaret told me to leave. I got so rough. I became like my clientele. It affects you. There's a reason why we have so many problems with policemen and their families. It's because you live in a negative world like that. When I was undercover I always stayed on the right side. But I operated right near the edge. And when you get to that stage, you've gotta make an assessment that it's time to leave. That's really why I never thought twice about leaving." It wasn't just dealing with hardened criminals that wore him down. He also saw first-hand how the children of addicts living there were treated. "There were kids being abused. Just little kids. I never saw them being physically abused but I knew they were. We did all we could to make sure they had food and that, and it's surprising what good policemen will do. But it really got to me."

Despite his stint as a union leader, his police career led to a firming up of his right-of-centre political views. He has long believed that the justice system has to be tough on criminals, and supports capital punishment as long as there is "direct" physical evidence proving the guilt of the accused, as opposed to hearsay or circumstantial evidence. His law enforcement experience also played a role in his opposition decades later to Prime Minister Justin Trudeau's plan to legalize and regulate the marijuana trade.

"I saw young girls coming down to the street. I'd talk to them. They were telling me that they smoked pot, but that it wasn't so bad. And the next thing you know, they were chipping heroin and doing other drugs, and the next thing you know they were addicted and they were hookers. It was terrible. You know it's a step that brought them there, and that's why my beliefs are as firm as they are in opposing legalization. If an adult wants to do it, well, it's not up to me to tell the world how to live. But let's not put anything into our society that would encourage those that haven't fully developed yet as adults." When it was pointed out that drug prohibition has done little to curb consumption, he replied, "If it stops just one, that's enough. That's a step in the right direction. Nothing in my world is justified just because they're already doing it."

St. Germain's single year on the Vancouver force marked the first time someone planted in him the idea that he might one day consider entering politics. He was required to take a mandatory swimming and life-saving course as part of working in a port city, and at a ceremony to mark their graduation he was asked to speak on behalf of his class. As St. Germain recalled, "One of the Vancouver aldermen came up to me afterwards and said, 'I guarantee you will be in politics someday.'"

3
∞

From Business to Politics

One summer weekend when St. Germain was seven his family visited an aunt and uncle in Oak Point, a community on the shores of Lake Manitoba about eighty kilometres northwest of St. François Xavier. The couple were renting a ranch. "There were these great big Hereford bulls, and I was totally in awe," St. Germain remembered. He already had a love of horses, and one of his favourite weekend treats was to be taken to the cinema to see a Gene Autry or Roy Rogers movie. For the next few months all he could think about was someday owning a ranch and being able to ride a horse through his fields while watching over a herd of cattle. One day that winter while he was home from school sick with jaundice, he wrote to another relative, his aunt Dorothy. *Dear Auntie Dora*, he began, before announcing that he was so sick he was *yellow as a lemon*. Clearly frustrated over being bedridden—his inability to sit still would be a lifelong challenge—he complained, *I do not no what to do with myself.* He concluded the short letter by announcing, *I am selling my bicycle and bying a poney. Come and see me soon. Love, Gerry.* This was the genesis of a lifelong love of cowboy culture and the "the dream," as he calls it, of one day owning his own ranch. While at various times in his life he aspired to be and then became a pilot, a police officer, a businessman and a politician, "the ranch was the dream, and everything else was filler."

When he and Margaret arrived in Vancouver in the early autumn of 1966 with their young family they had only $300 to their names. Margaret's relatives in the Vancouver suburb of Port Coquitlam knew two immigrant businessmen who had a problematic tenant who once fired a gun at them when they came to collect rent. The tenant was finally evicted and the two men, Ralph Zandbergen and Gerd Palm, agreed to rent the house to the young couple, a particularly attractive idea given St. Germain's police officer status.

Michele was four, Suzanne two and Jay an infant when the St. Germains moved in. A policeman's salary meant there was not going to be much beyond some loose change left to sock away to fulfill this wild fantasy of owning a grand ranch. The young couple struck up a warm—and ultimately highly lucrative—friendship with their landlords. Zandbergen was a carpenter from the Netherlands, while Palm was a plumber who had emigrated from Germany. As always with St. Germain, friendship would be accompanied by nicknames: Zandbergen became "the Dutchman" and Palm "Colonel Klink," the name of the bumbling German prisoner-of-war camp commandant in the TV series *Hogan's Heroes*. They naturally called St. Germain "Frenchman." Neither of the immigrants was particularly literate in English, and while pulling off various business deals they'd call on their new friend to help with the paperwork. Palm could see that St. Germain had a knack for business and was a natural salesman: "Frenchman, you're too good to work for someone else."

St. Germain kept that in the back of his mind, but with a young family and without much money to invest, he chose a more secure route after leaving the police force in the autumn of 1967. He convinced 3M to rehire him to be their Lower Mainland representative. Going back into the private sector was always part of his plan to hit it big as an entrepreneur. During this period, the St. Germains scraped together enough money to come up with a down payment

St. Germain went back to his previous job as a 3M salesman after he and Margaret realized his personality was being impacted by the dark experiences he had during his year as a police officer in Vancouver's Downtown Eastside. Here he's running a 3M booth at a trade show, with colleague George Specht, in Vancouver shortly after leaving the police force in 1967. LIBRARY AND ARCHIVES CANADA

on their first home, to be built on a vacant Port Coquitlam property. The new sales venture went well until 3M asked their bilingual star salesman to move to Quebec in 1969. "And I refused to go. That ended that career." He finally decided to follow Palm's advice to go out on his own. After leaving 3M he came up with the cash to become one of the first franchise owners in the BC-based Brownie's Fried Chicken chain. He located his business in a Port Coquitlam building owned by Zandbergen and Palm.

The outlet was a reasonable money-maker, especially on one crazy weekend. St. Germain's first hire was a remarkably clean-cut young man—a rarity in the hippie era—named David, who proceeded to bring in some equally straight friends to join him as co-workers. St. Germain soon realized he was surrounded by Jehovah's Witnesses who wanted to talk religion. He'd say in response, "I don't discuss politics or religion." One day David approached his boss with a tip. "You'd better order more chicken, Gerry." There was a Jehovah's Witness convention in Vancouver that weekend with thousands of people attending. David had made an announcement: "I told them that you have opened this new business in Port Coquitlam and you have hired all of us Jehovah's Witnesses to work for you and everybody should come and support Gerry and his new business." And they came in droves. The lineups grew longer and longer, but the new patrons remained patient. "I recognized that this was serious, and we cooked twenty-four hours a day for two days. The people in Port Coquitlam couldn't get over this, couldn't figure out what the hell was going on. And you know, the people in line wouldn't get mad, they would wait. And they said, 'Oh, we're not bothered, Gerry's such a good man.'"

But St. Germain would only stick with fried chicken for three months. "I hated cooking. I had already worked at Harvey's and said to myself, 'What am I doing back there?' So I found a couple of guys and they bought it." Meanwhile, next door to the Brownie's franchise was an appliance and plumbing store operated by Palm and Zandbergen. One day they had a truckload of appliances and asked St. Germain, who had been hired for a new sales job with a major corporation and was waiting to start, if he could sell them. St. Germain quickly delivered, finding an Italian businessman in need of stoves, fridges and dishwashers. "I got lucky. They bought my whole truckload, damn near. So the Dutchman and Klink, they got all excited." He told them he was now going to take a short holiday while awaiting the start of his new job. "And they said, 'No, we bought another truckload since you starting selling the last one.' I said, 'Oh no!'" Sensing St. Germain might not be so enthusiastic, they made an offer. "Okay, Frenchman, we'll give you a third of the business." St. Germain was surprised that it was only about $2,000 to become their partner.

By 1972 Zandbergen, who didn't have the patience to deal with mundane and frustrating issues like handling accounts receivable, had left the business to focus on building houses, although the three men would continue to work as partners on other business deals. And they still shared one concern: political uncertainty. A socialist

St. Germain's first experience as an entrepreneur, in 1969, was as one of the early owners of a Brownies Fried Chicken franchise. Despite initial success due to a wave of friendly customers from a Jehovah's Witness convention in Vancouver, St. Germain hated cooking and quickly sold the business. LIBRARY AND ARCHIVES CANADA

firebrand by the name of Dave Barrett was starting to look like he had a shot at becoming Canada's first provincial New Democratic Party premier. The premier at the time, W.A.C. "Wacky" Bennett, was an eccentric hardware store owner from Kelowna who would warn during election campaigns that the "socialist hordes are at the gates." St. Germain, a financial supporter of Bennett's Social Credit Party, feared that an NDP government would be disastrous for business people like him. But Zandbergen was beyond nervous, assuming

Barrett and his "make the rich pay" mantra would spell utter disaster for the economy. Zandbergen panicked just before the election, selling a swath of serviced Port Coquitlam residential properties to Palm and St. Germain. "He said, 'Holy smokes, these guys are going to destroy everything. The socialist hordes are actually at the gates!'"

British Columbians voted on a scorching hot August 30 of that year, and that evening St. Germain was driving along a street behind the Vancouver Golf Club. He turned on the radio to hear an announcer breathlessly informing listeners that the NDP had formed a majority government. Shocked and infuriated, he banged his hand on the steering wheel—and drove the truck into the ditch. He was uninjured but had to track down one of his business partners to come get him while he called a tow truck.

It turned out to be a classic if somewhat fluky lesson in the art of business deals: always buy when others are pessimistic, because prices will never be lower, and always sell when markets are filled with euphoric buyers. In a bizarre twist, the election of a party St. Germain had vociferously opposed led to his first huge financial break. A year after the election Barrett brought in legislation to create the Agricultural Land Reserve, a progressive initiative to protect from development 47,000 square kilometres of highly fertile land in BC, including large parcels in the Lower Mainland and the Fraser Valley. Left-leaning, anti-development intellectuals and BC's nascent environmentalist movement rejoiced at a decision that is still seen as possibly Barrett's greatest legacy. But the dramatic shrinkage of land available for residential and commercial development resulted in a windfall for landowners in areas still free for construction, resulting in a huge return for St. Germain and his partner when they sold their holdings. Each walked away with $360,000 in their bank accounts—a staggering amount in 1973 and the equivalent of $1.9 million apiece today. "We were made in the shade," he said. "I built a new home with a swimming pool. I bought Margaret a decent car. The curse of the NDP! I often say I should be more thankful to them."

The three kept doing business deals, mostly acquiring and

developing land during an era when inflation was sky-high. St. Germain got his real estate licence so he could also sell commercial and residential properties. In the late 1970s, however, St. Germain stumbled on a new business venture that didn't mean a lot to his bottom line but would lead to his forever being labelled, either affectionately or derisively, as "that chicken farmer." He happened to be raising Arabian horses on his South Surrey ranch, claiming it as an agricultural operation for tax purposes. Revenue Canada didn't see it that way, so St. Germain started looking for a way to maintain his tax break to help defray the cost of his horses. At the time his son Jay, then a young teen, was attending a private school in Burnaby. St. Germain learned that the father of one of his son's friends had a chicken farm for sale in nearby Langley. "I went and had a quick coffee and saw the guy that owned it and by ten o'clock I had bought it."

It took only six months for St. Germain to be voted in as chairman of the BC Chicken Marketing Board, which sets quotas in Canada's highly regulated and protected dairy, poultry and egg sectors. He made his mark with a strategic shift that is still in place today, convincing local producers to supply local supermarkets with fresh rather than frozen chickens. This innovation led to higher prices because producers in Alberta and Saskatchewan could no longer compete. It was also during this period that St. Germain helped the father of his future colleague in the Senate, Mobina Jaffer. One marketing board member told him that if they opened the door to Sherali Bandali Jaffer, it would lead to a takeover by brown-skinned foreigners. "I don't care," St. Germain replied. "You can't do this. You can't discriminate against anybody. He's got the money to buy quota. It's discrimination." It was one of the many instances when St. Germain's background influenced his decision-making: "I looked at that man sitting there and said, 'That could be my father.'"

In 1982 St. Germain struck a business deal that would be helpful a year later when he made the pivot into politics. One day he and Zandbergen made a handshake land deal to sell serviced lots to a trio of businessmen for $40,000 apiece. But in BC, vendors needed to issue a prospectus laying out all the necessary financial details. Once the lawyers eventually approved the final copy, "the bloody things were worth about $80,000." He and Zandbergen went to a restaurant to meet with the three buyers, who nervously flipped through the prospectus while wondering if their original deal would be honoured. Zandbergen was uncomfortable letting the properties go at a price that automatically doubled the buyers' profit. St. Germain started toying with the three men: "What would you guys do in a case like this? Tell me."

"That's not fair," they said.

"What do you mean, that's not fair? Tell me what you would do!" St. Germain repeated.

"To make a long story short," St. Germain recalled, "I go to the Dutchman to say I want to proceed with the deal, and he said, 'I'll hold my nose.' So I got up and teased them a bit and said, 'Go over and sign the documents—but bring your chequebooks. We will honour the deal but you're paying for these things right now.'" After the deal was completed one of the men, a lifelong supporter of the NDP, expressed deep appreciation for St. Germain's show of honour and suggested he should run for Parliament. A year later, he contributed to St. Germain's election campaign.

Like most countries of the western world, Canada was recovering during this period from two global oil price shocks: in 1973 as a result of the Israeli–Arab Yom Kippur War, and in 1979 as a result of the revolution in Iran. The result was a combination of high inflation caused by soaring oil and gas prices, and stagnant economic growth as a result of the damage done to businesses and consumers by those increases. In 1980, after Pierre Elliott Trudeau's Liberals won a majority government after a short-lived minority Parliament led by Tory Joe Clark, the new government took a drastic step in response to "stagflation." Allan MacEachen, the Liberal finance minister, introduced the National Energy Program (NEP) in his October 1980 budget speech. The policy, which included a variety of costly measures to wean Canada off dependence on foreign oil, was devastating for Alberta, which according to one estimate lost between $50 and $100 billion due to price limits placed on domestic oil.

The NEP was also ill-timed, as the global economy fell into a deep recession during the 1981–82 period, inflating the perception not only in Alberta but throughout western Canada that the Liberals—with just two seats west of Ontario and none west of Winnipeg—were hostile to western interests. Bankruptcies and unemployment were high as companies struggled under the weight of interest rates approaching 20 percent. St. Germain survived financially thanks to the inflationary impact on his real estate holdings. But he saw many other business people destroyed, and that steeled his determination to get rid of what he thought was the cause of Canada's economic woes.

Adding to the exasperation among many Canadians was Trudeau's decision during this economically troubled period to embark on complex and at times bitterly acrimonious negotiations to bring in a Charter of Rights and Freedoms as part of a series of measures in the Constitution Act of 1982. Once those goals were reached, Trudeau fuelled more suspicion he was uninterested in dealing with the struggling economy by undertaking a global peace mission that was widely viewed as futile. The early 1980s was also a time when the attention of the Canadian public, especially in BC, was focused obsessively on serial child killer Clifford Olson. The sadistic psychopath was caught and convicted in 1982 in the premeditated sex slayings of eleven children in BC between the ages of nine and eighteen. Support for capital punishment was high and St. Germain was among those Canadians who believed those convicted of the most heinous crimes should forfeit their lives.

These themes were pervasive during an enormously busy political spring of 1983 in BC, thanks to a May 5 provincial election to be followed just over a month later by a federal Progressive Conservative leadership race in Ottawa. St. Germain was deeply involved at both levels. He sat on the executive of the Progressive Conservative riding association for Mission–Port Moody, a working-class federal riding that was represented by New Democrat Mark Rose. Rose calculated that Dave Barrett's NDP was likely to win provincially, so resigned his federal seat to run in the provincial election. The move looked like a wise one during most of the campaign, as Barrett's New Democrats were widely seen to be leading the race against premier Bill Bennett's Social Credit Party. But the NDP leader blundered with just over a week until voting day, promising to get rid of public sector wage controls. The controls were popular at the time—and Barrett soon wouldn't be. Bennett's Socreds won their third straight majority.

While coveting Rose's vacated federal seat, St. Germain volunteered to do door-knocking and money-raising for Austin Pelton, the former Maple Ridge mayor who was running for the Socreds in the nearby provincial constituency of Dewdney. Pelton won the seat and was about to give his victory speech on election night when Gerry and Margaret St. Germain entered the room. "I'm walking in the door as he goes up to the podium and says, 'I just saw that young man Gerry St. Germain walk in. He should be the next Member of Parliament for this riding!'"

As the federal election approached, St. Germain was caught up in the notion that Canadians had to find a way to remove Pierre Elliott Trudeau, who had ruled Canada since 1968 with the exception of one brief interruption in 1979–80. But one of the challenges for the Tories had always been the party's own weak leadership. From the day Joe Clark became leader in 1976, in a surprise win over a field that included Brian Mulroney, he had been derided as ineffectual and, in comparison to the larger-than-life Trudeau, the "Joe Who?" of Canadian politics. St. Germain remembers doing work in the 1979 and 1980 election campaigns to help Clark when he was in BC. "But there was nothing exciting about him. He would show up and we did what we had to do." In the aftermath of his party's crushing 1980 election loss, Clark struggled with dissent within the party leading up to a lukewarm 67-percent approval from delegates at a convention. He announced he would voluntarily step down but then seek a new mandate as leader at a leadership convention in Ottawa on June 11, 1983. While there were eight official contestants, only three—Clark,

Mulroney and Newfoundland MP John Crosbie—were considered serious contenders for the crown.

There would be confusion decades later over whom St. Germain, viewed as an increasingly important power broker and fundraiser in suburban Vancouver, supported heading into that convention. He said he was leaning toward Crosbie, and dismissed any suggestion he may have supported Clark. But one of Mulroney's volunteer field organizers in BC, Ray Castelli, said it was widely assumed St. Germain was in Clark's camp because he was registered to stay at the prestigious Château Laurier Hotel in the heart of downtown Ottawa, a short cab ride from the convention arena. Since the party machine was controlled by Clark, his delegates were given the choice accommodation that had been reserved by the party. Castelli, who headed a sizeable contingent of young BC Tories working to support Mulroney, was pursuing perceived "soft" delegates they thought they could lure from other camps, and St. Germain was on the list.

It so happened that a few weeks before the convention Brian and Mila Mulroney were making an appearance in BC's Lower Mainland, so Castelli arranged for a private meeting between St. Germain and the ambitious Quebecer. St. Germain remembers being somewhat blasé about the meeting, as he was leaning toward Crosbie. But Gerry and Margaret stopped off at the hotel where the Mulroneys were scheduled to meet key delegates. Brian and Mila were late, and the ever-impatient St. Germain considered leaving. But he ended up staying for the meeting. "Tu parles français?" St. Germain asked Mulroney as they shook hands, and the two extroverts hit it off as they bantered in French. "His French was really better than mine, and he was as engaging as he always is—a typical Irishman." They also discussed the upcoming by-election in Mission–Port Moody. Mulroney, who promised St. Germain that he'd go to the riding to campaign for him, would later have a general recollection of his first impression: "I just thought he was a very likeable, straightforward, hard-working guy." As they left that meeting Margaret gave her husband's hand a tug and said, "There's the next prime minister of Canada." Gerry said, "Holy smokes, you think so?"

Shortly after that meeting, St. Germain and some other senior Conservatives formally joined the "British Columbians for Mulroney" camp, which included just two of the province's MPs, Tom Siddon and Chuck Cook. Castelli touted the St. Germain endorsement as a coup: "We wanted to show we had momentum, so we made a lot of hay out of it." St. Germain would almost immediately pay a price, getting a call from party organizer Scott McCord telling him the Château was overbooked and that he was being relegated to a hotel in Orleans, a low-income Ottawa suburb. But the discomfort of a bed in a cheap hotel and a long schlepp to the convention were small prices to pay, as St. Germain ended up backing a winner. For any aspiring young person in politics that's an automatic advantage, especially considering the fact that most incumbent MPs across Canada backed Clark. Now it was time for St. Germain to seek the nomination in the contest that would take place just a few weeks after the leadership convention.

Mulroney, meanwhile, had far bigger fish to fry. With a party divided into factions he needed to get his caucus and party supporters together to face one of the most dominant twentieth-century political parties in the developed world. Elmer MacKay, a long-time Tory MP in Nova Scotia, agreed to resign from his bedrock Tory riding of Central Nova so Mulroney could run in a by-election. As Rose had quit his post as MP for Mission–Port Moody, Trudeau called by-elections for both ridings to be held August 29, 1983. St. Germain was seen as a dynamic candidate with solid potential, though there were some awkward moments. He showed up at one political event in his working-class riding driving his silver-grey Mercedes convertible with a "SAINT" vanity plate on the back. His campaign advisers angrily ordered him to keep that car in the garage for the rest of the campaign. Despite his wealth, St. Germain managed to connect to residents of a riding that had the largest number of sawmills in the Lower Mainland. "He's a very outgoing guy and kind of charismatic, and he appealed to the kind of voters who were here," said Sandy Macdougall, a former journalist who worked in St. Germain's constituency office in 1988. "Big city-slicker politics weren't part of the game then."

St. Germain also needed work—lots of work—as a public speaker. Bob Ransford, his former political aide and speechwriter, remembers rehearsing the nomination speech with St. Germain in a one-bedroom apartment in downtown Maple Ridge on a steamy-hot summer afternoon. "Gerry was standing at the kitchen counter reading the speech. He had taken his white shirt off because he didn't want to get sweaty. He'd been out earlier in the day on the campaign trail meeting people. And he was fumbling and shaking. I remember thinking, 'Holy shit, this guy's really bad.' And I had to keep coaching him, get him to read each line over and over again, and telling him how to read it." But what St. Germain lacked in finesse he made up for with enthusiasm, energy and charisma. "He'd make you feel like you were a part of

St. Germain's chances of winning a seat in the 1983 by-election in Mission–Port Moody, a traditional NDP riding in Vancouver's suburbs, looked grim. But his campaign got a huge boost that summer when new Tory leader Brian Mulroney, after receiving a desperate phone call from St. Germain seeking help, left his own by-election campaign in Nova Scotia to barnstorm with his nervous Tory colleague. Mulroney would later say that his party had to win both seats to have any hope of unseating the Liberals the following year. BILL MCCARTHY

something that was going to be a lot of fun, and he was really positive and upbeat," Ransford said. "We were riding the wave of enthusiasm after Mulroney's win at the convention, and Gerry was the right guy for that because he knew how to sell. He's a born salesman, and that's what caught my attention. I remember thinking, 'This guy's not good at giving speeches, but when he meets up a constituent or potential party member, he really engages them and gets them on side.'"

After winning the nomination, St. Germain campaigned tirelessly but didn't have high name recognition and feared he'd lose to his only serious rival, New Democrat Sophie Weremchuk. "So I called up Mulroney, who's in Nova Scotia campaigning to win a seat, and said, 'Boss, I need you.'" While Mulroney's natural instinct was to immediately agree, he remembers considerable resistance among his top advisers. Trudeau, not adhering to a tradition of not contesting the by-election of a party's chosen leader, had sent in numerous high-profile ministers to campaign on behalf of Mulroney's Liberal opponent, Alvin Sinclair. Mulroney shared his recollection of this period in an April 2016 interview:

> It's traditional that the new leader of a party is given a pass into the House of Commons, as Pearson gave Mr. Stanfield and I gave Chrétien and so on. But the Liberals sent nine cabinet ministers into the riding to defeat me. So there was pressure on me from the National Campaign Committee not to leave the riding. I decided that if I was going to go to Mission–Port Moody that I would stop in Edmonton to speak to the huge Ukrainian-Canadian convention that was going on. This would take four or five days out of my campaigning, and they didn't want me to do it, and I said, "No, I told Gerry St. Germain that if he got the nomination I would come out and help him, and I'm on my way."

The arrival of Brian and Mila Mulroney was huge for St. Germain, and it was not merely an act of charity on the Tory leader's part. "Those by-elections were turning points for the Conservative Party," Mulroney recalled. "Had we lost one or both of them, it would have been lights out for us." The Mulroneys and St. Germains campaigned steadily for two days, drawing huge crowds and putting St. Germain's name on the map. It was terrifying for Margaret, a shy woman who was rattled by the masses of people and the burly security men around the Mulroneys. Mila, as skilled as her husband in working a crowd, took Margaret by the hand and held tight, assuring her, "You just stay close to me and you'll be fine." On the back page of *Maclean's* that week, prominent political commentator Allan Fotheringham predicted that Mulroney would win Central Nova easily: "More interesting is the battle in Mission–Port Moody, what should be a safe NDP seat just outside Vancouver. Mulroney chortled at what will happen if his candidate, Gerry Saint Germain, wins on the same day he takes Central Nova: it would increase the French-speaking contingent of the caucus by 200 percent."

St. Germain won the riding with 51 percent of the vote, ten points or 3,276 votes ahead of the NDP candidate. Later that year, in a speech to party members, he revealed in detail the impact of Mulroney: "I don't know if you realize what he meant to our campaign here. At the start of our by-election campaign they did a poll: I had a recognition level of 18 percent. I knew I was in trouble. I got on the phone to Central Nova and said, 'Brian, I need help.' Brian and Mila came out and campaigned dawn to dusk for two days. We all worked hard. They did a poll later and my recognition level was 83 percent." Mulroney's visit cemented a bond between the two rookie MPs. "Mulroney was the type of guy to build relationships and friendships quickly, and so clearly he saw something in Gerry," said Castelli. "Their personalities just clicked."

When St. Germain won the seat he immediately recognized he would very likely fall on his face if he didn't surround himself with staff who were strong in areas where he was weak. So he turned to Bob Ransford, the man who only a few months earlier had dismissed him as an unsophisticated cowboy. "Gerry said to me, 'I need you,' because I was the only one [among his volunteers] who had worked in Ottawa."

Ransford said he had no interest in a full-time gig on Parliament Hill, since he'd already worked there for BC MP Tom Siddon, but agreed to fly to the nation's capital to help set up the office for the wet-behind-the-ears chicken farmer.

St. Germain said he will never forget bursting with pride and nervousness as he walked into the House of Commons to take his seat on the same day as Mulroney. It was a special day in Canadian politics, and the public and press galleries that encircle the chamber directly above the MPs were filled with journalists, observers and family members leaning forward to observe Mulroney's first day in Parliament. First Mulroney was brought in by interim opposition leader Erik Nielsen and house leader Harvie Andre. After that raucous event, St. Germain was brought into the chamber with Mulroney on one side and Nielsen taking the other arm, as all members stood and

A 1984 photo shows St. Germain with Mulroney and deputy leader Erik Nielsen. Mulroney, recognizing he needed a bilingual MP with strong interpersonal skills, plucked a high-school drop-out and political neophyte to be chairman of the vast Tory caucus. Mulroney described the role as a "chief executive," and many Tory insiders said he had more access to Mulroney, and therefore influence, than all but a handful of Tory ministers. LIBRARY AND ARCHIVES CANADA

St. Germain is greeted by House of Commons Speaker Jeanne Sauvé on his first day in the House of Commons after he and Mulroney won their August, 1983 by-elections. He and Mulroney, both of humble beginnings in small-town Canada, were bursting with pride that day. "If you think it's a long ride from Baie-Comeau to 24 Sussex, it's not a shorter one, you know, from Gerry's beginnings to the floor of the House of Commons," Mulroney recalled. "This was a helluva big deal for him—and with good reason." LIBRARY AND ARCHIVES CANADA

applauded. "I've done a lot of things," St. Germain recalled in an interview more than three decades later. "I've flown jets, been close to dying. But this was really overwhelming for me."

During their time in politics Mulroney and St. Germain loved to crack jokes, even during tough situations, but Mulroney doesn't remember his friend and colleague dropping any one-liners as they walked up the green carpet toward Speaker Jeanne Sauvé. "I think he was very nervous and you know we all were, but Gerry in particular was. This was a huge moment for him. I mean, if you think it's a long ride from Baie-Comeau to 24 Sussex, it's not a shorter one, you know, from Gerry's beginnings to the floor of the House of Commons. This was a helluva big deal for him—and with good reason."

Before St. Germain finalized his move into politics he had some unfinished business. He approached his current partners in the property development business, Dave Harris and Gary Lycan, and had them buy out his interest. It was a decision he believes cost him tens of millions of dollars, as the properties they collectively held went on to soar. But their company was involved in zoning issues with local municipalities, and as an MP he wanted to avoid any hint of a conflict of interest. He ploughed the money into a 450-acre property in Pemberton, about 150 kilometres north of Vancouver, where he kept up to two hundred cattle, grew seed potatoes and usually had one or two farmhands on contract to run the operations. He finally had his ranch, though at this point his focus in life was shifting rather dramatically toward the nation's capital.

Ransford said the move to politics was consistent with his career trajectory. Long before he became more self-aware and proud of his aboriginal roots, St. Germain used to refer to himself in a self-deprecating way as a "dog-eater," a historical reference to starving Metis traders eating dog meat for sustenance. St. Germain's move to federal politics was "really about Gerry wanting to distance himself from the misery and humiliation of his hard childhood," Ransford said. "The success he achieved by being the big fish in the small pond of the Port Coquitlam collection of small land developers, contractors and local merchants didn't distance him enough from his childhood. It was still small-town, small-time. But he didn't have the credentials to move to the big leagues of business and the social circles of the 'downtowners' that come with the big leagues of business success. Politics was his highway out of his small-town, hardscrabble, dog-eater past."

4

∞

Caucus Discipline, from Opposition to Government

One of St. Germain's mottos is that if he had a choice between being good and being lucky, he'd take the latter every day of the week. Luck, combined with an ability to recognize and seize opportunities, did indeed play a key role in some major breakthroughs. Many disadvantaged Canadians, and in particular First Nations children whose parents and grandparents were emotionally damaged by the residential school system, don't necessarily have access to mentors and role models. But St. Germain had a father who taught him outdoor skills, a mother who pushed him to stay in school, other relatives who helped him become bilingual, and an inspirational teacher who kept him out of pool halls when his interest was drifting. Good fortune also blessed St. Germain when he hooked up with the two immigrant BC entrepreneurs who brought him into the business world, which in turn led to the financial windfall he enjoyed after the 1972 NDP election in BC.

And so it continued in politics. If St. Germain had entered the House of Commons at any time other than the early 1980s, chances are he would have had a tough time standing out from the crowd. He wasn't a particularly strong public speaker, he was a high school dropout and he had no public profile outside his community. But St. Germain's late-summer by-election win on the same day as Mulroney's gave him huge national exposure. In the traditionally NDP-leaning riding of Mission–Port Moody, it was also an indication that Canadians could expect dramatic change in the general election expected the following year. But of far greater significance for St. Germain were the historic events shaking Canada's foundation when he arrived in Parliament in September 1983. St. Germain, the Franco-Manitoban Metis, was accompanying Mulroney into a Parliament dealing with a national unity crisis tied directly to St. Germain's birth province of Manitoba.

It's easy to forget what happened during this period, since that final leg of the 1870–1985 Manitoba Language Crisis was obscured by the subsequent national unity crisis over the failed Meech and Charlottetown constitutional accords and the near-disastrous 1995 Quebec referendum. But when Mulroney and St. Germain arrived in Parliament that autumn, Canadians and especially Manitobans were bitterly divided. Four years earlier, in 1979, St. Boniface businessman Georges Forest, fighting the legality of an English-only traffic ticket in a province he believed should be officially bilingual, won his case before the Supreme Court of Canada. In doing so the court accepted that in 1890 the Manitoba government violated Canada's constitution by removing French-language rights in the province.

Instead, Canada's highest court accepted the validity of the Manitoba Act, which had received Royal Assent in the federal Parliament on May 12, 1870. That legislation was negotiated by emissaries sent by Louis Riel, then president of the Legislative Assembly of Assiniboia, in the wake of the Red River Rebellion of 1869–70. After forming a provisional government in March of 1870, Riel had dispatched a three-person delegation to Ottawa to negotiate the establishment of the new province of Manitoba, and the transfer of a 1.4 million-acre reserve to the Metis. The resulting legislation ensured public support for a separate French Catholic education system, and gave French and English equal standing in the legislature and the courts.

But almost immediately after the bill passed, Riel was a man on the run, due to the execution of Thomas Scott, an English-speaking Protestant resister to the provisional government, back on March 4, 1870. The Ontario government put a $5,000 bounty on Riel's head, sending him into hiding for more than a decade. Immigrants from Ontario and Europe flooded into the new province he helped create, resulting in French-speakers becoming a smaller and smaller minority. After his second attempt to lead a Metis uprising in 1885, Riel was captured and executed. The Conservative prime minister of the time, John A. Macdonald, refused to commute the sentence because he feared the wrath of Ontario's English-speakers more than he did Quebec's francophones. It may have been a tactically useful short-term manoeuvre, but Macdonald's party would pay a heavy price for most of the next century, as Riel's hanging became a permanent public relations albatross for the Tories in French-speaking Quebec. Things got worse for Franco-Manitobans in 1890 when the Manitoba legislature removed rights included in the 1870 law, a move that bitterly divided French- and English-speaking Canada.

In the 1983 Tory leadership campaign Mulroney had railed against the party's history in francophone Canada, and promised he would end the legacy of Tory failure in Quebec in particular. He had promised his party, and Canadians, that he was going to finally exorcise the Riel ghost. When Mulroney and St. Germain took their seats on September 12, 1983, the NDP government in Manitoba under Howard Pawley was attempting to bring in legislation to satisfy the 1979 Forest decision by the Supreme Court of Canada, as well as pre-empt a likely decision against Manitoba's language regime following a court case initiated by Roger Bilodeau. The provincial Progressive Conservatives, then sitting in opposition, bitterly fought the initiative with the help of some members of Pawley's government, and used procedural tactics to paralyze the Manitoba legislature.

Prime Minister Trudeau wanted to encourage Pawley to press ahead with the legislation. But it was widely believed at the time that he had a second, and far more political, motive. Trudeau had won a majority government in 1980 despite winning just two seats in western Canada, both in Manitoba. His power was in Quebec, naturally, where he took an incredible seventy-four of seventy-five seats. But the Liberal hegemony in that province faced a serious threat in Mulroney, especially since Trudeau was poised to retire and the party was expected to follow tradition by choosing its next leader from English-speaking Canada. Mulroney was fluently bilingual and even bicultural, because while both parents were Irish-Canadian anglophones he learned French growing up on the streets of Baie-Comeau, a remote pulp and paper town on the north shore of the St. Lawrence River. To be successful, Mulroney had to follow through on his 1983 leadership campaign promise to end the Liberal stranglehold in Quebec—but not at the risk of losing the support of his large western caucus, many of whom were unfriendly toward Quebec.

To kneecap Mulroney's grand plan, the Liberals went to work. On September 13, 1983, the day after Mulroney's arrival in the House of Commons with St. Germain, one of Trudeau's two Manitoba MPs, Robert Bockstael, stood up in Question Period. Every MP who has been in the House of Commons for more than a week knows what that almost always means: a staged question that the questioner has little if any role in preparing. Bockstael, noting the language crisis in Manitoba and the provincial PC Party's "extremism and hostility" toward the provincial NDP government's amendment, asked what the federal Liberal government could do to reinforce its position that francophone minority rights must be protected.

Sure enough, Trudeau rose with a kind of "funny you should ask" tone to state that he was considering proposing an all-party motion to the House of Commons urging the Manitoba legislature to respect Franco-Manitobans' rights. That, according to Mulroney, was a blatant attempt to "sow division between our party in Ottawa and our provincial cousins in Manitoba." Mulroney was naturally fearful that a small number of his more troublesome MPs would break ranks if there were a vote in the Commons. Worse, he knew any anti-Quebec, anti-francophone comments from one of his backbenchers would be seized upon by their political opponents and the national media, especially those representing French-language outlets. Mulroney sprang from his seat to say he'd be happy to meet with Trudeau and NDP leader Ed Broadbent to look for ways to address the standoff in Winnipeg. But before that meeting he assembled his MPs for a private caucus meeting to read the riot act. Mulroney couldn't recall specifically asking MPs like St. Germain to lobby the MPs known to struggle with Canada's "French fact." But he needed MPs to speak positively to the media about the caucus's support for Franco-Manitobans. "Gerry, of course, was particularly on-side in this, and he was particularly valuable as well because while he was a BC member, he also had a Manitoba background. So he was very helpful," Mulroney would say years later.

There was considerable hostility toward French-speakers in Canada, due in part to an accumulation of frustration with Trudeau's policies, including the Official Languages Act of 1969, which made Canada officially bilingual. Another sore spot in English-speaking Canada was the election in 1977 of Quebec's first separatist premier, René Lévesque, who was still in power in 1983. The Quebec media— and especially the nationalist Le Devoir newspaper—gave the Manitoba issue massive coverage. And Ottawa journalists, especially those representing Quebec media outlets, were keeping a close eye on the dozen or so "dinosaurs" of Mulroney's caucus, as they were known. One of the most outspoken was Dan McKenzie, a gruff military veteran nicknamed "Fighting Dan" later in Mulroney's first term, after slugging a Liberal MP in the House of Commons.

Mulroney avoided a potentially divisive and messy party split by convincing Trudeau to agree to a resolution that wouldn't require a vote, and would simply involve a hearty endorsement in speeches by all three party leaders. There was still a risk, however, that MPs like McKenzie might wander over to a TV microphone to shoot their mouths off. In a 1985 profile of St. Germain, the *Montreal Gazette* cited unidentified Tory sources indicating that the rookie MP earned his chops in the weeks after his by-election win by speaking out "strongly in support of Mulroney's commitment to bilingualism" at a time when "the new party leader faced the Manitoba language issue that threatened to divide the caucus."

Ransford would later remember St. Germain lobbying dissidents to stay in line: "I remember Dan McKenzie was the one that Gerry really focused on." St. Germain said he met regularly with his Manitoba counterpart, as well as other right-wingers who were deeply reluctant to just clench their teeth and accept concession after concession to francophones. "I said, 'We gotta get by this, we've won two by-elections and we want to form government. You guys better clean up your act,'" St. Germain recalled. "I told them we looked like a bunch of goddamned Orangemen. I talked to guys like McKenzie because I was originally from Manitoba, and I said, 'Dan, I don't give a damn what language you talk to me in. You supported Mulroney. Now is not the time to back off!'"

The efforts of Mulroney and his allies in caucus turned a potential disaster into one of Mulroney's early triumphs. The new Tory leader delivered two powerful speeches in defence of linguistic minority rights that won widespread praise from a skeptical media. Mulroney, who in his final years in power seemed to fear travelling to regions where crowds might be hostile, even went to Winnipeg in early 1984 to send the same message. He had to be surrounded by an extra-large contingent of Mounties because of the death threats. "Those speeches were probably the best speeches he ever gave, because he really cared about the subject, and also cared enough to get really involved in the process," former Mulroney policy adviser Jon Johnson later told author Peter Newman. The controversy eventually petered out when efforts by the Pawley government to pass the bill were halted due to obstructionism in the Manitoba legislature, and the matter was referred to the Supreme Court of Canada. In 1985 the court finally ruled that all Manitoba laws were invalid in their current state, but said they'd remain temporarily in effect until a suitable timetable could be established for resolution.

Dodging Trudeau's trap helped set the stage for Mulroney's spectacular election win in September 1984. "They had tried to sucker punch us and I wasn't having any of it," Mulroney recalled in 2016. "So Gerry was very helpful in that. I can't remember any specific requests of me saying, 'Well, would you go see so-and-so.' He just went. He knew that it had to be done and he went ahead and did it." The two men were already becoming close political friends and allies, but this experience would make sure that St. Germain was going to play a major role when a new government took over a year later. "I used to say to [deputy prime minister Don] Mazankowski, 'How could you not love a chicken farmer?'" Mulroney said.

The obvious chemistry between Mulroney and St. Germain reflected their personalities and backgrounds. Both were charismatic, wise-cracking extroverts and both were born in the late stages of the Great Depression in similarly humble circumstances—Mulroney as the son of a small-town electrician in a remote Quebec pulp and paper mill town, St. Germain as the son of a Metis trapper and construction worker on the outskirts of Winnipeg. Both married well and were bilingual Roman Catholics who had given up alcohol after recognizing their boozing was impacting their family lives. They also had chips on their shoulders, resentful of snobbish big-city intellectuals and business elites—especially from Toronto.

"Sure, Gerry was a poor boy, and so was I," Mulroney reminisced. "So I knew all about that, and I wasn't surprised that some of Gerry's sartorial leanings didn't inspire confidence on Bay Street. He had a chip on his shoulder too. I thought he handled it well. He wasn't nasty about it, but he would tell them to buzz off." Mulroney and St. Germain also needed each other, though obviously to vastly different degrees. Mulroney was like a brilliant four-star general heading into a battle against a tired but wily adversary, yet the new Tory leader was saddled with perhaps a few too many overly ambitious lieutenants and colonels—ex-leadership rivals and a host of other senior MPs with massive egos to manage—when what he really needed were disciplined corporals and loyal foot soldiers.

This challenge became obvious on September 4, 1984, when he won a majority that no one quite imagined was possible. He took 211 of 282 seats, including fifty-eight of seventy-five seats in the once-impregnable Liberal fortress of Quebec. Mulroney had indeed exorcised the ghost of Louis Riel from his party. In fact, this caucus appeared to be a grand and perhaps durable coalition between two groups united in their suspicion of a centralizing federal government: Quebec nationalists and western conservatives. But no one could deny the obviously huge culture clash. Many Quebecers were enticed by Mulroney's campaign promise to bring the province back into the constitution with "honour and enthusiasm" after the 1982 Constitution Act. The series of constitutional amendments made just two years before Mulroney's election included bringing in the Charter of Rights and Freedoms. But it was struck without the consent of Quebec's sovereigntist Parti Québécois government, embittering the province's political class.

Quebec is known for having a more left-leaning political culture, and many who supported Mulroney weren't necessarily conservative in nature. They were attracted to the idea of Mulroney as a fluently bilingual son of Quebec who was far more impressive than Trudeau's successor in the 1984 election, John Turner, who had served as finance minister in the 1970s. Turner's political instincts and ability to communicate in French were rusty after years working as a Bay Street lawyer prior to his return to politics. Mulroney also had the support of many prominent Quebec nationalists, among them Marcel Masse and future Parti Québécois premier Lucien Bouchard. And some of the successful Quebec Tory MPs were, as former senator and long-time party insider Marjory LeBreton pointed out, opportunistic former Liberals.

This group was now sitting in a caucus with a large number of western, rural Ontario and Atlantic Canada MPs, the vast majority of them unable to speak a word of French and uncomfortable with official bilingualism, Quebec nationalism, the metric system, the prohibition on capital punishment and "big government" social programs that led to yawning deficits and the resulting high taxes. Mulroney also had only thirty-nine ministerial posts—the largest cabinet in history—to sprinkle among his 210 MPs, "so you can imagine the frustrated ambitions," as he later described it. It wasn't an easy task saying no, as the prime minister recalled in his memoirs while describing a letter he received from the spouse of a devastated MP after naming his first cabinet. "Yesterday had to be the most exciting day for you and your family, especially your mother. For us, it was the saddest day of our lives," wrote the woman, describing the "death" of her husband's career in politics. "Perhaps the greatest toll is on our children—they are shattered."

As a newcomer to federal politics St. Germain had several things going for him: the Mulroney bond, a businessman's street smarts, a "man's man" sense of humour that worked well with the Tory crowd, and a bilingual and bicultural background that was obviously valued. But standing in his way in the autumn of 1984 were the 209 other ambitious MPs seeking Mulroney's favour, including eighteen in British Columbia. Regional considerations are always paramount for Canadian prime ministers selecting members of their cabinet, and four stood in St. Germain's way in his home province.

The most senior was John Fraser, one of BC's most respected politicians of the twentieth century. Born in Yokohama, Japan, where his father worked as a lumber salesman, he was a corporate lawyer and former officer in the Canadian military, and was first elected in 1972. Fraser ran unsuccessfully for his party's leadership in 1976, was environment minister in Joe Clark's short-lived Progressive Conservative government in 1979–80, and had deep connections in Vancouver's business and legal communities. He was also an avid fly-fisherman who had earned considerable respect from BC's powerful environmental movement. For Mulroney it was a no-brainer: Fraser would be sworn in as minister of fisheries and oceans, and would be Mulroney's "political" or "senior" minister in BC—the key voice on recommending patronage appointments, working with the business community and interest groups, dealing with the party apparatus, and acting as a liaison between the federal and BC governments.

The other slam-dunk appointee was Pat Carney, who was born in Shanghai, China, where her father had been a policeman and later a public health official. After getting degrees in economics and public planning at the University of British Columbia, she became a successful business columnist in the 1960s with the *Vancouver Sun*, working alongside future Mulroney cabinet minister Barbara McDougall. She picked up a lifelong understanding of how media works and what journalists look for in an interview—a huge advantage over most of her colleagues. Carney brought to the table a valuable asset when Mulroney was making his cabinet choices: she had lived and worked in Yellowknife as an economic consultant after leaving journalism in 1970, and had a deep understanding of the oil and gas industry. First elected to the House of Commons in 1980, she served as the Tory opposition energy critic during the 1980–84 Parliament and excelled at eviscerating the Liberal government's National Energy Program. While the hot-tempered Carney was unpopular among some colleagues, the new prime minister couldn't resist the opportunity to promote a bright, prominent and colourful western Canadian woman into a cabinet that was overwhelmingly male. She became energy minister, with job number one being to rapidly dismantle the NEP.

The third and final BC minister to get a post, albeit at the "junior" level of minister of state for science, was Tom Siddon. Always well coiffed and smartly dressed, the earnest, decent and ever-smiling Siddon sometimes looked like a man who'd never escaped the 1950s. The suburban Vancouver MP and native of Drumheller, Alberta, was one of a minority of Joe Clark's caucus members who publicly endorsed Mulroney in the 1983 leadership contest, meaning there was a political debt to be repaid. Mulroney appreciated the fact that Siddon was one of his more moderate supporters, especially when the Clark forces alleged during the 1983 leadership campaign that only the party's hard-core right-wingers were backing Mulroney. In his memoirs, Mulroney, in challenging that criticism, singled out Siddon as one of the several "accomplished and considerate" MPs who lent him their support. And Siddon, despite his occasional gaffes, was one MP you could never insult with the line "He's no rocket scientist" because, well, that's pretty much what he was. When he graduated from the University of Alberta in 1963 he did so as the winner of a gold medal in mechanical engineering, and he later earned both a master's and a doctorate in aeroacoustics from the University of Toronto's Institute of Aerospace.

Waiting in the bullpen as the obvious candidate to get the call if one of the three faltered was Frank Oberle, another foreign-born BC politician. Since 1972 he had quietly represented a vast riding that included the BC interior city of Prince George. A logger and gold miner before heading into municipal and then federal politics, Oberle had a background that was equally fascinating and heartbreaking. He was born in Forchheim, Germany, in 1932 and nine years later his family's life was turned upside down when his father's factory was disassembled, moved to occupied Poland and reassembled as a munitions factory during the early stages of the Second World War. Oberle and the other young children of the factory workers were placed in a kind of glorified Cub Scout program called Jungvolk, a precursor to the more sinister Nazi Youth program for teens. As the youngest and smallest member of his scout troop the nine-year-old Oberle was assigned on one occasion the task of presenting Hitler with flowers, and actually shook the hand of the twentieth century's most infamous war criminal. When the Red Army overran Poland in 1944, young Oberle's parents went missing. Oberle, who would emigrate to Canada at age nineteen, survived on stolen eggs and grass as he walked with a friend more than eight hundred kilometres to his hometown in the Black Forest, where he was reunited with his parents.

Despite his lack of experience, St. Germain had clung to hopes he'd be named to Mulroney's first cabinet. "His ambition and competitiveness always trumped his insecurities," said Bob Ransford, who joined him in Ottawa for the days leading up to the swearing-in ceremony, St.

Germain glued to his Château Laurier Hotel phone in hopes of a call. The phone never rang, so on the day of the ceremony the two friends headed out for a meal down the street from the hotel. While walking back to the Château after lunch they eyeballed a convoy of limousines barrelling toward them down Wellington Street past Parliament Hill and taking the sharp left to Sussex Drive en route to the swearing-in ceremony at Rideau Hall.

"Well," St. Germain deadpanned to his friend, "I can now tell you that I'm definitely not going to be in the cabinet, because as you can see I'm not in one of those cars." Later that evening St. Germain and his wife went with Ransford to the elaborate reception to mark the event at the National Arts Centre and stopped to observe, with no shortage of envy, the ministers in their limos being dropped off at the NAC's red-carpet entrance. The new minister of national defence, Robert Coates, was already inside when his chief of staff arrived in a defence department car. The military driver, new to the job and assuming the chief of staff was in fact the minister, saluted the political staffer after opening his door. "See, Bobby," St. Germain cracked, "they would have been saluting you if I was a minister!"

Mulroney had other plans for St. Germain. It was obvious to any student of Canadian political history that his vast caucus was a precarious assemblage of characters. Mulroney had learned about caucus perils as a young party activist during former prime minister John Diefenbaker's tumultuous leadership, and then as an important party player during the eras of Diefenbaker's successors Robert Stanfield and Joe Clark:

> I came up in a generation where the caucus revolted on Diefenbaker. That was one of the main reasons he had to go. They did the same thing to Bob Stanfield. They did the same thing to Joe Clark. And I said long before that, "This is not going to happen to me. I'm going to devote my time and my concerns and my attention to it, but I'm also going to have a chairman of caucus who is just like me in terms of his understanding of interpersonal

relationships and how much this means." And remember that in that election we had gone from one seat in Quebec to fifty-eight, and we had gone from 12.9 percent of the popular vote to, what, 55 percent or something. So I needed somebody as well who spoke French, but who preferably was not from Quebec. So Gerry was the guy.

While Mulroney chose St. Germain as caucus chair primarily because of his people skills, the political optics certainly didn't hurt as the new prime minister sought to cement his party's presence in Quebec. In a flattering February 2, 1985, profile in the *Montreal Gazette*, St. Germain was described as a "symbolic" figure who was a key part of Mulroney's bid to "break [Quebec] from its history and become a home to the two founding nations," as well as end the party's image "as the hangman of Louis Riel." The article said St. Germain was "uniquely qualified to chair" Mulroney's massive caucus because he could identify with both the Quebec neophytes and the hard-line Conservative veterans in the West:

> None of these veterans question St. Germain's conservative credentials. He's paid his dues as an entrepreneur and peace officer. He introduced a private member's bill last November that would reinstitute capital punishment. At the same time, when the new party leader faced the Manitoba language issue that threatened to divide the caucus, caucus sources say St. Germain spoke out strongly in support of Mulroney's commitment to bilingualism. He [also] spoke in French for Tory candidates in Quebec in the campaign last summer.

A similarly positive piece had appeared in the August 9, 1984, edition of *La Presse*, the province's main French-language newspaper. Published just prior to the 1984 election, the article focused on St. Germain's efforts in Quebec to convince members of the public that there was a home for them in the party they once shunned. The *La*

Presse writer noted that during St. Germain's speaking tour, franco-phone audiences in Saint-Jean, Quebec, "stared with wide-open eyes at this MP from British Columbia speaking to them in the language of Molière." Jean Charest, then entering his first term in Parliament at age twenty-six, remembers St. Germain playing an important role prior to Mulroney's landslide win:

> Gerry had a special significance for the Quebec members because his election had happened after the Manitoba debate on language, where Mulroney had laid down a very important marker that would be significant for his tenure as prime minister on the issue of language for him and for the party. Gerry came from Manitoba, spoke French, was elected to the House of Commons and was someone who represented something that the party wanted to be. The Liberals were portraying our party as not tolerant, not being able to represent francophones outside of Quebec. And here was the personification of exactly the contrary, and what we aspired to be. So Gerry was a very significant person for me.

Mulroney had a multi-pronged approach to running the country, securing his party's support base and avoiding destructive internal feuds. He advanced a number of policies to appease every component of his vast coalition, from dismantling Trudeau's National Energy Program to bringing forward Quebec-friendly constitutional reforms. Mulroney was also incredibly active at a personal level in keeping his caucus united, especially during Wednesday morning caucus meetings when he would regularly calm frayed nerves, ease tensions and rally his troops. Even when Mulroney was at his most unpopular, MPs—many of whom went into the weekly gatherings frustrated with the party's direction—would still emerge energized from those meetings and eager to confide to reporters that "if only" Canadians could see him in that setting, they'd learn to like him. Mulroney was also famous for remembering MPs' birthdays and anniversaries, and for calling when one of them experienced a personal loss.

But there were still day-to-day issues to manage, egos to stroke, scandals to avoid and ambitions to rein in. And this is where St. Germain's critical role came into play. As far as the public was concerned, St. Germain's only visible role would be to bang a gavel and call unruly MPs to order as he presided over the regular Wednesday morning caucus meetings, just prior to shooing the media away. But the job was much more than that. His office, formerly located in a building that required a minibus ride to get to the House of Commons, was strategically relocated in Parliament Hill's Centre Block to allow him access to the largest number of government MPs. At times he operated like a street cop, walking hallways and cornering MPs to smoke out any signs of unrest. When a problem emerged he then operated like a firefighter, rushing to the office of a disgruntled MP and, if necessary, lining up a meeting with Mulroney to ensure that burning embers didn't ignite into something far worse. With his background in sales and policing, he had the perfect combination of empathy, charm and subtle physical intimidation that helped him keep potential renegades in line. "I think Gerry was as important to the success of the Mulroney government as any of the ministers in cabinet," Ray Castelli told the *Vancouver Sun* in a 2012 profile marking St. Germain's retirement from the Senate. "He was almost a father-confessor figure because he had Mulroney's ear and trust."

5
∞

Chief Executive Officer

S t. Germain had more face time with the prime minister than almost any MP except Michael Wilson, the finance minister, and Don Mazankowski, the deputy prime minister who was dubbed Mulroney's "Minister of Everything." St. Germain met with Mulroney most Tuesdays when MPs were in Ottawa, often at 24 Sussex Drive for lunch, and always on Wednesday mornings prior to the weekly caucus meetings. St. Germain said he used those meetings to urge Mulroney to get his ministers to pay attention to MPs, many of whom were upset about their inability to get the attention of ministers on pressing issues in their ridings. "These bloody ministers aren't responding to the MPs. This can't go on," St. Germain complained to Mulroney. "He said, 'Who are they?' And I said, 'I'm not going to blow the whistle on anybody. Everybody should have a second chance.' But I told him to speak at caucus. And the next week he said, 'I understand that some of my ministers haven't been responding to MPs. I want you to know that as of now Gerry's going to keep track of this, and you let him know when there's a problem and we'll fix this.'"

Over his next three years as caucus chairman, St. Germain played a key role in keeping the lid on some of Mulroney's most trouble-some MPs. Some of the problem-solving was of a Keystone Kops variety. Canadians who followed politics during Mulroney's first term are aware of a number of scandals and cabinet resignations, but less is known about the minor ethical problems involving some of the inexperienced rookie backbenchers—especially Quebec MPs who never imagined they'd get elected in 1984. One day early in Mulroney's mandate a nervous-looking Quebec MP came to St. Germain with a real estate problem.

"Well, what do you mean, a real estate problem?" asked St. Germain.

"Uh, it's a serious problem."

"Well there's nothing wrong with owning real estate."

"It's my tenants."

"What do you mean?"

"C'est un bordel en haut."

"There's nothing wrong with that. You can't control what women do in their house if they're paying you rent."

"Ce n'est pas ça, St. Germain. C'est la commission!"

The ex-cop didn't initially see the problem with an apartment owner whose tenants were engaged in prostitution, but was horrified to learn the MP was actually getting a cut from the women's work. While prostitution itself isn't illegal in Canada, the MP was clearly violating the Criminal Code prohibition against "living off the avails" of prosti-tution. St. Germain jabbed a finger at the MP's face and ordered him to sell the apartment immediately.

One memorable behind-the-scenes showdown took place in October 1987 when the House of Commons voted overwhelmingly in favour of the Meech Lake Accord, an enormously controversial package of constitutional amendments that included recognition of Quebec as a distinct society. The vote was 242 to 16 in favour, and among the dissidents were two PC members, Pat Nowlan of Nova Scotia and Dave Nickerson of the Northwest Territories. Four other Tories abstained. Yet one MP who was deeply hostile to the deal, and was known for his outrageous comments about Quebec and official bilingualism, wasn't there. The last thing Mulroney wanted was to look behind him to the distant backbenches during the Meech vote to see Dan McKenzie—the MP who once called black South Africans too "primitive" and "immoral" to govern themselves—at the vote. What outrageous comments might he make in the media scrum afterward that might tarnish Mulroney's shining moment? So Mulroney ordered St. Germain to find a way to make sure the Manitoba MP was nowhere near Ottawa on the day of the vote.

St. Germain summoned McKenzie to his office and told him he had to be in Washington, DC, on the day of the vote to represent Canada at a military-related event. McKenzie, the parliamentary secretary for veterans affairs, immediately replied that he knew Mulroney was trying to silence him: "You and that goddamned Mulroney, you're nothing but Frenchmen."

"Mulroney's not a Frenchman, he's an Irishman," St. Germain replied.

"Bullshit. I can't trust you goddamned frogs. You bastard, you're trying to get rid of me!"

"Are you kidding? You are not going to vote against the boss! You gotta go to Washington."

"You know, every time I go on one of these goddamn trips it costs me money."

"Really, how much?"

"I don't know, it always costs me a hundred or so."

So St. Germain reached into his pocket, pulled out $200 and told McKenzie the limo would pick him up at seven a.m. "And that was it. He just scooped up the money as I handed it to him, and I said, 'Get out of here!'" Another MP who was constantly knocking on St. Germain's door was Alberta MP Alex Kindy, a psychiatrist who was frustrated by Mulroney's approach on everything from capital punishment to abortion. St. Germain remembers the day early in Mulroney's first mandate and prior to the launch of steps to privatize Petro-Canada, the Crown corporation, when Kindy rose at the closed-door weekly caucus meeting to essentially taunt Mulroney for not moving quickly enough. Kindy was born in Poland to Ukrainian parents, and spoke with a heavy accent: "Prime Minister, your office is a shithouse compared to [Petro-Canada president] Bill Hopper's! He's got an office that looks like a palatial estate. You just got a shithouse!"

On another occasion, a right-wing Ontario MP named Bill Domm pulled St. Germain aside to list a litany of problems he had with Mulroney. Fed up, St. Germain got on the phone and called Mulroney's secretary. Then he said, "C'mon with me." Domm's face went a little ashen as he was led upstairs to Mulroney's office, and he started protesting that the visit might not be necessary. St. Germain insisted, brought him in, and the prime minister and the backbencher had a lengthy talk. A smiling Domm walked out with a bounce in his step, and then St. Germain went in and asked what horrible grievances the MP brought up. "And Mulroney just laughed and said, 'Not a goddamned thing.'"

Walking the "beat" in Parliament was just one part of the caucus chairman's role. He also had to plan for, and then manage, the unruly weekly meeting of up to 211 MPs. Caucus members could be particularly grumpy on any given week if the government was in trouble, or if ministers weren't giving them the time of day to assist them in their ridings. St. Germain had to act as a meeting planner, finding out what the issues were and making sure Mulroney was ready with strong answers. He was also a choreographer: it was up to him to decide who got to speak and when their time was up. Charest said St. Germain was a maestro:

He had a quiet sense of authority. Maybe it had to do with him being a cop before. He wasn't loud, and he had a great sense of humour and timing, because you have to be an actor. The caucus chair is the arbiter; he takes the temperature of the room. There are caucus meetings that can be quite tense, and there are regional rivalries. When do you cut off someone? When do you intervene to say, "You know, we have talked about this long enough, we need to move on." It requires a deft hand in terms of managing people.

One of St. Germain's most sensitive assignments was to help BC caucus colleague John Fraser become the first elected speaker in Canadian history. The speaker's job is one of the most prestigious and sought-after positions in Ottawa, lording over all MPs including the prime minister in the House of Commons, and scolding them for bad behaviour. The speaker also gets extra salary, a limousine and driver, and is treated like royalty with staff on Parliament Hill and a lavish office with a well-stocked liquor cabinet. Another perk is an official residence called "the Farm," the former country estate of Prime Minister William Lyon Mackenzie King located across the river in Quebec's gorgeous Gatineau Hills.

On the one-year anniversary of the 1984 swearing-in, the CBC's program *The Fifth Estate* broke the "tainted tuna" story—a sensational report disclosing that John Fraser approved the bulk sale and shipment of canned tuna produced at the StarKist company's plant in St. Andrews, New Brunswick, even though federal inspectors had declared it "unfit for human consumption." Fraser, an empathetic man who always wore his heart on his sleeve, was under tremendous pressure from both the company and New Brunswick premier Richard Hatfield, as well as local Tory MPs, to keep the plant open. They argued that the inspectors were too severe and that the tuna was safe to consume. Fraser, fearful of devastating job losses in a region with few other major employers, agreed and overruled his inspectors. The story was leaked and Fraser was forced to resign.

St. Germain remembers going to Mulroney to discuss the huge loss for the party on the west coast as a result of Fraser's resignation. "I said this guy has a real presence in BC—he is one of the symbols of conservatism out there," St. Germain recalled telling Mulroney. "So he said, 'We've got to do something for him. Ask him about the position of Speaker of the House.'" St. Germain approached Fraser, who said he wasn't interested and added, "I can't win it anyway." Fraser's ability to speak French was limited, and this was to be the first time in Canadian history that a speaker was to be chosen by secret ballot rather than be appointed by the prime minister. It was widely assumed that the bilingual Marcel Danis—the choice of former prime minister Joe Clark—would get the job.

"So then in the summer Mulroney called me and said, 'You gotta find Fraser and talk him into it, because we gotta get his credibility back in BC.'" St. Germain headed up to the Chilcotin region in the BC interior, where Fraser was fly-fishing, and persuaded him that if he ran he would get the job, replacing John Bosley. "I told him that we would see to it that he won." On the day of the vote in late September 1986, Mulroney confidently told St. Germain that everything was in order. Mulroney said, "I talked to Joe and he wants Danis to run on the first ballot, and he will then ask him to withdraw." Shortly thereafter, there was panic: the first ballot took place and Danis made it clear he was keeping his name on the ballot. St. Germain rushed upstairs to Mulroney's fourth-floor office.

"What's happening?" he asked. "You told me, Prime Minister, that he will pull out. What the hell is happening?"

"You get down there and fix it," Mulroney replied.

"Fix what? This guy could win it if all the Quebec MPs go with him."

"Get your ass down there and fix it."

"I'm going to have to make some deals."

A long-time Mulroney aide was in the room at the time and later told St. Germain, "I've never seen a guy argue with the prime minister." St. Germain rushed back down to the House of Commons lobby and cornered Pierre Cadieux and Pierre Blais, the two senior Quebec MPs viewed as having the ability to control the Quebec caucus's vote. "Boys, you're not voting for Marcel Danis!"

"What do you mean? He's our colleague from Quebec!"

"Boys, this is the way it is. You go talk to your people and turn it around."

St. Germain had a similar conversation with Ontario supporters of Doug Lewis, who was also running for the speaker's job. No specific reward was on offer. "But I insinuated there would be good things coming their way." While Cadieux was already in cabinet, Blais and

Lewis, both articulate and media-savvy lawyers, were named junior ministers a year later. St. Germain would later say both men were deserving of their promotions regardless of any special considerations: "They were valid guys."

Reflecting on these times, Mulroney would have trouble identifying a single incident where St. Germain pulled an iron out of the fire, because such events happened so regularly—and often without him knowing the fire had even existed. "This was a regular occurrence. This was not something that he did once or twice," he said. "Gerry played a major diplomatic role on my behalf. He was kind of like a chief executive officer of a vital part of our operation." Castelli said St. Germain performed a remarkable feat in preventing any caucus defections during the first term:

> I think Gerry did an incredibly effective job of identifying when somebody was at risk, by being able to read them and sit down

Mulroney cracks up as St. Germain, chairman of the vast Progressive Conservative caucus at the time, regales MPs with his masterful story-telling skills. To Mulroney's right is Tory whip Chuck Cook, while to St. Germain's left are deputy leader Erik Nielsen and House leader Ray Hnatyshyn. SCOTT GRANT

with them and project his proximity to the PM and soothe whatever that wound was, and keeping people in line and figuring out what they needed. That's the beauty of Gerry St. Germain. We all knew shit was happening and people were unhappy, but somehow he found a way to keep the lid on it, particularly with the Quebec guys. And Gerry has a sort of enforcer look. People saw him as an extension of the prime minister when they were talking to Gerry. If they had a frustration, he would draw it out of them and find a way to fix the problem.

In only the first year of Mulroney's tenure, there had been several cabinet-level resignations in a government that promised to end Liberal corruption. Every Tory slip—whether major or minor—triggered a cacophonous response led by the hyper-aggressive Liberal "Rat Pack" of shrill MPs like Sheila Copps and John Nunziata. But a more serious problem was slowly but assuredly eroding the party like rust on an abandoned bike. Many in the party, including people who were publicly viewed as devout loyalists, were troubled by Mulroney's apparent drift toward the political centre. St. Germain's personal journals of that period show that he shared some of the frustrations of grumbling MPs during a time when a second consecutive Tory win didn't seem at all likely.

During the 1984–88 term, Mulroney made a number of moves that generated positive headlines but upset the party's core voters. Among these decisions was legislation to bring forward a costly national daycare strategy, though the bill died on the order paper when the 1988 election was called. Another was Mulroney's decision to toughen Trudeau's 1969 Official Languages Act, which pleased Quebec MPs but triggered an internal caucus revolt involving mainly MPs from Ontario and the West. Mulroney's 1984 decision to name former Ontario NDP leader Stephen Lewis as Canada's ambassador to the United Nations, while cheered by Canadians who wouldn't dream of voting Tory, left a bitter taste throughout the party. "We made him an international star," St. Germain scribbled into his journal.

But two policy decisions stand out. During the 1984 campaign the Liberals tried to frighten Canadians by accusing Mulroney of having a hidden agenda to impose cuts to—or perhaps even "Americanize"— Canada's public health care system. Mulroney was never hesitant to use rhetorical excess when a simple "No, that won't happen" would suffice, so after a string of Liberal attacks and PC denials Mulroney decided to describe Medicare as a "sacred trust." A Progressive Conservative government would "vigorously defend the integrity of universal health care," he declared during the 1984 campaign.

That promise would come back to bite Mulroney a year later when finance minister Michael Wilson introduced a budget intended to satisfy the concerns of many Canadians—and especially bedrock Tory supporters—who believed in small government, low taxes and a return to balanced budgets after the Pierre Trudeau era. One of the measures in the May 23, 1985, budget was to partly remove inflation protection from Canadian pensions, which triggered a torrent of protests led by the Liberal Rat Pack, declaring Mulroney had broken his "sacred trust" vow. At a Parliament Hill protest Mulroney tried to engage a sixty-three-year-old pensioner named Solange Denis, who was not about to succumb to his Irish charm. While TV cameras were rolling, she declared, "You lied to us. You made us vote for you and then it's goodbye, Charlie Brown!" That line then became an integral part of a narrative that Mulroney was a threat to all social programs, and not just health care.

"It was a typical press gallery distortion," Mulroney would later fume to author Peter Newman. Wilson and many in caucus continued to support the measure despite the criticism. But Mulroney was already wobbly when confronted by Denis, and the confrontation led to capitulation. "If the notion of fairness is offended we're going to try to take a serious look at that because it's important," he said. The subsequent reversal didn't just infuriate the right-wing caucus members St. Germain was assigned to keep happy, but also then external affairs minister Joe Clark, Mulroney's long-time rival. Clark, according to Newman's *The Secret Mulroney Tapes*, sent a private memo to Mulroney warning him to avoid encouraging the growing view that he "undercuts" his cabinet colleagues. The issue is also mentioned a number of times in St. Germain's diary as a source of caucus frustration.

The second misstep, and one that played a direct role in ultimately destroying the PC Party, took place the following year. On October 31, 1986, the Mulroney government announced that a lucrative maintenance contract for CF-18 fighter jets would be awarded to Montreal's Canadair. In doing so Mulroney overruled the recommendation made by an independent panel assembled to evaluate competitive bids. That panel had determined that Bristol Aerospace of Winnipeg had submitted a bid that was both technically superior and a better deal for taxpayers.

St. Germain wasn't part of the decision, but attended a meeting with Mulroney and a number of senior government and party officials to be briefed on how to sell it to a skeptical public. This group included Norman Atkins, who ran Mulroney's 1984 and 1988 election campaigns. Atkins was part of the "Big Blue Machine" political apparatus in Ontario, behind one of the most successful premiers in Canadian history, Bill Davis. Due to his suspicion of big city "suits" and eastern elites schooled at Upper Canada College and Osgoode Hall, St. Germain held a deep resentment toward the "BBM," as he referred to the Big Blue Machine in his journals. But on that day both he and Atkins were in agreement that the prime minister should not to go ahead with the CF-18 decision. They feared the blatant show of favouritism toward Quebec could cause immeasurable damage in the West. "It's not often that I agreed with Norm Atkins, but we were together on that. We said to Mulroney, 'Don't do it.'"

But Mulroney went ahead, and the decision set the wheels in motion for Preston Manning, the obscure, squeaky-voiced son of one-time Alberta premier-preacher Ernest Manning. Both father and son had for years advanced the notion that Canada needed a truly right-of-centre party that married both social and fiscal conservatism. As the furor erupted in western Canada, Preston Manning started calling around to various contacts who were concerned about the direction Mulroney was taking the country. "It's time," Manning told one of them, future Alberta MP Bob Mills. In 1993 Mills was one of the fifty-two MPs who were elected for Manning's Reform Party in an election that reduced the federal Progressive Conservatives into a two-seat rump. "I spent a lot of time with the Reform guys after they got in," St. Germain later recalled. "The majority of them say it was the CF-18 that got them into politics. That was the straw that broke the camel's back."

For some reason St. Germain, who kept meticulous handwritten notes during his term as PC Party president from 1989 to 1995, left for the archives only one journal from his time as caucus chairman. But that diary, which starts on January 28, 1987, and ends in the fall that same year, reflects the deep concerns he and many Tories felt that year. It was a time when many Canadians, and not just grumbling Conservative backbenchers, were looking to replace Mulroney after more than two years of scandals and a string of forced and unforced errors. Misgivings about Turner's leadership skills, however, resulted in Canadians contemplating a radical step. A shocking party preference poll released in early May 1987 had the NDP, for the first time in Canadian history, in first place with 37-percent support. Turner's Liberals were next at 36 percent, while the Tories were at 25—exactly half their total in 1984. The resulting slide in morale had MPs constantly knocking on St. Germain's door.

In his first entry, on January 28, 1987, he referred to the frustration he and other MPs had with cabinet ministers who were both botching their files and failing to listen to MPs. He made a reference to the Quebec caucus and underlined the names Roch La Salle and Marcel Masse. The former was a long-time Quebec MP, and one of the few who had previously won a seat under Clark's leadership. The previous month La Salle had fired two aides because of their criminal backgrounds. Masse, meanwhile, was the elitist communications minister who publicly expressed concern in 1986 that Mulroney's initiative to strike a free trade deal would harm Canada's culture industries. "How far can these people go without being thrown out of cabinet?" St. Germain asked himself. La Salle would resign from cabinet only a few weeks later over bribery and conflict-of-interest allegations, while Masse would resign from cabinet in 1987 after the RCMP began investigating allegations of campaign overspending (he was eventually cleared and returned to cabinet).

St. Germain also wrote that ordinary Quebec MPs were being ignored by cabinet ministers and "overrun" by unelected political organizers. He noted that the national caucus was "polarized" along regional lines—an obvious reference to the aftermath of the CF-18 decision, which Quebec MPs like Masse vigorously defended. St. Germain then listed off a number of Mulroney initiatives that had drawn controversy, including the launching of a commission of inquiry into Nazi war criminals in Canada, contemplating legislation to protect the rights of homosexuals and offering compensation to Japanese-Canadians interned during the Second World War. "Why did the Liberals leave such issues alone? Because politically they're divisive and you can't win." He added that the "general feeling" in caucus was that the government wouldn't have so many problems if MPs had been listened to before decisions were made.

He suggested that unless there was imminent change, some MPs would bolt: "The general attitude is we have three or four weeks to change direction. Most are saying, 'If we don't count so be it. Tell us and we will just go home.'" He complained again of ministers ignoring MPs, singling out Masse. "His total ignorance of caucus has been damaging." Speaking more broadly, he expressed concern about his government's drift. "We must do something significant that shows decisiveness and leadership to bolster PM's image," he wrote. "We must take action to re-establish support with our traditional conservative base." St. Germain also complained about senior ministers speaking out publicly. "We are [perceived as] a bunch of bunglers. It is one thing to have Alex Kindy or Pat Nowlan [two outspoken dissidents] making conflicting statements. However, when we have Marcel Masses, Jake Epps and John Crosbies at odds with each other, or with the government, how do you expect me to keep my caucus in line? And ministers are travelling all over the bloody world—Clark, Masse, etc. [Meanwhile] the local scene is a shambles." He complained that neither of Mulroney's top rivals for the leadership, Clark and Crosbie, "think of the PM's well-being. They just truck along."

While St. Germain bided his time as caucus chairman, his path toward cabinet slowly but gradually became clearer. That process had begun with Fraser's resignation from cabinet in 1985. Pat Carney became political minister for BC and Tom Siddon moved to fisheries. Still, no space had been created for St. Germain because the more experienced Frank Oberle slipped into the vacated junior science portfolio. In June 1986 Carney, who by then had completed the NEP demolition, was shuffled to international trade with a mandate to strike a historic free trade deal with the US. "Now you watch Pat Carney go," Mulroney boasted. "She's got the ball and you just watch her run." Siddon, who was kept in fisheries, was perceived as a "bit

Brian Mulroney, Margaret and Gerry St. Germain, and Mila Mulroney attend a summer party in 1986 for MPs at 24 Sussex Drive, the official residence of Canada's prime ministers. St. Germain's close personal as well as professional relationship with Mulroney played a crucial role in his political success. BILL MCCARTHY

of a bumbler" due to his difficulty with the media, according to Ray Castelli.

In fairness, Siddon and his government faced enormous public pressure in Newfoundland, where the cod fishing industry refused to accept warnings from federal scientists that over-fishing could destroy that fishery. Every day in the House of Commons, Liberals Brian Tobin and George Baker hammered the government over cutting cod allocations, which in turn led to capitulation by Mulroney's senior Newfoundland minister, Crosbie. "Well-intentioned, fair-minded and thoughtful, Siddon was from day one outmuscled by a trio of large-lunged political bulldozers: Crosbie, Tobin and Baker," Alex Rose, author of the 2008 book *Who Killed the Grand Banks: The Untold Story Behind the Decimation of One of the World's Greatest Natural Resources*, recalled in April 2016. "This was a time when politics utterly trumped science, resulting in the catastrophic collapse of the Grand Banks cod. DFO scientists were silenced, sidelined or fired. The once world-respected agency had become intellectually bankrupt, as it remains to this day. Siddon didn't stand a chance."

Referring to a rumoured cabinet shuffle, St. Germain indicated in his journal that he urged Mulroney to "clean house" to deal with ministers who misbehaved or ignored MPs, with both those last two words underlined twice. "As PM you are saying that the ministers will be brought to task. However, nothing is done. My people are saying 'We have to toe the party line but Crosbie can challenge a government?'" While St. Germain doesn't remember the particular transgression by the Newfoundland minister, he does recall Crosbie angering the caucus's right-wingers in 1986. A year earlier a parliamentary subcommittee on equality rights, after cross-country hearings heavily attended by gay and lesbian rights groups, recommended that the Canadian Human Rights Act be amended to include sexual orientation as prohibited grounds for discrimination. On March 4, 1986, Crosbie told the House of Commons that the government would "take whatever measures are necessary to ensure that sexual orientation is a prohibited ground of discrimination in relation to all areas of federal jurisdiction." This was never going to fly in a Tory caucus with a powerful social conservative wing, and in fact it wasn't until 2016 that Conservatives agreed at a convention to accept the reality of same-sex marriage in Canada.

Another issue that drove the so-called "dinosaurs" bonkers was Mulroney's insistence that the federal Parliament amend, and toughen, Trudeau's 1969 Official Languages Act. Trudeau's original bill, which gave French and English equal status in the federal Parliament, the federal courts and "throughout the federal government system," needed updating in order to comply with the 1982 Charter of Rights and Freedoms. But anglophone Tory MPs, responding to complaints that first Trudeau and now Mulroney were shoving "French down our throats," publicly resisted the effort and waged a noisy campaign in hopes of watering the measures down. "Areas of irritation must be dealt with," St. Germain wrote on February 2, 1987. "Upcoming items [like] official languages must be handled better. The same for [homosexual] equality rights." And repeating a mantra throughout his journals, he says cabinet had to "do less but do it better"—a reference to the chaotic approach Mulroney's first administration took in seeming to want to resolve all of Canada's problems instantaneously.

In notes prepared for one of his many meetings with Mulroney, he attempted to give a broad-brush characterization of the criticisms from within the party: "Your image is one that you are no different than Trudeau. We are perceived as being led left of centre. Our voters are saying they thought they elected a right-of-centre party, and that is the way they want to be governed by us." The next day, in a veiled criticism of Mulroney's closest advisers, he wrote, "Political bungling is killing us. Morale is affected. We are being [portrayed] as incompetent managers. [It's] time to tell you the truth. You are not being told the truth." In terms of patronage and cronyism—the idea that the government was rewarding its friends with largesse—"we look worse than the Trudeau Liberals."

On April 8, 1987, in one of his many warnings of the impending threat from Manning's Reform Party, St. Germain noted the nervousness over Mulroney's disciplining of outspoken Alberta MP David Kilgour, who had criticized his own government for ethics breaches and poor treatment of western Canada. There was fear at the time that Kilgour might quit politics, forcing a by-election that Reform could very well win. "Alberta [MPs] do not want to lose Kilgour because they do not want a by-election at this time," he wrote.

Later that month, Mulroney struck a unanimous deal with all ten provincial premiers to endorse the Meech Lake Accord, which would among other things recognize in the constitution that Quebec is a distinct society within Canada. The agreement, described as essentially symbolic by its supporters in English-speaking Canada and portrayed as a potentially powerful tool by Quebec Liberal premier Robert Bourassa, was initially popular. Canadians seemed relieved that the national unity issue had apparently been resolved. But enthusiasm for the deal started to slide due to growing criticism from people like Pierre Elliott Trudeau. St. Germain says today that he still supports the principles behind Meech, but at the time warned Mulroney that he could boost Meech's chances of success by backing off on the plan to amend the Official Languages Act. "The feeling is that the [languages bill] could jeopardize [Meech] if it is brought forward at this time."

Things remained grim in early September as polls continued to show the Tories in third place. St. Germain wrote that he was urging the party to deal with its fading support in western Canada by pushing for the reform or abolition of the Senate. "This was suggested as a diversionary tactic to focus attention away from the PM's image . . . caucus not facing the real issue of the PM's image. Issues are not the situation we must deal with . . . the reason for his unpopularity, true reason, is the perception he is untrustworthy . . . Lifestyle is too presidential and lavish Gucci shoes."

The journal ended in November 1987 with a comment about the failure of the Western Diversification Program, an economic initiative intended to convince western Canadians that the government cared about them. He wrote that it was "not working" due to excessive expectations. That was a bit of an understatement. The program was hailed by the government in 1985 as a half-billion-dollar means of diversifying the economy away from natural resources. Subsequent budgets, however, showed that the program was far more modest in its ambitions than the Atlantic Canada Opportunities Agency, which acted as a funnel for federal dollars to the east coast. St. Germain, who would later be accused by aide John Baldwin of sometimes being overly pessimistic, didn't mention free trade much in these journal entries. But the signing of the historic Canada–US Free Trade Agreement in October 1987, at around the time St. Germain's journal entries ended, turned out to be one of the most brilliant strategic plays by a prime minister in the twentieth century.

6

∞

The Boss Wants to See You

As the PCs began the final year of their mandate in 1988, Mulroney had a new chief of staff, Derek Burney, who had played a key role the previous year in nailing down the Canada–US trade deal. The free trade issue was critical in rallying both pillars of Mulroney's government: the westerners who always championed greater access to US markets, and Quebec nationalists who saw the deal as a way to reduce the province's dependence on the Ontario market. "Mulroney instinctively saw that free trade offered him a ticket to political salvation," wrote John Duffy in *Fights of Our Lives*. "His intuitive stroke of genius was to understand the opportunity he could seize by embracing this risky policy." The beauty of the deal was that it played to Mulroney's portrayal of himself as a strong, decisive and daring leader, in contrast to a Liberal opponent whose fumbles were so consistent that a 1988 book on John Turner's time in office, by Greg Weston, was called *Reign of Error*.

While the Tories were beginning to rebound heading into that autumn election, Mulroney had a particular problem in BC. The province at the time was ruled by the Social Credit Party, more popularly known as the Socreds, under charismatic but erratic premier Bill Vander Zalm. A populist and social conservative, "the Zalm" lived in a theme park called Fantasy Gardens, leading many pundits to dub his administration "Fantasyland." He was leading a party that like its successor, the BC Liberal Party, was a coalition of federal Conservatives and Liberals united under the singular goal of keeping the NDP from forming government. The free-enterprise Socreds, therefore, were a natural ally for Mulroney despite the presence of federal Liberal supporters in the provincial party.

But there was a bit of a culture clash between the two governments that started at the top. Vander Zalm was a simple man, an immigrant from the Netherlands who survived Nazi Germany's brutal occupation of his country as a child and arrived in Canada as a young teenager. After finishing high school he went into the tulip and gardening business, making flowers his lifelong career outside politics. Bob Ransford, who served as Vander Zalm's executive assistant between October 1986 and mid-1988, said Vander Zalm had a difficult relationship with Mulroney. For instance, the BC premier resented the way Mulroney pressured him to agree to the Meech Lake Accord in 1987. "He didn't like his high style," Ransford said, recalling the evening when the premier returned from the Meech negotiations and walked into his office. "Do you really think this is a good deal?" Ransford asked Vander Zalm.

"Just between you and me: no, I don't."

"Well, why did you support it?"

"It felt like I was going to be the odd man out and I didn't want to be the odd man out. And Mulroney put so much pressure on us."

While Meech was initially popular among a large portion of Canadians who were relieved Quebec was finally in the constitutional fold, it didn't last. Trudeau came out of retirement to attack the deal, and key opponents were emerging at the provincial level—provincial Liberal leaders Clyde Wells in Newfoundland and Frank McKenna in New Brunswick, and Progressive Conservative premier Gary Filmon in Manitoba. Any impression that Quebec was getting special treatment was never going to go down well in BC, where there was a long-standing antipathy toward the province. "As people turned against it, so did Vander Zalm," said one senior BC government insider. "Many were whispering in his ear from the right who latently thought it a concession to Quebec and therefore not in BC's traditional interests. So it became a struggle between us on the inside, trying to hold firm to our agreement, and those on the outside who were against it."

Vander Zalm's anxieties over Meech were taking place while his own government was starting to sputter. His Socreds won by a land-slide in the 1986 election, riding the euphoria of his own popularity and a spectacularly successful Expo 86, which lifted BC's spirits and self-confidence. But things started to unravel in January 1988 after a Supreme Court of Canada decision struck down Canada's abortion law. The premier triggered a huge controversy by launching an initiative to defund abortions except in life-threatening situations. Asked about pregnancies arising from rape and incest, Vander Zalm covered his ears: "Don't ask me those questions. I don't want to hear them." One of his MLAs, future Tory prime minister Kim Campbell, would publicly break from her leader. Fumbling the abortion file, *Vancouver Sun* columnist Vaughn Palmer noted, "started the party on the road to ruin."

One of the ways Vander Zalm chose to deal with his slipping popularity was to look to a tried-and-true political tool for BC premiers dating back to the former colony's entry into Confederation in 1871: "fed-bashing." While he didn't move to rescind his legislature's support for Meech prior to the accord's death in 1990, he found a different way to distract voters away from his own growing problems. "He wanted to show his BC populist roots so he started making statements against Ottawa," said the former senior government insider. "He wanted to have it both ways."

In March 1988 Vander Zalm seemed to be trying to settle a score with an unusual Throne Speech. It complained bitterly that Victoria had supported both Meech and the free trade negotiations (as if a free-enterprise government like Social Credit wouldn't back greater

Canada–US business activity) but wasn't getting anything in return. "My government has been patient, but we have seen too many inequities and the allocation of too many grants, subsidies and federal resources to central and eastern Canada," said Lieutenant Governor Bob Rogers, speaking on behalf of the Socred government. "The result has been a deepening feeling of alienation in our Pacific region. For too long, British Columbia has been out of sight and out of mind of successive federal governments. Even now, that vision of western Canada appears to encompass only Prairie grain and Alberta energy."

BC was trying to get hundreds of millions of dollars for a natural gas pipeline to Vancouver Island and a new particle accelerator at the University of BC's TRIUMF facility. Remarkably, there seemed to be a veiled threat in the Throne Speech that Canada could have a new problem child of Confederation along with Quebec: "We will monitor and evaluate British Columbia's standing within the federal system." According to *Vancouver Sun* columnist Vaughn Palmer, Vander Zalm went too far: "I've reviewed throne speeches back to 1950 and couldn't find a single outburst of fed-bashing as extensive, as aggressive, as just plain rude as what we heard in Victoria yesterday."

The speech came at a time when the Mulroney government had been hearing steady complaints from Victoria that the province was not only not getting its fair share of the spoils, but that the province's MPs in Ottawa were neither accessible nor delivering the goods. According to a former insider, the latter situation developed after Fraser lost his cabinet post and Carney emerged as the senior minister. "When Carney was left on her own I think things degenerated . . . there was not much effort on Carney's side to develop real relationships with the Socreds." Carney likely cemented that view in Victoria when she told the *Vancouver Sun* editorial board that the 1988 Throne Speech was a "petulant and very whiny" document.

Things got so tense after the Throne Speech that Mulroney, at Vander Zalm's request, set up a federal–provincial "Council of Ministers" to deal with BC issues. As a sad commentary on the mood at the time, Alberta minister Don Mazankowski was designated the lead minister on the federal side. "And it is my understanding this was the result of Vander Zalm's concerns about having an effective senior minister take the lead on the federal side," said Doug Eyford, a former Manzankowsi aide who worked in the government's regional office in Vancouver during the period. "I recall Vander Zalm was complaining publicly that BC wasn't getting its fair share from Confederation, and he repeatedly delivered that message to Mulroney." Carney, Siddon and Oberle sat on the federal side of the table while Grace McCarthy, Stephen Rogers and Brian Smith were the provincial members. St. Germain, not in cabinet at that point, was named the federal caucus liaison.

It so happened that these tensions were taking place while federal Tories in BC were growing anxious about the coming election and the apparent surge in support for the NDP. Ray Castelli, then the lead Tory field organizer in the province, sent an urgent message to his bosses in Ottawa about the need to bring in St. Germain. "I said, 'Look, we're going to be screwed in BC. Carney's a smart lady and she definitely knows the trade file, but she has no business running the political side of government.'" He also felt that St. Germain would be able to smooth over the tensions with the Vander Zalm government. "Vander Zalm liked Gerry because he could talk at Vander Zalm's level." Castelli and others started advocating for a "split" regional minister, with Carney remaining the BC representative on the priorities and planning committee but St. Germain taking over the political job and federal–provincial relations. "We needed to have a specific political minister in the run-up to the election because we needed to raise money. We needed to recruit candidates and set up nomination meetings and policy conferences," according to Castelli. Siddon was "up to his ears" on fisheries matters and while Mulroney liked him, "he didn't trust his political instincts." Oberle's base in distant Prince George was impractical. "The party needed attention, and there was really nobody else but Gerry."

Ransford, who worked in both governments and would go on to consider himself good friends with both St. Germain and Carney, said the change was needed due to a personality clash between Vander Zalm and Carney. "Carney was never close to him. I recall him dealing with her on the softwood lumber dispute and he was always cordial with her, but he felt she was a bit of a bully and always abrupt." The late David Poole, Vander Zalm's principal secretary, "probably dealt with her more and he used to joke with me about her abrupt way." There are questions today about who held the actual title of senior or political minister, or whether they were split. But most observers say the reality on the ground was clear. "Gerry may not have been officially a co-regional minister, but he played a significant role communicating with Zalm and Poole, often through me," Ransford said.

Mulroney's memory is also clear. In a 2016 interview he stated that St. Germain was promoted to political minister in 1988 in order to deal with a situation that needed fixing. "It was very vigorous out there and Gerry was a business guy and he had a good relationship with Vander Zalm. Moreover, there was also the fact that the political apparatus of the party wanted more sensitive representation. Carney had been looking after it as the senior BC minister and it was time for a change." Asked if in fact there was a split senior role between Carney and St. Germain, he replied in the negative: "It was me saying to Gerry that he was my senior political minister—okay?—and everybody knowing it in my office."

St. Germain, meanwhile, had started to lobby for a promotion heading into the first of two 1988 cabinet shuffles that year. "Gerry had done a great job in caucus, and on a couple of occasions he had staff express frustrations to me about him being behind the scenes doing all this work trying to keep caucus together and keeping things from falling apart, and doing all this extra party work in BC, and meanwhile all these cabinet ministers are doing fuck all," Castelli recalled. "I think when Gerry went into caucus, he didn't really aspire to be a cabinet minister. I think he was very proud about being the caucus chair. Maybe he didn't feel like he had the policy depth, and a lot of people questioned whether he did or not. Nobody expected him to be a minister. But I believe Gerry started looking at the cabinet after two or three years of getting more confident and being close to Mulroney, and seeing minister after minister after minister screw up and resign, he decided he was ready."

On Wednesday, March 30, St. Germain finally got the call that would confirm all expectations that he was a player on the rise. "The boss wants to see you," Derek Burney informed him. St. Germain's heart began to race. He was in his basement-level office on Parliament Hill's Centre Block when he got the call from the second most powerful man in Ottawa. Years later Burney wouldn't remember this particular moment, as he made many calls like it. But he said St. Germain was rightly being rewarded because he, unlike more than a few of his colleagues, was "a doer, not a whiner":

> What I can say is that Mr. Mulroney did value highly Gerry's political judgment on BC issues, more so than some others! For me, the caucus had several "mavericks" who required inordinate attention, and some who were consistently attentive to the government's agenda. Gerry fit the latter category to a "T" and was inevitably a pleasure to deal with, meaning he could be relied upon to work for solutions and not come with problems. That is undoubtedly what earned him a cabinet appointment.

St. Germain took a few deep breaths after his brief phone conversation with Burney, then put on his overcoat to shield him from the cool breeze on that day in late March of 1988. He exited through Centre Block's lower-level entrance, then walked briskly along the promenade past a few tourists milling about near the Centennial Flame. He walked down the sidewalk to Wellington Street, named after one of Britain's greatest military heroes, and turned left and crossed the street to enter the Langevin Block, the headquarters of the prime minister and his staff, and location of the Privy Council Office—the heart of the federal bureaucracy. Only vaguely aware at the time of his aboriginal roots, St. Germain had no idea the building facing the vast lawn in front of Centre Block was named after Hector Langevin, a Father of

Confederation. Langevin, a Quebec-based Conservative minister, was one of the architects of Canada's residential school system. In 1885 Langevin tried unsuccessfully to persuade Prime Minister John A. Macdonald to block the hanging of Louis Riel.

St. Germain was led up to Mulroney's second-floor office, which overlooked the Parliament buildings, and was greeted by a prime minister offering him three choices—to be the minister of either fisheries or Indian affairs, or to serve as junior minister of transport under senior minister Benoît Bouchard. The first two were full cabinet positions, coming with a higher salary and much larger staffs. But both portfolios had historically been political death traps due to often hostile constituencies and impossibly difficult mandates. The third option was a junior cabinet position as minister of state in an area where he had some expertise. So St. Germain, the former military and commercial pilot, grabbed it. "And Mulroney said, 'Why that?' I said, 'The other two are tough, and I haven't got experience as a cabinet minister. Transport would be an excellent opportunity.'"

St. Germain knew he would be working under Benoît Bouchard, a Mulroney favourite and a popular and charming former high school teacher from Roberval, in the heart of Quebec's very sovereigntist Saguenay–Lac St-Jean region. St. Germain immediately volunteered to focus on the implementation of a 1984 campaign promise that was dragging along at a snail's pace—the transfer of airport operational management to local authorities. "You should do that," Mulroney responded. "We promised we would do that and it hasn't happened and we've gone through a couple of ministers." So after checking with Bouchard, St. Germain planned to put the issue at the top of his agenda in his first meeting with his top bureaucrats.

The announcement the following day that St. Germain would be the junior transport minister was accompanied only by the vague indication that he would be helping Pat Carney prepare for the coming election. At a news conference Carney dismissed a reporter's suggestion that the shuffle was in response to Vander Zalm's frustrations over BC not getting its fair share. But it was clear among those on the inside that his role was a little bigger than assisting Carney. Vander Zalm didn't make a secret of his delight, telling the *Vancouver Sun* after the shuffle that St. Germain "was the one person that we've always been able to get through to if there was a bit of a hang-up on anything." In 2016 the ex-premier would say he couldn't remember specific details, only that there had been issues with Carney: "Gerry was extremely good, we could always go back to Gerry. He listened and responded. I think that was a problem back then, getting a response."

Carney didn't appreciate the characterization of herself as an inaccessible minister. She also didn't appreciate the sources of the criticism. She was never a fan of social conservatives like Vander Zalm and St. Germain, with a particular dislike for St. Germain. "I am a Red Tory and he is NOT," she declared in a 2016 email. When Carney was a senator in 1996, she urged the party to shut the door and click off the lights in response to the emergence of the Reform Party. "I'm glad to get rid of the right," Carney said at a time when her party was left with two

Mulroney chats with St. Germain after naming him to cabinet in 1988. The Tories were in deep political trouble prior to that year's election, so Mulroney assigned St. Germain the task of smoothing over relations with the erratic Social Credit government led by Bill Vander Zalm, who lived in a theme park called Fantasy Gardens. BILL MCCARTHY

seats in the House of Commons to Reform's fifty-two. "I sat in caucuses for years with the right, arguing about the metric system, arguing about social policies, arguing about French on cereal boxes. I can't begin to tell you the relief I have as a Conservative that the right wing split off and formed Reform. And there are a lot of Conservatives like me."

In her 2016 email, Carney responded angrily to the assertion that St. Germain's 1988 ascendancy was connected to concerns expressed by federal and provincial party officials about her performance. She also launched a personal attack on St. Germain. "I dislike him—and all the other men like him who demeaned my work, annexed my achievements and still do," she said, pointing out in particular John Crosbie, who replaced her as trade minister prior to the Canada–US Free Trade Agreement getting passed in Parliament. She went on:

> I am not denying that St. Germain was asked by Mulroney to take a party role. I was very sick, and spent more than a year on disability. I am refuting your suggestions denigrating my role and contribution as a regional minister . . . I co-chaired along with Jean Guilbault the national leadership review of the Conservative Party in 1983, and [also co-chaired] the following leadership [convention] which elected Brian Mulroney. That year I campaigned with St. Germain in his first election, showing him how to sit in a café facing the door, etc. As political minister I shared responsibility for the creation of Haida Gwaii [national park] and other nation-changing federal–provincial initiatives . . . I had excellent and productive relations with provincial ministers . . . BC has had great federal ministers, for example John Fraser. St. Germain was not one of them. He was a chicken farmer in a cowboy hat— an amusing sight to me, the daughter of a BC homesteading, cattle-raising family—who represents a facet of the Conservative Party I abhor. And so do other Canadians.

In fairness to Carney, she was dealing with arthritis and other issues while also handling by far the toughest file on the government's agenda at that time. If Carney, after dealing with the abrasive Canadian free trade negotiator Simon Reisman all week, wasn't enthused about going to a Tory pancake breakfast in Vernon that weekend, who could blame her? It just wasn't part of her political brand. Capilano–Howe Sound MP Mary Collins, a Red Tory backbencher when Carney was minister, suggested her colleague wasn't the ideal conduit between Mulroney and Vander Zalm. "Pat is crusty—always has been and still is," Collins said, adding that she was among those MPs called in to do party work because "Pat wasn't available." She said it made sense for Mulroney to bring in St. Germain to deal with a provincial party led by a man with a similar ideological bent. "Gerry was brought in to be a fixer."

Doug Eyford candidly assessed the different assets of Carney, who was more prominent and skilled with the BC media and Vancouver business community, and St. Germain, who "was more involved in fundraising than Pat and could be counted on to show up at political and community events. Gerry was particularly effective in meetings in rural parts of the province. He was well respected by his caucus colleagues." Bob Plecas, a senior provincial deputy minister in charge of intergovernmental affairs during the period, said St. Germain provided a low-key but valuable service to the province. He compared him to Jack Austin, Pierre Elliott Trudeau's one-time principal secretary who later served as cabinet minister from 1980 to 1984. "Gerry around this time, like Jack Austin did with Trudeau, was able to talk to the PM and represent BC at the centre, and explain BC, its issues and Vander Zalm, whose style and reputation confused Ottawa," Plecas said. "And he was very helpful."

St. Germain was also crucial in helping his Ottawa counterparts understand that apparently hostile actions, like the hyper-aggressive Throne Speech, were politically motivated and not intended to sever relationships. "It is always essential that messages of bottom-line intent, not just public posturing, be understood between governments," Plecas said. St. Germain would prove to be a low-profile but energetic and productive minister. But for him the seven-plus months as minister—giving him a limousine and chauffeur, fancy suits, status as a power player in BC political circles and most importantly even greater distance from his humble beginnings in St. François Xavier—would turn out bittersweet.

7
∞

Election and Defeat

As he sat down for his first meeting after the March 1988 shuffle with senior officials and a heavy briefing file on his desk covering a multitude of issues, St. Germain realized that acting as the junior transport minister might not be as easy as it sounded. The last thing the rookie minister wanted to do was get swamped with numerous priorities when his forte in life was sticking to manageable and achievable goals. He was a born salesman with a laser-beam focus on closing deals. "I said to them, 'I want to talk about the devolution of airports.'" There was immediate resistance. "The bureaucracy, they were insisting that they had the people in place to do this, and I said, 'Well, why hasn't it happened?'"

"Minister," one replied, "you don't realize there are lots of issues we are dealing with."

"I know there's lots of files. This is something that we want done."

St. Germain later recalled, with a sprinkle of hyperbole, the sorry state of Canada's airports when they were managed by the federal bureaucracy: "You have to remember that at the time those airports [Vancouver, Calgary, Edmonton and Montreal] were just big concrete bunkers with bad coffee at five dollars a cup." St. Germain had been part of a parliamentary delegation to Memphis to see how devolution of day-to-day management to the private sector would work. "It was a big economic generator in the community," St. Germain recalled.

When he realized the officials were not willing to push ahead he reached for the phone and dialled the number for Ginette Pilotte, Mulroney's long-time secretary. "I said 'Ginette, is the boss in?' Whenever I called her she said, 'I'll put you through.'" That got the attention of Glen Shortliffe, who was then deputy minister of transport and would later become Clerk of the Privy Council, the most senior position in the federal public service. St. Germain said his top political aide, Doug Eyford, was taken aback by his boss's hardball approach with the bureaucrats. "He said to me later, 'Geez, Gerry,'" and I responded, 'If they don't do what I want to do, then there's no point in me being here. This has been on the agenda for a period of time, it just hasn't gotten done.' I was being aggressive, but I wanted them to know that I was going to ask the prime minister [to step in]. But it never got to that."

Shortliffe and his deputies immediately assured St. Germain they would do his bidding, so he told Mulroney's secretary, "I don't think I have to bother the PM," and hung up. St. Germain considers Canada's modern airports part of his legacy, and especially BC's gorgeous facility—ranked eleventh out of one hundred in a 2015 Skytrax World Airport Awards ranking. The Vancouver International Airport, located across the Fraser River in nearby Richmond, is filled with sushi bars and high-end gift shops, natural light and spectacular local art including *The Spirit of Haida Gwaii: The Jade Canoe*, a six-metre-long, four-metre-high sculpture by legendary Haida artist Bill Reid.

While St. Germain's personal objective was in transport, his primary mandate was to improve relations with the government's Socred cousins. One of Ottawa's frustrations at the time was the lack of clarity about what among the big-ticket items on BC's wish list was the priority. One day it would be a request for help in subsidizing a natural gas pipeline to Vancouver Island, the next it would be a plea for assistance in funding the new particle accelerator at the University of BC. Finally, after the furor over the Throne Speech, it was confirmed that the pipeline was the key priority. The $250 million, 528-kilometre pipeline, to be built by a Westcoast Energy Inc. subsidiary, was being pushed by the provincial government as a way to bring cleaner and cheaper energy to Vancouver Island residents and industries, including pulp mills. The Vander Zalm government advanced the argument that the pipeline construction would generate plenty of jobs—especially in ridings Mulroney's PCs were targeting.

But the project would go nowhere without government handouts, so the proponents sought a major Ottawa contribution even though the federal government was struggling—thanks largely to double-digit interest rates—to bring down the deficit inherited from the Trudeau Liberals. St. Germain went to cabinet with a request for a $100 million grant and a $50 million loan, double that of the provincial government's $25 million loan. The $75 million being lent to the company had sweetheart terms: no interest would be charged, which was a big deal at the time given that bank prime rates were around 12 percent. The loans would be repayable only when the line began turning a profit, and Westcoast would have to contribute no more than $75 million up front for the project.

It was a deal that caused a lot of anxiety at finance minister Michael Wilson's department, which was trying to find an economic justification for such a huge commitment. But St. Germain said Mulroney was always supportive on issues like the pipeline. And the newly appointed BC minister had allies among the three top western Canadian ministers—deputy prime minister Don Mazankowski of Alberta, Indian affairs/western economic diversification minister Bill McKnight of Saskatchewan and health minister Jake Epp of Manitoba. "I went to cabinet and presented the case. Jake Epp, I remember, spoke up on my behalf and said, 'I think that's a good idea, Prime Minister.' And McKnight said, 'You really need this?' and I said, 'It needs to be done.' And he said, 'Okay, I support it.' And Maz said, 'I know all your staff have done a lot of good work on this.' And Mulroney said, 'It's done.'" The pipeline, far less controversial than such a project would be twenty-five years later, quietly began operation in 1991 and was later sold by Westcoast to a predecessor of FortisBC Energy Inc., which took on the loan. The final payment on that loan was scheduled to be made on Canada Day in 2016.

Another priority for St. Germain was dealing with bureaucratic opposition to the city of Kelowna's pleas for an airport runway extension. In 1988 there was plenty of anxiety in the Okanagan over the pending Free Trade Agreement, as the wine industry wasn't aware at that point that it would thrive rather than suffer due to the removal of tariffs protecting vintners on both sides of the Canada–US border. City officials, anxious to improve tourism as well as help its fruit industry get products to international markets, wanted to extend its 1,600-metre runway by 594 metres. But Transport Canada bureaucrats said any available dollars in its budget for airport expansion in BC should be focused on the Vancouver International Airport. Safety was also a concern. "I went into Kelowna [in the summer of 1988] and they had been asking for their runway to be lengthened. I couldn't believe that we weren't doing this because Kelowna had been growing so much. I was asked to speak at the Chamber of Commerce lunch. I got up and said that it sure was nice to be in a city that had a runway that was two thousand feet too short. And the place just exploded!"

There was one problem with St. Germain's support, though. Cabinet hadn't approved the expenditure, which would end up totalling $4.5 million. St. Germain remembers an aide hissing to him under his breath, "You can't do this, you crazy bugger!" and his own response of "I just did it!" When St. Germain pointed to a fund in the department designed for such projects, the aide responded, "Yeah, but you have to have the authority to do it." St. Germain shot back, "Tell [the bureaucrats] if they want to be the minister they should run. And if they don't want to do it, I quit." In late August the deal was announced. It was a classic example of St. Germain's deal-making style—and his ability to lever his friendship with Mulroney.

A few days later he made a similar though less spectacular announcement that Ottawa had approved a $336,700 grant to pave and extend the Pitt Meadows Airport runway and install lights and pavement markings. St. Germain remembered this grant well as one that would save lives, explaining that it was widely felt in the flying community that it was risky to land aircraft there. Another major project St. Germain pushed for was the establishment of a rail line from Port Coquitlam to Vancouver, serving the many commuters who lived in St. Germain's riding but worked in downtown Vancouver. With former transport minister Don Mazankowski's help, Ottawa and Victoria cut a deal with CP Rail to use the company's existing facilities to begin operations the following year. Ottawa's contribution was $16 million.

Despite his frantic deal-making and higher profile, St. Germain had little if any hope of winning a seat three tries in a row. In Mulroney's 1984 sweep, the PCs won nineteen of twenty-eight BC seats with 46.5 percent of the vote, well ahead of the second-place NDP's eight seats and 35.1 percent. In that same election St. Germain did one point better than the provincial average in Mission–Port Moody, getting 47.5 percent of the vote—to the second-place NDP candidate's 40-percent vote share. Clearly the Tories weren't going to do as well in 1988 after four years of scandal and controversy, regardless of what St. Germain managed to do locally.

The Progressive Conservative vote share in BC dropped to 34.4 percent in 1988, thirteen percentage points worse than 1984. The NDP, while gaining only a couple of points to 37 percent, took advantage of favourable vote splits thanks to a boost in Liberal support. Ed Broadbent's New Democrats ended up with nineteen of thirty-two seats, to the PCs' twelve and the Liberals' single seat for leader John Turner. The combination of the thirteen-point drop in Tory support in BC, and the two-point gain for the NDP, added up to a fifteen-point shift in provincial voting to the NDP against the Tories, double the 7.5-point margin of victory St. Germain had in 1984. In other words, he never really stood a chance. Despite his new status as BC's most powerful minister and a rainmaker in terms of federal handouts, he lost to the NDP by four points, 44 percent to 40 percent.

St. Germain was also forced into the new riding of Mission–Coquitlam, created through the redistribution of new seats by Elections Canada to fast-growing BC. It remained an area that was historically NDP-friendly and he was running against New Democrat candidate Joy Langan, a gravel-voiced typesetter who came out of the labour movement. While she was not a star candidate, her campaign was helped by a major NDP effort to bring down a Tory incumbent closely identified with Mulroney and the free trade deal. The area had plenty of sawmills and was dependent on the heavily unionized lumber industry, which had been hammered by protectionist duties imposed by US interests during Mulroney's first term. While the free trade negotiations were intended to facilitate cross-border trade, the US assault on Canadian lumber producers was cited by the NDP as evidence that Mulroney was promising something he couldn't deliver.

The NDP brought out extra campaign workers and the party's big guns to make sure Mulroney, even if his party were to win another mandate, wouldn't retain his BC lieutenant. Provincial NDP leader Mike Harcourt, the popular former Vancouver mayor who would become premier in 1991, was one of them. Normally one of the true gentlemen of Canadian politics, Harcourt was convinced to drop the gloves and aim his punches below the belt, going after St. Germain at one campaign event over the federal promise to help fund the commuter rail project. Harcourt argued that Ottawa's contribution was inadequate and that CP Rail was getting an overly favourable deal.

"Gerry St. Germain is a total flop," Harcourt declared. "He's shown that he's a captive of the CPR." Harcourt said that for the budget being estimated, CP Rail could "gold plate" the rails. "It's outrageous," he went on, "that that company, which has ripped off Canadian taxpayers, particularly westerners, for decades, is allowed by this very junior minister—who is proving that he is unfit for elected office—to get away with that kind of nonsense." (When St. Germain was defeated, the project no longer had a political champion and went into hiatus. It finally got built in 1995, without federal aid, when Harcourt's NDP was in power and nearing the end of its first term.) In a 2016 email

Harcourt, asked about his memory of the event, replied: "I guess it was election time . . . Gerry's a pal now, so I feel a twinge of remorse for those remarks."

Bob Ransford said St. Germain was jarred by the nastiness of the election campaign, which was an emotional and—it seemed at the time—existential battle across the country over how free trade would impact Canada. St. Germain, thanks to his role as caucus chairman, had spent an inordinate amount of time in Ottawa riding herd on that vast caucus. When he started his on-the-ground campaign in 1988 he quickly realized it was much different than his experiences in 1983 and 1984. "We were in a shopping mall in Port Coquitlam, and it was an outdoor mall and we had just gotten out of the car," Ransford recalled. "We were on the edge of the parking lot and there was a woman way over by the stores and she recognized him and yelled at him, 'You're an asshole, St. Germain! You're supporting free trade!' That really shocked him, because up until then we felt there was a lot of support in the riding."

Whether it was fair or unfair, St. Germain lost—and the setback was devastating. "I was bitter. Really, really bitter." Part of St. Germain's frustration was that he felt he and his government got little credit or thanks for their efforts. There is indeed a tendency in BC political culture for British Columbians to grumble and complain about the lack of attention from Ottawa—and then shrug cynically when the goodies arrive because it's assumed that other regions, and especially Quebec, got far greater largesse. "The Vancouver Island gas pipeline was one of the big ones and the strange thing was I did that $150 million announcement around the same time I did a $5 million announcement in Quebec," St. Germain recalled. "And you know in Quebec it was as if I was a celebrity. There were mayors greeting me, big cars driving me around. You'd think I was the Pope. That's the difference. Quebecers just love that stuff. In BC we got nothing—there is more of an entitlement mentality."

A sad component of his loss was that he had spent the previous five years as an MP and minister working twelve-to-fourteen-hour days, seven days a week, while leaving the raising of his two daughters and son to his wife Margaret. "Family pays a huge price, too much," he said grimly in a 2012 interview with the *Vancouver Sun* as he retired from the Senate. "They needed me at critical points in their lives, when they were making decisions on education and things like that, and I just wasn't there. And that's really a sad part." During the many interviews done for this book, St. Germain said he was always a workaholic, and Margaret seconded that. Even when he was a policeman in St. Boniface working union-mandated regular shifts, he'd go out in the evenings to attend union meetings and volunteered at the golf course in order to play for free. St. Germain pointed to his desperation to rise above his poor background:

> When I was a policeman I wanted to be the best. Same with the air force. And when I went into business I was relentless, it was just day and night. The harder I worked the more successful I got. And when I went into politics I took that ethic with me. But I was leaving people behind—my wife, my kids, everybody. I had to give my head a shake a few times to get back on the ground, because I was so obsessed. I'd wake up in the morning and my feet were moving before they touched the ground. I couldn't stop because I just kept thinking about where I came from.

In December 2015 St. Germain finally opened up about one of the family "prices" he was alluding to in the 2012 *Vancouver Sun* interview. Three decades earlier, in 1985, he got a disturbing phone call as he was scurrying down Parliament Hill corridors stamping out Mulroney's fires. Margaret informed him that their youngest child Jay, then nineteen, had been busted by police on a drug charge. This would be disturbing enough for any parent, but it was particularly problematic for St. Germain, as this innocuous story that would never be reported on in most other families could easily be made into a career-threatening event for a politician. How could an ex-cop, who always took a tough stand on law-and-order issues, have a son in that situation? St. Germain knew he was potentially walking into career oblivion when he headed with Margaret to the Langley courthouse, where his son was to plead guilty and be given a conditional discharge.

"I'm standing there," St. Germain recalled, "and there's one media person there, and this reporter comes up to me and says, 'You're Gerry St. Germain, aren't you?'"

"Yeah," St. Germain said.

"Well, what are you doing here?"

"That's my son."

The reporter, scribbling notes, said, "I know, but you don't have to be here."

"Yes I do, he's my son and if he's fallen by the wayside maybe I'm partly responsible."

"That takes a lot of courage."

"No, it takes a lot of love."

The reporter took his stenographer's notepad, ripped the pages out, tore them in half and gave them to St. Germain. "I don't know who it was, and I wish I did. I'll never forget that reporter. He could just see the anguish and the pain Margaret and I were in . . . Some people in the community knew about it, but it never made the media." As St. Germain shared the story in December 2015, he noted that his son had called him a week earlier to proudly declare that it had been thirty years to the day since he quit drugs and alcohol after that court appearance. Although St. Germain and Jay became closer in later years, former aide John Baldwin said it should be no surprise that St. Germain has regrets: "Every person who has had the type of success that Gerry has had has paid a price in their personal life. He is not an exception, but he has been working ever since he got out of politics to recoup some of those moments and time he missed with his family."

There was nothing unusual about Margaret being the one to inform her husband of the family setback. The former hairdresser from a low-income Winnipeg family was the glue that kept the family together. "I should have spent more time with them, but everything was a rush with me. Margaret raised the kids, and I am so grateful to

Gerry, Margaret, Michele, Suzanne and Jay holding their dog Kermit. St. Germain felt Margaret and their children paid too high a price for his work-related absences. A few years later, at age nineteen, Jay would be arrested on a drug charge. Clean of drugs and booze for more than thirty years, Jay, with his father, now runs a vast ranch in Hedley, BC. GSC PERSONAL COLLECTION

her. When I was with Klink we'd start at six a.m. and we'd be stacking warehouses until ten or eleven at night. I'd come home just for dinner. If it hadn't been for Margaret there's no way that I would have experienced the success I did, because she put up with my baloney and my insensitivities, whereas most other women would have said, 'Hey, you're out of here.' There was a day of reckoning [in 1988] when she said she wanted to talk to me and I said, 'Don't you realize how busy I am? I'm a cabinet minister!' That was it. She laid the law down on me and said, 'You have become . . .'" St. Germain paused, and was asked to finish the sentence: "'. . . an asshole.'

"And I said to her that I'd better change. One thing I had the ability to do was to recognize when I had to change, whether it was drinking, gambling, family relationships, whatever." Margaret wasn't the only one who noticed how St. Germain's rapid ascent in the 1980s had impacted him personally. A fashion consultant was hired to get him into the slick downtown suits that he so abhorred when he arrived in Ottawa. Sandy Macdougall, the former *Maple Ridge News* journalist and one-time municipal councillor who worked as St. Germain's constituency assistant in 1988, wasn't impressed: "Gerry's a very outgoing guy and kind of charismatic, and he appealed to the kind of voters who were here. But he forgot where he came from. He really did. He started saying stuff like, 'You people in British Columbia, you don't know how lucky you are.' And that's not the way you act even in private conversations. I don't want to make the guy look like a bozo. Gerry's a good guy essentially. I think he was just believing his own press notices and drinking his own bathwater." Macdougall also acknowledged St. Germain's achievements in the riding, including the expansion of the Pitt Meadows Airport and millions for shake and shingle mills to market their products after that industry was hammered in the mid-1980s by devastating US duties. "It's not much now but it was huge money in those days. He did some great things during the time he was there. I think that's what pissed him off, that people weren't too grateful."

What made the loss particularly frustrating for St. Germain was that he felt he was a politician on the rise. Despite his success on various files, he remained low-profile relative to Carney, a media magnet. But she had opted out of running for re-election in 1988, putting more pressure on St. Germain to step up as BC's voice in Ottawa. "The seat is important to the Tories because St. Germain figures prominently in their plans for the future," *Vancouver Sun* columnist Jamie Lamb wrote during the campaign. "The Tories have adopted a system of powerful regional ministers to oversee their political fortunes. Thus Manitoba has Jake Epp, Saskatchewan has Bill McKnight, Alberta has Don Mazankowski, and BC has . . . has . . . well, there's the problem. We don't have a powerful cabinet minister charged with overseeing political and policy decisions affecting the province. Pat Carney has retired, John Fraser is running in his Speaker's robes and therefore unable to speak out on issues, Tom Siddon is burdened with the fisheries portfolio and Frank Oberle has his own problems in the Interior. St. Germain was supposed to emerge as the government kingpin in BC but it hasn't happened. Not yet, anyway."

While it's true he wasn't yet at the level of his prairie colleagues Mazankowski, McKnight or Epp, there should be no doubt that, had he won, St. Germain would have had a major cabinet portfolio and the lead role for his province in a post-1988 cabinet. Kim Campbell, who won Carney's vacated Vancouver Centre seat, was a rising star. But as a former MLA who butted heads with Vander Zalm on abortion, she had her own issues with the provincial government. She also had no real experience with the PC Party at the grassroots level. Campbell would have been the media star, but Mulroney would have assigned the political and intergovernmental work to St. Germain.

Despite his success in twice winning a challenging riding for the Conservatives, St. Germain struggled to get over the voters' rejection in his third campaign. Most painful was his trip back to Ottawa with Margaret after the loss. Defeated MPs always make one last visit to the nation's capital to close down their offices, thank and say goodbye to staff, and attend one last caucus meeting with their former colleagues—most of whom were basking in their party's second straight majority victory. John Baldwin, his aide at the time, was with him on the flight back to Vancouver:

Margaret and I were trying to carry on a conversation and keep Gerry up, but it was a hopeless task. He was horribly depressed and did not know what he was going to do, even though he was rich as Croesus and never had to work again if that was what he chose. The plane was relatively empty and I took advantage of this by leaning across the aisle and telling him to snap out of it. I told him that he had a lot to be thankful for. He had a great run and was leaving Ottawa at the top of his game, his family was still intact and he had his health, which was way more than most people who had been through what he had in business, not to mention Ottawa, could claim. We both knew many politicians who had started screwing around [i.e., having affairs] and lost everything, and he had been to Ottawa and was leaving with everything and everybody that was close to him he had gone there with, plus much more. I told him that his defining trait as a person was that when things were tough there was no one I would rather have in my corner, but when things were good he was a pain in the ass because he could never enjoy the good times and was always waiting for the next shoe to drop. Margaret clapped her hands and said, "Yes, that is exactly right. You listen and smarten up." He started talking and I turned on a movie and put on some headphones to let him and Margaret be alone. He seemed a lot happier when we got off the plane. When I talked to him later he said that he was looking forward to spending more time with his kids and he was going to get Jay set up and going in business.

Gerry and Margaret St. Germain meet Ronald and Nancy Reagan at a 1987 reception hosted by Jeanne Sauvé, then the Governor General of Canada, who is standing to Reagan's right. Reagan was impressed with Margaret's beauty and would later crack to Mulroney that he hadn't told him and Nancy about one of Canada's "national treasures." BILL MCCARTHY

There was one problem, though, with this notion of riding back west and into the sunset to return to his old life. Like so many who enter the business, he was hooked on politics and the adrenalin rush of being close to some of the world's top power brokers. His leader had played a key role in freeing Nelson Mandela and changed Canada forever by bringing in free trade. St. Germain regularly breakfasted at 24 Sussex, and he and Margaret were introduced to and briefly chatted with Ronald and Nancy Reagan at the White House. Was it really going to be possible to go back to the Lougheed Highway diners to swap stories and cut land deals with his cronies?

8

∞

Trouble in Paradise

Despite their personal chemistry, Gerry St. Germain and Brian Mulroney were different political animals. St. Germain had pretty unshakeable conservative values, and Mulroney was nothing like that. During the 1983 leadership campaign he convinced many Tories that he was an attractive right-of-centre alternative to Joe Clark, but he moved sharply to the centre as leader to capture what he thought was the "sweet spot" of Canadian politics—the large number of traditional Liberal supporters who found the NDP too left-wing and potentially dangerous for the economy, and the PCs too right-wing on social issues and not to be relied on when it came to the task of keeping Quebec in Canada. Mulroney's centrist leanings were not just noticed by Canadian conservatives. Margaret Thatcher, Britain's prime minister from 1979 to 1990 and a hero for a generation of young Tories that took power under Stephen Harper, once quipped about Mulroney and the Progressive Conservative Party he led, "Mr. Mulroney puts too much emphasis on the adjective and not enough on the noun."

But despite their differences, St. Germain was a discreet and committed loyalist. So once his wounds had healed after the 1988 defeat, it was no surprise when he decided to keep his toe in federal politics. St. Germain figured the party had a chance for a third term, and he was hoping to launch a comeback. Mulroney was delighted to accommodate, and began by appointing St. Germain and former Liberal cabinet minister Francis Fox to a bipartisan commission to reform the pay packages for parliamentarians. When that project was done, Mulroney urged his former minister to seek the presidency of the PC Party. St. Germain was acclaimed for the job in 1989. In some ways the presidency was similar to his job as caucus chairman. His chairman post had required him to keep tabs on more than two hundred MPs and given him a remarkable insight into the country. As party president he had to go several levels deeper, connecting with senior party officials across the country as well as riding presidents and financial donors.

As Ray Castelli noted, St. Germain had a "father-confessor" style that tended to lead senior party members to confide in him. It didn't hurt that St. Germain, despite his loyal and deep admiration for his prime minister, personally agreed with many of the critiques suggesting the Mulroney agenda wasn't sufficiently conservative. So as the months passed after the November 1988 electoral triumph, the Tory Party office on Slater Street in downtown Ottawa was receiving regular calls from Tories around the country providing earfuls about how the party was playing with Mr. and Mrs. Front Porch. It wasn't pretty. "There's trouble in paradise," St. Germain wrote on the margins of his diary during his first year as president. Two straight majority governments might have suggested the PCs could rival or even supplant the Liberals as the "natural governing party." But instead St. Germain had received a front-row seat to witness a political cancer eat away at the party's internal organs and ultimately destroy it.

In retrospect, the old PC Party's demise shouldn't have been all that surprising. The second majority was thanks not to a popular leader backed by a strong party, but rather to a determined and tactically brilliant prime minister who won by pushing through the controversial Canada–US Free Trade Agreement and then making it

the centrepiece of the 1988 campaign. With the Liberals and the NDP
starkly warning that the FTA would destroy Canada, the public polarized and the election effectively turned into a single-issue referendum.
A slight majority of Canadians (52 percent) voted for one of the two
major parties opposed to the FTA, which meant the anti-Tory vote was
split. In Canada's first-past-the-post electoral system, an opposition
split is a gift for a governing party. The PCs under Mulroney took 57
percent of the seats in the House of Commons with just 43 percent
of the vote. Free trade was a fantastic issue for Mulroney's troops, as
it united most of the party's factions, in particular the free-enterprise
westerners and the nationalist Quebecers. The issue also re-energized
the party's grassroots. Jamie Burns, then an executive assistant to
senior Mulroney-era minister Don Mazankowski, grumbled privately
to St. Germain after the 1988 election that "free trade was the only
issue we had from '84 to '88 that was conservative."

But the reckoning came in the months after the 1988 election.
Preston Manning's Reform Party had by then become well-organized,
and had it not been for the free trade dynamic it seems likely the party
would have won seats in Alberta in the 1988 election. During that election Manning challenged Joe Clark in the Alberta riding of Yellowhead,
and the Reform leader was defeated easily. "All of the issues for which
the Reform Party came into existence . . . were sideswiped by the
whole free trade thing," Manning's campaign manager would later
complain, as quoted in John Duffy's *Fights of Our Lives*. "People here
wanted free trade and there was only one party to vote for." The fact
that free trade only temporarily cut the marauding Reformers off at the
pass was underscored in March 1989 when Deb Grey, a schoolteacher
and devout Christian who finished a distant fourth in Alberta's Beaver
River riding in 1988, cruised to victory in a by-election after the elected
Tory candidate died.

Mulroney would long remain bitter that Manning ran candidates in the free trade election, which ended up costing Tory seats
and could have led to the trade pact being scuttled. But in the grand
scheme Manning's timing was impeccable. Canadians were angry

and tired of the dismal drama surrounding the Meech Lake Accord as the June 23, 1990, deadline for ratification by all ten provincial legislatures approached. The premiers of New Brunswick, Newfoundland and Manitoba were all hold-outs, and Mulroney frequently resorted to insinuations that anyone not supportive of the accord was putting the country at risk and was not adequately patriotic. With overwhelming support from Canada's political, business and intellectual elite, all this hectoring and guilt-tripping led to a populist revolt among people frustrated that they were being force-fed something even the politically astute struggled to understand. Meech critics from Pierre Elliott Trudeau to Manning to feminist leader Judy Rebick planted seeds of doubt regarding what exactly it would mean to entrench in the constitution Quebec's status as a distinct society.

A second problem for the Conservatives was a growing global economic slowdown that would continue into the early 1990s. The decline in government revenues meant that the promise by the Tories to sharply bring down the federal deficit was not being realized. Finance minister Michael Wilson had in fact balanced the "operating" deficit—that is, he managed to bring spending down to the same level of revenues coming in via taxes. But the actual deficit remained stubbornly in the $30 billion range due to the double-digit interest rates the government of Canada was paying on that accumulated debt.

A third issue was the government's 1989 announcement that it planned to introduce a new value-added tax to replace the 12.5 percent tax on Canadian manufacturers, which was widely viewed by economists as an inefficient tax that hurt the ability of companies to compete internationally. The new Goods and Services Tax (GST) was a 7-percent charge on everything from restaurant meals to haircuts. While it wouldn't be enacted until 1991, the courageous but high-risk announcement of a plan to replace an invisible tax with a highly visible one upset many Canadians, especially those in the Tory-leaning small business sector who would have to deal with both the administrative red tape and grumbling customers. As with free trade, the opposition seized on the development to demonize Mulroney. By November 1989, a year after the free trade election, an Angus Reid Group poll showed the party's support had fallen by close to half. But it wasn't entirely unfamiliar territory for Mulroney. At 23 percent, that level of support matched a previous all-time low reached in early 1987—a fact that allowed the always optimistic Mulroney to push the notion that they could pull another rabbit out of the hat.

There were a host of other irritations, from Mulroney's toughening of the Official Languages Act, to musing about taking action to legally entrench gay and lesbian rights, to the government's handling of the 1988 Supreme Court of Canada abortion decision, to the Tory policy of keeping immigration levels high despite a weakening economy. Reform candidates also became obsessed about MP perks and pensions, with many treating a 1991 book on the subject by Robert Fife and John Warren, *A Capital Scandal*, as a kind of bible or handbook on what needed fixing in Ottawa. And then there was Mulroney's personality. As veteran political observer Geoffrey Stevens noted in a 1991 *Toronto Star* column, Mulroney's detractors viewed him as untrustworthy as well as "shallow, rodomontade, insincere, vain, unprincipled and besotted with the sound of his own rich baritone. To them, he is quite simply the worst prime minister Canada has had."

For the Progressive Conservative Party's powerful Red Tory wing, which believed in an activist federal government with an approach not particularly different from that of the Liberals, the Mulroney government's centrist bent wasn't a huge problem. But the party's core constituency was heavily populated by fiscal and social conservatives who believed in small government, low taxes and policies friendly to traditional nuclear families—Dad at work, Mom at home, kids, dog, white picket fence. In fact, one Reform campaign brochure in the 1990s actually featured a supposed traditional Canadian family smiling in front of their white picket fence. Many grassroots lifelong Tories found Manning's appeal irresistible. The folksy son of a famous Alberta premier would hold huge rallies that would begin like a hockey game, with a thunderous rendition of "O Canada" that seemed to involve everyone in the audience—some singing proudly, others angrily. After Manning's policy-heavy speech, which would address "common-sense" solutions and a government "of the people, by the people and for the people," volunteers would pass around empty Kentucky Fried Chicken buckets to collect donations. It was populist, modest and tactically brilliant. The contrast with Mulroney was palpable.

St. Germain's diaries during his presidency bring to life a back-room world of patronage deals, internal party backbiting and his own deep frustrations over what he felt was the unwillingness of Mulroney's top ministers and advisers to recognize that Manning was a legitimate threat to the party of Sir John A. Macdonald. The entries begin just before the Conservative convention in late August 1989, when several thousand members gathered to discuss the party's policy direction. At the time, party members were grumbling about the GST, and the large Tory social conservative wing was pushing the government to come up with an abortion law after the Supreme Court of Canada struck down the old one in 1988.

In August 1989 St. Germain met with Mulroney at the prime minister's Harrington Lake official summer residence, a thirteen-acre estate across the Ottawa River in Quebec's Gatineau Park. The two were meeting a few weeks prior to St. Germain being acclaimed president at a party convention. One of the ideas being floated at the time, and pushed heavily by Mulroney, called on each MP to sign up one thousand new members. St. Germain had documented how nervous MPs were about that idea, especially in the West. Jack Shields, who represented Fort McMurray, privately told St. Germain, "A thousand members are no problem at this time, but my members are steadily defecting off to the Reform Party." At another point he noted that Vancouver-area MPs Kim Campbell and Mary Collins were expressing concern that if they signed up that many members, those newcomers could become part of a ploy to challenge them for their nominations in the next election. St. Germain was concerned that PC Caucus Services, the entity designed to assist MPs, did not appear to be tracking Reform.

St. Germain would also be disappointed in Mulroney's recent

promotion of broadcaster Patrick Watson to the post of CBC chairman. Watson was the former co-host of the anti-establishment *This Hour Has Seven Days* series. The program was highly controversial in the mid-1960s and a favourite of the Canadian left. It broadcasted ground-breaking items that were critical of the government and damning of US policy in areas like race relations and the Vietnam conflict. The show was so hot it was forced off the air in 1966 by Lester B. Pearson's government. It's hard to imagine that Watson's appointment won Mulroney much public support, and it certainly didn't go over well with traditional Tory supporters. St. Germain's notes described the appointment as the "equivalent" to Mulroney making New Democrat Stephen Lewis UN ambassador in 1984.

St. Germain viewed patronage as a tool best used to ensure the support of key party backers, and it was a regular concern for him while the Tories were in power. He mused about the possibility that long-time BC Social Credit minister Grace McCarthy—like many in her party increasingly uncomfortable serving under Bill Vander Zalm—might get named as Canada's consul-general in Los Angeles, though she never was. On October 3, 1989, St. Germain wrote about Mulroney wanting to "help the Zalm as much as possible," presumably to keep him on side during the dicey Meech Lake drama. Brian Smith had resigned as BC attorney-general in June 1988 after alleging that Vander Zalm had interfered with the administration of justice, and was seeking an opportunity to leave provincial politics. Nothing more is written about the matter, but St. Germain's papers include a letter from Smith to St. Germain six weeks later thanking him for his "kind letter regarding my appointment as chairman of Canadian National Railway." Mulroney's favour to Vander Zalm, Smith would recall in a 2016 interview, was timing the CN appointment to ensure it was consistent with the BC premier's plan to call a by-election in Smith's Victoria-area riding.

The problem of continuous negative media coverage was also one of St. Germain's preoccupations at this time. At one point in late 1989 he referred to an unidentified woman in Kim Campbell's office who was "believed to be part of the conspiracy" to expose two Tory MPs who were facing heat in the media after it was leaked that they had hired each other's daughters. The snitch must have been from Ottawa because St. Germain wrote, "Never hire anyone from the Ottawa region. They're not competent politically. If they don't carry a PC [membership] card fire them!"

On November 4, 1989, St. Germain criticized himself for delivering a weak speech at a party gathering in BC's Saanich–Gulf Islands riding, where he was peppered with angry questions about the "GST, government spending and their mistrust of politicians." He then expressed comments along a common theme in his diaries: his frustration over the penchant of his Tory colleagues in central and Atlantic Canada to shower contempt and ridicule on Manning's Reformers. "When criticizing the Western Reform we are criticizing Tories who were totally disillusioned by the lack of conservative direction the PC Party took after the 1984 election." By early 1990 St. Germain's attentions were consumed by the descent into hell that was the lead-up to the June 23, 1990, deadline for the provinces to pass the Meech Lake amendments to the constitution. This period was also the beginning of the end for the PC Party as it staggered for another three years toward the grim fate that would be delivered in autumn 1993.

In one February 1990 note St. Germain lamented the fact that Marjory LeBreton, Mulroney's head of appointments or "Patronage Queen" would "not leave the PMO." St. Germain was a LeBreton critic who felt she only told Mulroney what he wanted to hear. He presciently wrote at one point "Senate?" as a possible place for her to be dispatched. In one entry in mid-March 1989 he appeared more demoralized than usual in the wake of a grim Gallup poll. "The great unwashed had high expectations [after a recent party convention] but nothing appears to be happening. Ministers are not out in the field. Tough to get things rolling when party is 19 percent in the polls. There is a need to define the role and direction of the party." St. Germain cited one of the pet theories he was floating at the time, which was to have the Mulroneys establish an official residence in western Canada. "Western residence is an absolute must to dispel the myth of non-representation." He also fretted about the controversy at the time over allowing Sikh RCMP officers to wear turbans, describing it as a "major" issue along the lines of the CF-18 maintenance contract fiasco. He lamented the state of the party in Alberta, saying there were serious problems with an unhappy and undisciplined caucus. "Someone from outside has to come in and take control of them."

On March 18, 1990, just under three months before the Meech deadline, he again complained of his party's inability to deal with Manning, who at the time was drawing huge crowds across the country that were deeply hostile to Mulroney. Under the heading "PM Western Canada" he wrote, "Westerners don't feel they have a voice in Ottawa. Preston Manning is capitalizing on this view [of Mulroney] as another Trudeau. Trudeau shoved bilingualism down their throats and Mulroney is doing it with Meech Lake." There are similar entries leading up to Meech's formal failure. "Ship is rudderless," he wrote, before taking a shot at the "suits" advising Mulroney that he so deeply resented—chief of staff Stanley Hartt, secretary for federal–provincial relations Norman Spector, and Senator Lowell Murray, Mulroney's minister responsible for federal–provincial relations. "Hartt, Spector, Lowell Murray et al. have screwed it." The party seemed mortally wounded. In addition to the growth of Reform in western Canada, a new pro-independence federal Quebec party called the Bloc Québécois was created under the leadership of Mulroney's former friend and cabinet minister, Lucien Bouchard. On June 26, three days after the accord died, St. Germain wrote of the state of the party, "Maritimes is in a state of collapse." He also noted that Mary Collins, a Vancouver Tory MP, "called me and sounded desperate."

In early July 1990, just a few weeks after Meech's collapse, St. Germain—when he probably should have been at a lake with the kids—was stuck in humid, sticky Ottawa somehow thinking there was a way out of this mess. He visited the "centre" of Canadian political power—the Prime Minister's Office and its bureaucratic arm, the Privy Council Office, in the Langevin Block. St. Germain wanted to know what "line" he and party members should use when approached by journalists in the wake of the Meech collapse. "Utter chaos on the deck of PMO-PCO," he wrote. The only official there, Tom Trbovich, offered blunt advice to the party president: "There's no line available and the strategy is to do nothing." St. Germain complained in his diary that chief of staff Stanley Hartt had gone off to Europe for a North Atlantic Treaty Organization meeting, while senators Lowell Murray and Marjory LeBreton—"Where the hell is Marj LeBreton?" he scribbled—were on holidays. Norman Spector, meanwhile, was in his office "trying to work on something."

St. Germain noted in retrospect that Mulroney had dispatched Spector, Murray and Hartt to meet with Elijah Harper, an aboriginal NDP member of the Manitoba legislature who held up an eagle feather as he denied unanimous consent to allow a vote on Meech. "When they sent the three intellectuals to Winnipeg I knew we were finished . . . this did not stand a ghost of a chance of working." St. Germain didn't mention it, but presumably he had to be questioning why he—a Metis from a poor Manitoba community and professional salesman with a down-to-earth nature—wasn't asked to meet with Harper. "The PM surrounded himself with academic lawyer nerds. [Clerk of the Privy Council Paul] Tellier is a Grit and dangerously uninformed of the street. Spector is a . . . bureaucrat who has no respect for elected people . . . Lowell Murray is smart academically but it really stops there. Hartt [is] a real lawyer. Mike Wilson recommended him. A disaster."

A few days later St. Germain learned that Mulroney wanted him to brief cabinet on the state of the party in August—at the same time he was planning to finally spend some quality time with Jay. At that meeting, St. Germain later recalled, Mulroney asked him "what I was hearing on the street" about newly elected Liberal leader Jean Chrétien. Mulroney and many party insiders and media pundits—naively as it turned out—viewed Chrétien as "yesterday's man" and not strong or bright enough to be prime minister. "I told him nothing, but warned him about the Reform Party in western Canada." St. Germain also lamented in his diary about the Oka Crisis in Quebec, involving armed

Mohawks who took over some land and shot dead a Quebec provincial policeman, which had resulted in solidarity roadblocks elsewhere in the country, especially in BC. In August the journal entries once again delved into patronage and especially Mulroney's plan to appoint Pat Carney to the Senate. "I reaffirmed my solid opposition to the move and that there was no way I would approve of such an appointment." Near the bottom of the page he referred to Mulroney again bringing up Carney, and he wrote to himself in block letters: "THIS COULD BE THE END, IF HE APPOINTS CARNEY."

In late October of 1990, St. Germain wrote another journal entry after a discussion with MP Lorne Greenaway, the BC caucus chairman and a close ally. They discussed Kim Campbell's prospects as an up-and-comer for a party that desperately needed one. "Many good things about her, but she does not seem to realize how one gets elected," St. Germain wrote about his future leader and prime minister. "She like all the rest has been overtaken by the trappings of cabinet." Mulroney's decision in 1991 to name future separatist Marcel Masse to the defence portfolio was "a true insult to the military," St. Germain wrote. "After they have succeeded so well at Oka and in the Persian Gulf, why Masse in defence? Everyone considers this appointment bizarre. No one opposes a Quebecer [getting the job]—but not Masse." In June 1991 he wrote one of a number of entries complaining about the senior party official he appeared to have the most contempt for, Progressive Conservative Canada Fund boss David Angus, who apparently was not letting St. Germain have any role in fundraising or budgeting. "Party is run by the PCCF because I'm being held hostage by David Angus. Absolutely no input into the process. Our entire national executive has and will continue to be ignored."

St. Germain would proudly remember Mulroney returning his calls, both as an MP and minister as well as when he was party president. But there was clearly a period when this wasn't the case. In a lengthy June 5, 1991, entry he wrote, "Anyone who challenges him in any way is ostracized and given the silent treatment." A few lines later it's clear he was basing that assertion on personal experience as he vented frustration over his party's refusal to take the Reform threat seriously. "In the fall of 1989 and spring of 1990 I attempted to motivate or instigate an operation to deal with the Reform Party. The reaction was totally non-existent at the ad hoc committee on reorganization chaired by [future Toronto mayor] John Tory. I tried to activate some interest and only Peter White [a former senior PC insider] would respond positively." It wasn't until the spring of 1991, when the Reformers started making inroads into Ontario, that the "whole party came to life." He ended the rant by writing, "After having challenged [Mulroney] on the Carney appointment he has virtually ignored me."

But that didn't last. On August 4, 1991, he "called the PM [who] took the call immediately." Mulroney was at this point clinging to a theme that he would carry for the rest of his life—that he was unpopular because he spent all his "political capital" to make unpopular changes that were good for Canada, like free trade, Meech Lake and the GST. St. Germain wrote that Mulroney was quoting Churchill, who once said, "You have enemies? Good. That means you've stood up for something, sometime in your life." Mulroney was speaking to St. Germain about the upcoming party convention in Toronto, where he hoped to breathe some life into the suffocating party. "With a little bit of luck, with St. Patrick saying a few prayers, we're going to bounce into the election in 1993 with prosperity all over," Mulroney told his troops in a speech that was widely panned by the media.

The party further distanced itself from traditional members who were flocking to Manning, who was taking a hard line against Mulroney's pandering to Quebec and close relationships with Quebec nationalists like Bouchard and Masse. Delegates voted by a wide margin to recognize Quebec's right to self-determination, which *Toronto Star* columnist Geoffrey Stevens described as something "that would have been heresy to right-thinking Conservatives." St. Germain took some criticism during the convention when former party president Dalton Camp, famous for leading a revolt in the 1960s against leader John Diefenbaker, complained that St. Germain shouldn't be re-elected as president due to a lack of public profile. It was the kind of comment from a "downtowner" that ate up St. Germain. "My reply," he wrote in his diary, "was that since I never frequented the Albany Club"—an exclusive private club in Toronto that proudly proclaims on its website that it caters to "leaders in Canada's business and conservative political spheres"—"it would be hard for him to see me as I work rural Newfoundland and Saskatchewan."

St. Germain lauded Mulroney for "performing like a true champion" at the various convention events, and even praised Stanley Hartt for his work as co-moderator. "Grassroots left feeling their voices had been heard for the first time in the life of the party." But by October 22, 1991, St. Germain was describing the convention as "good but is only a start." He quoted a party member from New Brunswick prophetically suggesting the Tories faced the same kind of annihilation suffered by his province's PCs under Richard Hatfield, the flamboyant premier who lost every seat in the legislature to Frank McKenna's Liberals in 1987. "New Brunswick prepared to stick with him, but they feel he has to make a move immediately to move the party out of the tank. Most people are looking for solutions as to how to repackage [Mulroney] so as to make him more resalable."

That same month there was a "major confrontation" between St. Germain and David Angus during a meeting over control of the party's budget. When one of St. Germain's rivals at the meeting made a statement about the party's spending plans, "I jumped all over him, and Angus allowed the whole meeting to break down. A shouting match erupted, the rest is history. [Mulroney] got upset but the entire direction of the party and PCCF changed. Angus's stock went down from there. Marj LeBreton was the only one who actually stood up for me." A deal ended up being struck as "LeBreton and I negotiated a peace agreement."

By early 1992 it was clear the Tory survival strategy, which as it turned out exaggerated Canadians' willingness to accommodate Quebec, was to highlight the perceived vulnerability of Mulroney's opponents. On January 15 of that year St. Germain wrote, "Stay the course. Exploit Jean Chrétien's weaknesses. Inform English Canada that Chrétien is very unpopular in Quebec and does not have the answers in dealing with the Constitution." The approach for the NDP was to "lightly marginalize" the party's struggling new leader, Audrey McLaughlin, who in 1989 had replaced Ed Broadbent. But later that month St. Germain's pessimism returned, as he complained that "those that are screwing up are being rewarded and the loyalists are being shafted." He noted that Joe Clark's performance as national unity minister had been "dismal" and also grumbled about the lack of support for fundraising. He asserted that Clark, who was engaged in negotiations to strike a new unity accord, "has no bloody idea what he's doing and does not appear to be listening to anyone." He warned that Alberta Tory MPs were demoralized. "No one federally is fighting for Alberta." He also reported around this time that Carney, whose Vancouver Centre seat was won in 1988 by Campbell,

St. Germain proudly introduces Mulroney to his father-in-law, Herman Schilke, who St. Germain nicknamed "Herman the German." Back when Margaret and Gerry began dating she wasn't looking forward to having her father meet her new boyfriend, due to her dad's prejudices against aboriginal people, but their relationship was one of love and respect. The last words Margaret and Gerry ever heard from him as they left a nursing home were, "I love you, Gerry!" BILL MCCARTHY

was introducing Campbell at events "as the next PM"—even though at that point Mulroney hadn't made it known that he wouldn't run for a third term.

St. Germain was also frustrated that patronage appointments, by not being used strategically to entice or at least not alienate party donors, were "just undermining every attempt to raise funds." He cited as one example Jack Munro, the late and legendary BC union leader. A prominent New Democrat and a personal friend of Pat Carney's, he was named to the board of Canada Harbour Place and the Japan–Canada Trade Committee. St. Germain mentioned his nemesis LeBreton being in control of patronage appointments, and suggested that his influence was being roadblocked by her. "I gave up all business to do this for [Mulroney], and now I couldn't get consideration for anything. I sometimes feel I am in the wrong party, or that we have been totally taken over by the 'politically correct.'"

But one sad moment for St. Germain represented a reminder of why Mulroney, despite his unpopularity with the Canadian public, was able to preserve the loyalty of his key followers. St. Germain's beloved father had just passed away:

Dear Prime Minister and Mila:

Margaret and I would like to thank you for your kind thoughts and considerations at the time of my father's passing. Prime Minister, in spite of your very onerous responsibilities one of your greatest attributes is the kindness you always have extended to those of us who have been so privileged to work with you. I have not written or called on a regular or frequent basis Prime Minister, knowing full well that the challenges we face as a nation are all-consuming. However, I have kept a close eye on the party and continue to work closely with those that you have chosen to prepare for the next campaign. Your government budget under Maz's leadership has gone very well and will hopefully improve our fortunes in the minds of the electorate.

But on June 2, 1992, he wrote again about the party's ongoing inability to deal with Reform, and added that "We are in trouble in the Maritimes." He correctly predicted that a referendum on constitutional amendments then being negotiated by Ottawa and the provinces—the Charlottetown Accord that would be defeated in a referendum in the autumn of 1992—"is a non-starter in the West." He described Moe Sihota, BC NDP premier Mike Harcourt's young constitutional affairs minister, as an "unmitigated disaster." That assessment was long before Sihota, in the days leading up to the October national referendum, made one of the biggest blunders of the campaign by saying in a speech that Quebec premier Robert Bourassa "lost" in the negotiations with his fellow premiers. That comment blew a huge hole in the Quebec leader's credibility as he tried to sell the deal to his skeptical citizens.

On October 26, 1992, Canadians defeated the Charlottetown Accord, with a strong turnout of "No" in Quebec and the four western provinces. The deal was going to, among other things, recognize Quebec's distinct society, put aboriginal self-government in the constitution and create an elected Senate with equal representation for all provinces. St. Germain, writing during a flight to Ottawa while Canadians were still voting, said he was "harbouring deep resentment" over the "completely exclusionary" thinking of Mulroney's referendum team, which he said was dominated by Ontario's "Big Blue Machine" of Bill Fox, Tom Trbovich and Paul Curley, and BC ally Jerry Lampert. St. Germain warned them that the polarization of opinion in BC was particularly dangerous. "Prior to going to a national referendum I told them it was sheer lunacy to proceed. Calls were made to [senior Tory strategist Harry Near] and later [Mulroney] but the die was cast, there was no stopping them." He said Mulroney's chief of staff Hugh Segal had been enthralled with Mulroney's performance in the negotiations. "They were oblivious to the outside. They were drinking their own bath water."

He added that Mulroney had been "wild" with anger over unity minister Joe Clark's alleged "bungling" of the negotiations, and added that Mulroney should have let provincial governments run their own referendums. "I clearly stated that our unpopularity would be reflected in the outcome [and that] it would be a chance for people to vote against him." However, he was also frustrated that he wasn't better utilized by the "Yes" campaign. "We were never given a role, we were [seen as] too partisan." St. Germain, one of the best-connected small-c conservatives in the province and someone who understood the mindset of Reform-oriented voters, was left twiddling his thumbs. One of the top organizers "once said they were going to try and establish a role for me, but they never called." He said his isolation appeared to begin when Hugh Segal asked if Bert Brown—an Alberta farmer who had campaigned for a reformed Senate and had given a lukewarm thumbs-up to the accord—could be trusted to be part of the campaign. "My only comment was, 'Would you sleep with a rattlesnake, Hugh?' That was the end of me. I had shown a slight moment of partisanship."

Unsurprisingly, St. Germain also suggested Carney played a role in the accord's flame-out. Carney declared in a front-page *Vancouver Sun* article in late July 1992 that British Columbians had been "sold out" by Joe Clark and his BC counterpart Moe Sihota. "I do not support this Moe and Joe fiasco," she said. Carney's point—and many experts have taken the same position over the years—was that a more democratically legitimate and therefore more powerful Senate, with equal representation from each province, would be bad for Canada's three wealthiest provinces. BC, Alberta and Ontario would have been outnumbered in Senate votes by representatives of Quebec and the six other "have-not" provinces: "The fact is the Maritimes always have their hands out. As an energy minister and a trade minister, I have learned that."

St. Germain wrote in his diary that this was a huge setback for the "Yes" forces. "My belief is that Carney really triggered the avalanche against the deal when she went after [Harcourt's NDP] . . . The irony of it all is that I was against Carney's appointment to the Senate, and also against the referendum. I had never given [Mulroney] any bad advice but he opted for the advice of 'Yes.'" St. Germain had other criticism for his boss's tactics. One of Mulroney's blunders at the start of the campaign was classifying the accord's opponents as the "enemies of Canada." The campaign in favour of the "Yes" side also erred by running a dramatic television ad showing water boiling over, to suggest that Canada would be destroyed by a "No" vote. St. Germain was right in his prediction about his home province of BC, where popular media and political figures were leading a populist revolt against the initiative. More than 68 percent of the province's voters gave their thumbs down to Charlottetown, the highest margin of opposition in the country.

For his part, Mulroney would reject many years later the criticism of second-guessers that he ignored the Reform threat:

> I didn't need Gerry to tell me that. When you're being smeared every day of the week by Preston Manning and his acolytes, saying everything from personal attacks on one's honour and one's commitment to Canada, and then the implication that we had bankrupted the country, and that when they get to Ottawa there's going to be reform, they won't be eating meals in the parliamentary cafeteria, they won't be living in Stornoway [the official residence of the leader of the opposition], they won't be accepting parliamentary pensions, you know all of this stuff, all of which they repudiated as soon as they got their hot little hands on the levers down there. And then look what they did when they had a government. So no, I didn't need Gerry to tell me that. I knew we were being savaged every day.

Mulroney repeated his longstanding argument that he did more for western Canada than any other Canadian prime minister by bringing in free trade, dismantling the National Energy Program and the Foreign Investment Review Agency, moving the National Energy Board from Ottawa to Calgary, establishing the Western Economic Diversification agency and headquartering it in Edmonton, giving huge rescue payments to western wheat farmers and making sure western politicians like Alberta's Don Mazankowski were central to his government's operations. He also cited the GST, deeply unpopular when it was brought in, as being critical along with free trade in helping the Liberals erase Canada's chronic deficit in the 1990s.

Despite his protestations, other Tories agreed that the party should have paid more attention to St. Germain's warnings and launched some sort of counterattack against Preston Manning. Jim Prentice, the party's treasurer at the time and the only other westerner on the national executive, said they both tried with little success to convince their eastern colleagues that a new approach was needed. "There was never really much clarity about what we should do," Prentice said. "They wanted to stay the course. Meanwhile, Gerry and I were connected with the grassroots in the West. There was a developing sense that this government wasn't their Conservative government, it wasn't reflecting their values. And we were telling them that this isn't working, that we have to change our approach. We could see the political base of the party eroding out from underneath us. It was unfolding in real time. And we weren't very satisfied with the approach they were taking."

Mulroney's later defence for his approach to Reform would be illustrative of the attitudes many in the East had about Manning's party. "I was leading the fight against apartheid and for the liberation of Mandela. There were people in the Conservative Party and in the conservative movement who didn't think this was a great idea, that Mandela was a communist and we shouldn't be on this side, that we should be on the other side, that kind of thing. And so, what do you do? Do you embrace a different philosophy to please some people in Lethbridge?" But St. Germain recoiled at the tendency of establishment Tories to denigrate and dismiss people who were once inside the Tory tent as bigoted kooks. While there were certainly a number of intolerant Reformers on issues like homosexual rights, the driving force for Reform's success was the legitimate concern in western Canada with the Mulroney government's approach to fiscal and national unity issues. St. Germain's frustration with the attitude of his Tory colleagues toward those in western Canada who had abandoned the PCs would eventually lead to a bitter and highly personal rupture between him and the Tory establishment.

9
∞

The Campbell Collapse

M ulroney naturally considered resigning after the Meech failure. Instead, he chose to hang on due to events such as the Oka Crisis and the first Gulf War. But the death of the Charlottetown Accord on October 26, 1992, would be the final nail. "I look forward to the enthusiasm and renewal that only new leadership brings," he told assembled reporters and a group of party supporters, including Mila and his two youngest sons, on Parliament Hill on February 24, 1993. He spoke of a recovering economy, half-jokingly referred to polls putting his party in a "strong" second place behind the Liberals, and predicted that the regional Reform and Bloc Québécois parties would "continue their decline." It was "very clear that the next election will be fought between the Liberals and ourselves," he said, declaring that his party was prepared "to wage perhaps the most effective campaign that Canada has yet seen."

It was typical Mulroney hubris, as a recent Gallup poll had just put the Liberals at an astounding 49 percent, the PCs a distant second at 21 percent and the NDP not far behind at 16 percent. But he was correct that both Reform and the Bloc Québécois appeared, as Gallup indicated, to be in decline in their respective regions. And he was certainly right in tacitly acknowledging it was time to leave. The day before his announcement, the *Edmonton Journal* had just published an editorial under the headline "Mulroney stays and stays and stays," responding to his previous musings that he might seek a third term. "The decision by Joe Clark not to run in the next election, and the decision of a host of other Tories to call it quits, raises a certain question about Prime Minister Brian Mulroney," the editorial began. "As wildly unpopular as he is, as bereft as his government is of new policies, why would he choose to lead his party into an election that promises to be a disaster for the Tories?"

At that point in Canadian history there shouldn't really have been any discussion about a future Tory government any time soon. There was a running joke during the early 1990s that Mulroney's support levels, which at times hovered around 14 percent, were consistent with the percentage of people who believed Elvis Presley was still alive. Mulroney's self-aggrandizing personality, the emotional roller-coaster of the constitutional wars, and the imposition of the GST—the "tax on everything" as it was dubbed—when the economy was weak represented a lethal combination for the party brand. Yet something remarkable was happening. A refreshing and relatively young newcomer to politics was dazzling the political world. Kim Campbell, first elected in 1988, seemed to be defying gravity as she soared like an eagle above the rotting PC carcass. The bright Vancouver lawyer and former Social Credit MLA had gained some media attention for opposing Vander Zalm's bid to restrict abortion access in 1988. She had been elected to the federal Parliament later that year, catching Mulroney's attention with her fiery defence of free trade, and had received positive reviews as justice minister. Even St. Germain, according to Campbell, was on the bandwagon: "When I agreed to run after the '88 election had been called, he totally kissed my ass and said I was the Gretzky of the BC team!"

In early November 1992, when it was widely assumed there would soon be a leadership race, Campbell's star rose even higher after a breathtaking photograph was published on the front page of the *Ottawa Citizen*. Headlined "Doing justice to art," it showed Campbell holding up her legal robes with only her bare shoulders visible. She was quite possibly stark naked for all the observer knew—though in fact she was fully clothed below her shoulders. The photo was taken in 1990 and was on display as part of an exhibit at the National Arts Centre presented by photographer Barbara Woodley, who had travelled across Canada in a van taking portraits of important Canadian women. The story got coverage around the world, giving her the kind of celebrity status that's highly unusual in Canadian politics. "She may read Tolstoy in Russian and play a mean Bach on the cello, but it was bare shoulders that put Avril Phaedra 'Kim' Campbell on a fast track to be Canada's next prime minister," gushed an April 3, 1993, report in the British newspaper the *Independent*. "Not since Pierre Trudeau was snapped sliding down a banister in Marlborough House—he was attending a Commonwealth leaders' conference shortly after being elected prime minister—has so much Canadian public attention turned on one photograph."

When Mulroney finally announced he was stepping down, almost every cabinet heavyweight who had considered the leadership deferentially stepped aside in the face of the Campbell juggernaut. Among them was Perrin Beatty, who was ambitious, reasonably bilingual and seemed destined for leadership after going from Queen's University straight into the House of Commons in 1972 at age twenty-two. By 1979 he'd become the youngest cabinet minister in Canadian history, and by 1993 he'd served in numerous senior cabinet posts. Yet his ambitions melted in the face of Campbell's steamroller, so he chose instead to endorse her. "At a subsequent cabinet meeting I watched with amusement when he stood as Kim Campbell entered the room and quickly moved to get her a coffee," Mulroney recalled in his memoirs. "This gesture brought home to me my new status as an outgoing prime minister." The only serious candidate who didn't wilt was young Jean Charest, and that was only after some spine-stiffening pressure from people like Mulroney who wanted to see an exciting race.

The rest has been well documented. Campbell, in a shaky leadership campaign, barely won over Charest in the June 13, 1993, vote,
despite a massive early lead. Less than two weeks later the transfer of
power was to take place, with Mulroney finally exiting federal politics.
But he had some unfinished business, and one item on his to-do
list involved his old friend from the west coast. Back in 1991, when
Mulroney asked St. Germain to serve a second term as president, there
was some hesitation because St. Germain planned to get back into the
real estate and development business.

"Is that really what you want?" Mulroney countered as the two
had lunch at the prime minister's favourite table in an alcove of the
parliamentary dining room. St. Germain, realizing at that time that he
wouldn't have an opportunity to run again for a seat in the House of
Commons, was resigned to leaving politics. "I said, 'I really enjoyed
working with you, Brian, but it's not to be.'" Mulroney countered that
he needed the bilingual westerner around while he tried to salvage the
national unity mess created by the Meech collapse. "Is there anything I
can do for you?" Mulroney asked. St. Germain, after promising to talk
over the notion of a second term as president with Margaret, said he
had only one request—the right of first refusal if a BC Senate vacancy
appeared. "That's all?" Mulroney replied. The promise was made but
St. Germain wasn't holding his breath, since there were no scheduled
retirements of BC senators in the near future.

In mid-1992, however, a vacancy did open up when Liberal George
Van Roggen, a long-time champion of Canada–US free trade when
it wasn't popular, got cancer and quickly died. The spot wasn't filled
for a full year and was still open in late June as Mulroney prepared to
finally step down. St. Germain was driving along Vancouver's Hastings
Street near Commercial Drive when he got a message on his pager
from Margaret. St. Germain stopped the car and went into a Greek
restaurant to use the public phone. Mulroney's secretary, Margaret
told him, had called and said the prime minister wanted to thank him
and say goodbye. "So I called the PMO and asked for the boss. And he
comes on the line and says, 'Well, Ger, thank you for everything, thank

St. Germain, then party president, addresses the Progressive Conservative national executive prior to the disastrous 1993 federal election. Watching him are Kim Campbell and party executive director Tom Trbovich. St. Germain, who initially compared Campbell to hockey superstar Wayne Gretzky, lost faith and didn't vote for her in the 1993 leadership contest. The two clashed after the Tories took a historic drubbing in the general election later that year. LIBRARY AND ARCHIVES CANADA

you for serving as you did. I hope you stay on as president but that's your choice. I really valued your loyalty and hard work for me and all of Canada.' I said, 'It's easy to work for someone you really like.' I said, 'Good luck to you and God bless you,' and he said, 'Okay, Ger, goodbye.' And then he said, 'Oh, by the way . . .' I said, 'What would you like, sir?' And he said, 'I appointed you to the Senate today, as you requested. God bless you too, Ger.'"

While polls suggested in the summer of 1993 that Campbell had a shot at winning a majority in the upcoming autumn election, thanks to a wave of excitement in Quebec over Canada's first female prime minister, the whole enterprise imploded. Her French-speaking ability didn't come as advertised. Prior to and during the campaign she made several gaffes, and she appeared devoid of serious policy initiatives. The party somehow thought that her gender and her promise to offer a more consultative approach would be sufficient. A final, desperate TV ad campaign launched by her team, which appeared to mock the facial deformity of Liberal leader and election winner Jean Chrétien, was the final straw. With francophone Quebecers flocking to the separatist Bloc Québécois, and western Canadians moving en masse to Manning's Reform Party, Mulroney's grand coalition was blown to smithereens. On October 25, 1993, the PC party went from 169 seats won in the previous election to just 2. The pair of survivors won only on the strength of their huge local followings—the bilingual and bicultural Jean Charest in Quebec's Eastern Townships, and eccentric social conservative and former Saint John mayor Elsie Wayne.

There was one saving grace for the party: Campbell had lost her Vancouver Centre seat, making her inevitable departure less painful since she wouldn't be sitting in Parliament. Charest was still there, and it had been clear even before the end of the leadership race that he was the superior politician, a smooth speaker whose popularity in

St. Germain, according to Jean Charest, was a key Mulroney ally in convincing Quebecers that the PC Party was shedding its century-old image as a party hostile to French-speaking Canada. St. Germain "was the personification of exactly what we aspired to be," the former Quebec premier recalled in a 2016 interview. LIBRARY AND ARCHIVES CANADA

his home province was unquestioned. The party would have taken a pounding regardless of who was leader, but many felt that with Charest there would have at least have been the dozen seats required for official party status, extra funding and some reserved time in Question Period. Wishful thinkers thought Manning was a loopy western hayseed advocating policies of intolerance, and would be a flash in the pan. It seemed inevitable that Charest would step in and begin the painful rebuild, perhaps getting into a position to win power two elections down the road. While some leaders have hung in after a tough loss, with John Turner in 1984 being an example, Campbell's failure was of such epic proportions that it was widely assumed she would soon be history.

Or so they thought. Campbell had loyal campaign staff and a large contingent of followers, many of them women, who were huge admirers of hers and thrilled to be part of history in helping to choose Canada's first female prime minister. Many were devastated by her loss. Campbell gave one of her best speeches of the campaign after the results came out on election night, ending with a glowing smile and a message to her supporters to "consider yourself hugged." And that was it. There was no mention of any plans to leave, either then or in the election's immediate aftermath. This would seem odd in today's politics, as leaders suffering from defeats far less decisive—like Paul Martin in 2006 and Stephen Harper in 2015—almost immediately vacate the scene. In her memoirs Campbell wrote that she expected to resign, and implied that her departure was inevitable. But in fact nothing in that autobiography indicated that decision was a certainty. "From my own self-interested perspective it made sense for me to go," she wrote. "However I wanted to make sure that it didn't seem as if I was just cutting and running. If it had made sense for me to stay on for a while I would."

After the concession speech she gathered with her top aides at a suite in the Pan Pacific Hotel overlooking Coal Harbour in downtown Vancouver. Campbell was with Pat Kinsella, her closest campaign adviser and a veteran election organizer from BC. St. Germain was in a grim but decisive mood as he arrived in room 2336 of the Pan Pacific. He would later describe the scene in his diary:

> Met by a mob. She was insisting that her and her people would be sitting down to develop plans for the party, et cetera. Advised I was prepared to work closely with her but that I planned on taking over with an advisory board. She actually ignored what I said, but to be fair to her she was under extreme stress. But the one aspect of her that was dominant is, she really does not want to listen to anybody.

Three days after the election, on October 28, 1993, St. Germain had a telephone chat with Mulroney to brief him on the state of the badly wounded and heavily indebted party, and of his first post-election meeting with Campbell. Mulroney said she should have resigned as leader the day she stepped down as prime minister, and that Charest should have taken over the leadership, a view St. Germain shared. The diary then confirms a longstanding rumour that Campbell's leadership campaign debt might be used as leverage if she tried to stay on. "We should use [Campbell's] personal leadership debt"—assumed at the time to be $140,000–$200,000—"to pry her out," St. Germain wrote, suggesting that a senior member of Campbell's leadership team "should be the messenger."

The next day Campbell went to party headquarters to visit employees and try to lift their spirits. All but two out of eighty were about to lose their jobs due to the party's massive debt, combined with doubt in the minds of financial supporters about the party's viability, especially with uncertainty over Campbell's departure. St. Germain later drove to an event to honour veteran Tory MP Bob Layton, father of future NDP leader Jack, with Jean and Michèle Charest. "[Charest's] general feeling is that Kim Campbell has to go," St. Germain wrote in his diary. St. Germain noted that Charest got a "standing ovation" after he was introduced at the event.

Like pretty well every Progressive Conservative in the country, St. Germain was in a bitter and sour mood over the performance of

Campbell and her campaign team. In the days after the disaster he was already trying to think about a renewal of the party from the grassroots up after the once-mighty Tories had their lunches handed to them by a brand new Quebec party and an upstart western movement categorized as "fringe" by many in the media and establishment. He mused in his diary about creating a conservative-oriented policy think-tank and wrote in a November 2, 1993, diary entry that the Tories needed to start "rebuilding from the ground up. After nine and a half years in power we became totally top-down [and run by] a few insiders and so-called power brokers." The Prime Minister's Office became "arrogant and vindictive." These same insiders, portrayed by many media admirers as brilliant rainmakers because their polling and attack ads in the 1988 election had snatched victory from the jaws of defeat, "had risen to the level of godliness through polling, and no longer had to go out and listen to the grassroots."

He also criticized Campbell's campaign message, which began with a warning that unemployment wouldn't come down below 10 percent for another seven years—or close to two terms of government. The Liberals seized on that comment as a sign that the Tory campaign lacked a message of "hope," and Campbell never recovered. When reporter Robert Fife questioned her during one campaign event about that lack of an aspirational message, she snapped that one of Ottawa's most senior and accomplished reporters needed a hearing aid. St. Germain knew as a former salesman that her vague message about structural change, and promise to crack down on the deficit, weren't grabbing Canadian political consumers. "We tried to sell the car on its engineering value as opposed to the visual sex appeal, styling and gadgetry that has sold cars from the very beginning. We also started out by saying that there was an inherent problem in the car that would take time to isolate, locate and repair—that is, no marked improvement in unemployment until the year 2000." He also had some specific criticisms about Campbell, who in both her leadership and election campaigns complained of physical and mental fatigue and the lack of time to recharge her batteries. She had "no physical stamina,"

St. Germain recounted in a discussion he had with Tory campaign manager John Tory. And she could not speak fluent French "in spite of the fact that she left the perception out there that she did."

His final shot in his journal was that Campbell, despite her time in the Vancouver school board and in the BC legislature and federal Parliament, didn't understand the political "game" and "had to be coached." He also criticized comments she made during the campaign that didn't appeal to the party's social conservatives: "she alienated traditional conservatives, made light of marriage and joked about her failed marriage." He also seemed to criticize her openness to gay and lesbian Canadians, a political necessity given she represented the riding with the largest concentration of homosexuals in the country. She "appeared to endorse the non-family lifestyle of the riding she represented." St. Germain also noted that she "spoke of her lack of a sex life as a single person" and joked about the "evils of the papacy."

Campbell, in her 1996 autobiography *Time and Chance*, wrote at length about the process that led to her dragged-out resignation. She noted that she had heard "rumours" that Charest was under great pressure from his wife Michèle to leave politics. Where she heard those rumours is unclear. Quebec journalist André Pratte's 1998 biography *Charest: His Life and Politics* dissects this period and explores the tense relationship between the two Tories, with no mention of Charest considering retirement from politics. Pratte did note that Charest was being urged by Mulroney to stick around, and was told that in two elections he would be handed the front-door keys to 24 Sussex Drive. In a 2016 interview Charest made clear he never seriously considered any option other than remaining to help lead and rebuild his shattered party.

But Campbell seemed determined to explore the possibility that one of the party's two MPs might jump ship, so she met him twice for lunch to see if he wanted to take over. "If I resigned immediately . . . it seemed to me that this would have made it harder for him to go," Campbell wrote in her memoirs. "If Jean were not available to take over the leadership, the party would have to be led from the Senate, which seemed an unappealing idea." She said she asked him if he was leaving, but he remained coy. So Campbell kept quiet about her future heading into the first formal Tory gathering after the debacle—a major fundraising dinner in Toronto in November, exactly a month after the crushing election. Earlier that day a nervous St. Germain had gone to her hotel room, as Campbell recounted in *Time and Chance*:

> Gerry and I had never been close, although we were both from British Columbia. He was a true Mulroney loyalist. I knew he would be one of the custodians of the Mulroney reputation, which meant that the sooner I threw myself on the funeral pyre, the happier he would be. He paced up and down my room, explaining that when he lost his seat in 1988, he "wasn't rational" for at least two years afterwards. Watching him, I wondered about his current state of mind. As he kept assuring me that I could count on him to tell me the truth, I remembered all the reports I'd heard of his bad-mouthing me over the past few years, all the while professing friendship in person, and assumed it was business as usual.

St. Germain has a different recollection of that meeting, straight from his diary entry while on a November 30, 1993, flight to Ottawa. "My meeting with her was bizarre," he wrote. "She became very irritated when I was trying to tell her that when the inevitable would happen she would be treated properly. She spoke of a job at Harvard, writing a book and having a role in rebuilding the party . . . It was as though she was obsessed with telling people what she was doing instead of building a consensus."

Later that evening Campbell headed to Toronto for what was originally billed as the "prime minister's dinner," a fundraiser where she was to deliver her first major post-election speech to party members. She began by saying she took "full responsibility" for the election results, but she "also took responsibility for rebuilding the party." She spelled out a plan she had previously floated right after the election, that she wanted to launch a commission to look into ways to rebuild the party.

Then Campbell made a bombshell statement that caused several jaws to drop around the room. This commission, she declared, would report to *her* in June, eight months after the worst electoral drubbing in the history of federal politics in Canada. Her sharp mind may have been impacted by the after-effects of the shocking electoral defeat, because in her memoirs she suggests this was a harmless slip. "Since the question of my resignation had not been determined, I wasn't sure whether to say that the report would be presented to 'the leader' or to 'me.' I chose the latter, not realizing the consternation it would cause."

The prime minister of the day wasn't wrong in concluding that the president of her party was hardly a fan. St. Germain confirmed that widespread assumption, and acknowledged he voted for Charest in the 1993 leadership race. "Campbell was a different kettle of fish," he said. "She wasn't like Pat Carney, but she was oblivious to what other people said. She'd be late for everything." While the views of Mulroney, Charest, St. Germain and others were interesting, they weren't as decisive as those of the people the party needed to bankroll them out of their $10 million debt. St. Germain said he and others were convinced by long-time donors that they weren't prepared to "throw good money after bad" by funding a party led by Campbell. She had to leave, and fast.

Campbell acknowledged in her memoirs that her speech's reference to staying on until June "accelerated" the movement to give her the boot. Rumours began circulating that "the executive had refused to vote me a salary, which would have been necessary if I were to stay on. I had never asked for a salary and was offended by the gratuitous insult." She said her plan was to finally tell Canadians she was stepping down in mid-January, close to three months after the election, while leaving in her stead a legacy initiative—the commission—to revive the party (though St. Germain pointed out that she hadn't consulted with the party and didn't have a mandate to initiate such a move):

Finally, I came to see that the original plan I'd worked out with my advisers—in which I would step down around January 15, leaving

the plan in place as a parting contribution—would not work . . .
Over several weeks, I spoke to my closest supporters to be sure
that they were comfortable with my intention to resign sooner
rather than later. I finally decided that what I owed to all the people
who had worked so hard to support me for the leadership was not
to debase myself. Staying on, even if the party executive agreed it
was appropriate, would be a non-stop process of pulling knives out
of my back.

She then noted in her memoirs what St. Germain and Mulroney
discussed on the phone two days after the election—that she "became
aware of another problem—I owed the party money" from her leadership campaign.

I began to hear of rumours in the party that not only did I owe the
party money, but I was making my resignation as leader contingent on my debt being written off. This was completely untrue,
since I insisted that the party not say it would pay my debt. Given
the enormous debt the party was facing, the rumour was designed
to turn party members against me. I told [campaign finance chair]
Robert Foster that my debt had to be paid and, thanks to his quiet
efforts, it now has been.

Jim Prentice had an interesting perspective on the fallout. He served as
St. Germain's treasurer on the party executive at that time. He was also
a prominent Campbell supporter, and in fact nominated her at the party
leadership convention in June. Prentice said he has no memory of the
debt being used to pressure Campbell to leave. But he did remember the
day shortly after the election when he and St. Germain approached her
while she was still prime minister, to tell her the party had serious financial problems and that the leadership debt had to be repaid:

Gerry and I attended a very difficult meeting with her, he as president and me as treasurer. We had an obligation to meet with her to

tell her that the party would have to be repaid. I recall that meeting quite vividly. I don't know if it was the first time she heard about that, but it was a difficult and emotional meeting for all of us. There was no attempt to suggest it would be used against her, it was just to apprise her of fact of the debt. But she appeared hurt by it. She was still the prime minister at the time, so it was quite emotional.

Campbell, who didn't mention that meeting in her memoirs, concluded at this point that St. Germain and others, including Mulroney, "seem to take my continued presence at the helm of the party as a personal affront. In their view, all our problems were my fault, and the party would never be able to raise money or recover as long as I was there." Finally on December 13, 1993, she marched into the National Press Theatre in Ottawa to sit uncomfortably next to St. Germain before a packed room of journalists to announce her resignation. "Afterwards he read a statement accepting my resignation with the obligatory regret," Campbell recounted in her memoirs. "I tried to be upbeat and positive, but Gerry's expression confirmed everything that had been rumoured about the shabby treatment I had received from him and others."

Noting that Chrétien's triumphant Liberals had offered her an office and a secretary to organize her papers for six months, she wrote that the "short-sightedness of the national executive created considerable resentment against the party, particularly among women, which could only hinder the rebuilding process. Watching the frenzied activity of those individuals after the election was like watching a group of pygmies running around in a tizzy." It was an obvious shot at St. Germain, and her resentment of him has endured. In a 2016 interview she said St. Germain, whose "loyalty was only to himself," was part of a Mulroney-led effort to make her wear the defeat even though more sympathetic observers felt she was handed a poisoned chalice. "For some people the election result must be laid at my feet in order not to acknowledge other realities." St. Germain, used to being dismissed as a lowly chicken farmer, would have to shrug off the criticism of people like Campbell that he was a frantic and less-than-rational pygmy. He had a fractured party to rebuild and only a handful of people left to start the process.

10

∞

The Aftermath

In late 1993 a kind of nuclear winter set in for what was left of the once-mighty Progressive Conservative Party of Canada. Winning just 2 of 295 seats was a disaster, leaving one of the two great ruling parties of Canadian history far short of the dozen required for official party status in Parliament. That status is an afterthought for every established party in Canada—that is, until the moment when they don't have the twelve seats. Parties below that threshold not only lose the extra staffing to fund researchers and media specialists; gone as well is the guaranteed slot to ask a few questions in Question Period, the only time of day when the majority of the national media pays close attention to the House of Commons. The parliamentary press gallery also occasionally covers committee meetings, where MPs from parties without status are forbidden from questioning witnesses.

But for the PCs in late 1993, the lack of formal status was far from the biggest worry. The party was $10 million in debt, morale among the few who hadn't abandoned ship was rock-bottom, finger pointing was rampant, and the brand was brutally and perhaps permanently discredited. It was easy for Jean Chrétien's new Liberal government and the two main opposition parties, Reform and the Bloc Québécois, to point fingers at the Tory legacy to explain why times were tough. Canada's economy was weak, the public was still grumbling about paying Mulroney's GST, a Quebec referendum that could break up the country appeared imminent, and the federal budget deficit was at crisis levels. Cutbacks were coming, and the Liberals—despite their own legacy of leaving Mulroney in 1984 with a massive structural deficit—would blame the pain of those cuts on the PCs.

Yet while Kim Campbell may have been wondering about the possibility that Jean Charest might want to flee from this nearly sunken ship, to Charest that wasn't an option. He confided in a 2016 interview that his wife Michèle would have appreciated having her husband spend more time with her and their three young children after that election. But "Michou," an intelligent and radiant blonde who would laugh at his jokes during public speeches like she'd heard them for the first time, was as politically savvy as her husband. When the results rolled in on election night, Charest felt a burst of pride that he managed to win his seat easily despite the carnage for established Tory MPs across Canada. "I thought this was a bit of a compliment!" Charest recalled. "And I turned to her and there were tears in her eyes. I said, 'What's wrong, aren't you happy?' And she said, 'This means you're going to have to stay.' And her instinct was that this was going to be difficult, and it was. It ended up being quite challenging."

Charest would also get considerable pressure to stay from Mulroney, who had been in regular contact with him and St. Germain, and who was desperate to protect his legacy by keeping his party alive. St. Germain was a kind of second-in-command in saving the party from total annihilation. There had been some speculation, penned in a newspaper column by future senator Mike Duffy, that he might seek the party leadership. "I never took that seriously," St. Germain said. "I knew the limits of my capabilities."

As Michèle Charest predicted, the leadership was a hellish project. Charest had lived the good life as a cabinet minister in the Mulroney government, which spared no expense to ensure ministers and their entourage travelled first class, in limousines while in Ottawa and occasionally via the fleet of government jets. What a contrast to his grim post-1993 task in trying to reassemble the pieces of a party that had shattered like a wine glass dropped on a ceramic floor: "In the first years I'm sleeping and eating in the homes of volunteers and supporters. We were dirt poor." Charest gave speeches to small crowds on a Vancouver Island tour arranged by St. Germain, being transported from one town to another via a small airplane. The cowboy-boot-wearing pilot—a friend of the senator's—was playing loud country music as they entered the aircraft. Charest sat in the front next to the pilot, while a Quebec journalist travelling with him sat behind them. "And the pilot asked me to hold the door closed, because it wouldn't shut."

On another occasion Charest was brutally questioned by BC open-line host Rafe Mair, a harsh critic of Mulroney's pandering to Quebec, and Mair's listeners over the state of the country following nine years of Tory rule: "It was rough." Charest would also recall an arduous life touring the country, trying to boost morale while bringing in democratic reforms to make grassroots members feel it was their party. St. Germain said there was some grumbling that Charest didn't have the passion and work ethic to pull it off, but St. Germain said he wasn't part of that.

"I never tolerated any criticism. I was so grateful he was doing what he was doing. Who tries to fly a plane that is wrecked? Sure there was criticism that he didn't work hard enough. But I am eternally grateful to both him and Elsie [Wayne]. They allowed us to regenerate a party that had been annihilated." St. Germain was doing similar work, travelling the country and meeting with supporters and donors trying to convince them the PC brand could be revived. "To be a leader and have no support, you've got to have the courage and commitment to keep going, and it's an ugly job. I know what it is to get off an airplane and there's no one to meet you. It makes a huge difference when you have to do everything yourself."

St. Germain was supportive of his leader but the two didn't have much contact. Instead, St. Germain focused on managing the other half of the Tory caucus, the New Brunswick firebrand Elsie Wayne. The former Saint John mayor rose to prominence as a blunt-talking but often humorous housewife upset over annual flooding in her area of town. She parlayed that exposure to get elected to city council, and then to the mayor's office, before taking advantage of her enormous local popularity and name recognition by seeking a federal seat in 1993. Once she got there she discovered she had more in common with a lot of Reform MPs, who shared her views on matters like abortion, than she did with her leader. "I was busy babysitting Elsie, renting cars, driving her here and there. She was alluding to the fact she was being courted by the Reform Party. I wanted to make damn certain she didn't [accept]. I had two MPs and I didn't want to lose either one of them."

In those early years there was some media speculation, often encouraged by Mulroney in private chats with columnists, that the PCs would inevitably rebound to their rightful place as soon as the Reform Party lost its lustre. That speculation at times seemed credible. Preston Manning, thanks to his domination of the political landscape in BC and Alberta, arrived in Ottawa with fifty-two seats—a historic breakthrough and a remarkable achievement, though frustrating for him because it was just one short of the Bloc's fifty-three-seat total, which resulted in Canada getting its first leader of the opposition dedicated to breaking up the country. The grassroots party vowed to bring in a bottom-up rather than top-down approach to politics, and preached the notion that MPs should be their constituents' voices in Ottawa, rather than their party leader's voice in their riding. That sounded great in theory, but it meant that party members felt they had licence to say whatever popped into their heads, or whatever they heard in the local coffee shop back home. That was fine for some of Manning's more polished and loyal MPs, like Chuck Strahl in BC and Deb Grey in Alberta. But for others it was a tough transition adapting to the so-called "politically correct" demands of Ottawa, where anyone questioning Quebec's place in Canada as a "distinct society," the established immigration policy, official bilingualism and other mantelpieces of a century of centrist governing were considered heretics.

Manning must have felt like he was leading fifty-two soldiers through a minefield while his critics —not only from the other parties but also from the parliamentary press gallery—sniped at them from a safe distance. Myron Thompson, a US-born former Alberta school-teacher with a heavy American twang who could have passed for a Texas rancher, was one who bore watching. At one jam-packed gathering of party members, the topic for discussion was the Liberal government's plan to amend the Canadian Human Rights Act to prohibit discrimination on the basis of sexual orientation. Thompson boomed, "God made Adam and Eve, not Adam and Steve!" to thunderous applause.

Another incident that had many pundits wondering if Reform was a one-term wonder, and speculating that the smooth Charest could bounce back, was the one that sent Manning and his party into a tailspin in early 1995. Vancouver Island Reformer Bob Ringma said in a *Vancouver Sun* interview that he would fire or "move to the back of the shop" a homosexual or member of an ethnic minority whose presence turned off bigoted customers. Reform plunged to a low of 14 percent in the polls in the aftermath of that controversy, which no doubt played a role in a pessimistic Stephen Harper quitting politics and returning to Calgary in early 1997. But media speculation missed the mark in suggesting the party was going to fade away.

Despite Reform's challenges, neither Charest nor St. Germain needed to be convinced that the challenge of retaking lost ground would be incredibly difficult. St. Germain was known in the party for sensing the pulse of grassroots conservatives, whether they were Reformers or PCs: "I knew where Reform's strengths were. The Reform base was solid . . . but the only way we were going to resolve this was by negotiating a [merger] deal. These were all our people, but they were disillusioned with the direction we took." Charest said he also recognized there was no easy route out of political purgatory: "You learn the hard way that success can't be based on the business plan that your adversary is going to fall apart. We had taken a huge beating in 1993, and were reminded every day after that of what we'd done wrong. When I became leader in December 1993 it was like being put in charge of a train wreck. We knew this was going to take some time. There was no assumption Reform would go away."

Still, St. Germain's spirits began to lift when Charest started to build momentum heading into the 1997 federal election. It began when two staffers were brought in from then Ontario premier Mike Harris's government, which in 1995 had replaced Bob Rae's NDP with the most ideological PC government in the province's history. Signalling a shift to the right and an end to Red Toryism, the federal platform they wrote called for low taxes and less government. As *La Presse* journalist André Pratte noted in his Charest biography, the strategists were adamant that there be no reference to Quebec's status as a distinct society. Their tax cut theme failed to generate much excitement during the early stages of the campaign, so Charest pivoted. First, he began attacking the Chrétien government's employment insurance (EI) reforms, which were deeply unpopular in Atlantic Canada. Then, in the only dramatic moment during the high-profile leaders' debate, he vowed to do as his father had by passing on a united Canada to his children. There was a sudden surge in the opinion polls, and while the Liberal lead was insurmountable the PCs looked to have a shot at second place and official opposition—jumping to 25 percent in the polls against Reform's 18 percent.

But then the ground shifted. Manning, advised at the time by Rick Anderson, uncorked a desperate new strategy that threw Charest, whose key adviser on polling was Rick's brother Bruce, for a loop. Reform began running television ads featuring the faces of four Quebec francophone leaders—Chrétien, Charest, Bouchard and Gilles Duceppe, who had taken over as leader of the Bloc Québécois when Bouchard moved to provincial politics. Each face had a red circle and single diagonal cross over it, with the declaration that Canadians were sick and tired of being led by Quebec leaders. Suddenly the election polarized. Even though unemployment was by far the biggest public concern, all talk shifted to Quebec's place in Canada. Chrétien, Charest and the Quebec nationalist movement accused Manning of intolerance

and bigotry, but the ads resonated with many western Canadians who
were tired of being held hostage by central Canadian promises to keep
Quebec in Canada with what seemed like never-ending bribes.

Charest ended up being on the wrong side of a squeeze play,
winning just twenty seats, only three of them west of Quebec. The
criticism of Chrétien's cuts to jobless benefits won over many voters in
Quebec and especially Atlantic Canada, but in crucial Ontario Charest
took a single seat out of 103. Especially for St. Germain, the 1997 result
was a classic illustration of the futility of a divided conservative movement. Reform and the PCs each took around 19 percent in Ontario, but
together they ended up with one Tory MP heading to Ottawa. Going
from two to twenty seats seemed like a strong incremental gain for the
PCs, but it was far short of official opposition. Worse, the way the party
got there left considerable bad feelings. Ontario Tories were furious
at Charest for pivoting from the tax cuts to national unity. He in turn
was bitter at Ontario premier Mike Harris for taking a publicly neutral
position toward Reform due to fears that he would alienate Ontario
Tory party members who liked Manning's ideas.

Charest recognized that his dream of becoming prime minister of
Canada was over. The party was once again divided and fingers were
being pointed at him. Worse, for people like St. Germain, Charest
seemed to take the anti-Quebec Reform ads personally and ruled out
the notion that the two parties could ever unite. "The only coalition I
see emerging is between the Reform and Bloc," he declared bitterly
to Global TV. "After what [Manning] has done, it is very difficult to
envision [a merger]. I don't see that happening. This is as close to
the word 'never' as I could ever get." In the spring of 1998 he finally
succumbed to the pressure from federalists in Quebec and elsewhere
in the country to take over the leadership of the Quebec Liberal Party.

St. Germain was deeply troubled at this point. While he had
stepped down as president in 1995, he remained involved in Tory
politics, holding his annual summer barbecues and helping the party
organize. But unlike Charest, he neither saw Reformers as bigots
nor did he believe an indefinite cold war would do anything other

than ensure Liberal rule. He remembered being impressed, as most political observers were, with the bright, bilingual young man from Calgary with the sleepy eyes and odd hairstyle, the stark outlook laced with occasional dry humour. Stephen Harper had been Manning's top policy guru since Reform's founding in 1987, was elected during the Reform sweep of BC and Alberta in 1993, and up until his split with Manning in 1996 was considered the leader's heir apparent. The media often described him as the party's "moderate" voice, something that bemused Harper given his firm right-wing views. But he did come from the libertarian (in favour of small government and free markets) rather than social conservative (anti-abortion, anti–gay marriage) wing of the Reform Party, and came across as a sophisticate in the context of "turnip truck" caucus members like Stetson-wearing MPs Myron Thompson and Darrel Stinson.

So St. Germain made a trip to Calgary, where Harper was head of the right-wing National Citizens Coalition, and spent a day and a half with Stephen and Laureen Harper, trying to convince Stephen to return to his former party to run in the 1998 PC leadership race. "I spent a lot of time talking to him," St. Germain recalled. "I knew we needed new blood. I went over every aspect of it one afternoon for four or five hours. I told him, 'I've seen you around, I've seen you perform,' and I said, 'There's no perfect horse, but I think you are ready for the race.'" The next morning he came back and Harper said, "Gerry, it's just not the right time to go." St. Germain took note in his journal of a direct quotation from Harper: "Preston is prepared to work towards reconciliation but he is not prepared to put his leadership on the line or to relinquish his position." He also wrote on the same day his own assessment of PC leadership candidates Hugh Segal, Brian Pallister and Joe Clark. He seemed to be leaning toward Clark as he scribbled down a barely lukewarm endorsement of "We won't do much but we should hold our own."

Despite his initial coolness toward Segal, St. Germain ended up supporting the former Mulroney chief of staff and party insider from Ontario's Big Blue Machine. During the leadership campaign St.

Germain was approached by a reporter and asked about Segal's senior role with one of the most unpopular prime ministers in Canadian history. He answered as honestly as he could, saying a candidate's past service for another leader shouldn't be held against him. He never anticipated the blast he would receive more than a month later in a private letter on Senate stationery. It was from his old nemesis Marjory LeBreton, who had worked in the office of every Conservative leader dating back to John Diefenbaker in the early 1960s. The letter—complete with a *coup de grâce* under her signature on the final page—represents the nastiness that can occur between politicians in the same party:

September 21, 1998
Dear Gerry:
I'm writing to you to raise an issue that will surely not come as a surprise since I have been unrelenting in my comments in caucus, to the media, in public and indeed in personal conversations with whomever will listen—and that is the timidness, lack of courage, backbone, or what have you, on the part of a great many people in our party to a) defend Brian Mulroney & b) defend the record of the government he led.

Our inability or unwillingness to defend our government has caused all of us collectively a great deal of difficulty—especially since had we done so from the moment Brian Mulroney left office in June 1993, we could have been first off the mark in holding the Chrétien crowd accountable and legitimately made the claim from the outset as we now finally do—that it was the courage, foresight and planning of our government that produced the favourable results so valuable to the present government. There's no way they should have had such a free ride.

But it is on the first point (lack of defence of Brian Mulroney) that I really get agitated. I find such conduct so offensive, so cowardly, so disrespectful and stunningly ungrateful.

By and large, the media, our adversaries and political enemies have had a field day by simply injecting into their question the name "Brian Mulroney"—so successful have they been in keeping the anti-Mulroney or Mulroney-bashing industry alive and well. Why have our detractors been so successful? We need to look no further than ourselves. I'm reminded of the great quote of Pogo which goes something like—"I have seen the enemy and it is us."

The sad conclusion of all of this is that in not challenging these attacks and fighting back we have left the impression that what our enemies say is true.

How can anyone who was part of Mulroney's government be party to such nonsense, especially when we saw first-hand the level of activity, the hard work, the innovative programs, the radical structural changes, the courageous efforts to bring constitutional peace to our country—all while subjected to "the most intense and unrelenting campaign of denigration that any Canadian government has faced since at least this side of the Second World War" to use George Bain's words in his book *Gotcha!* Thanks to "Rat Pack" tactics, special-interest lobby groups, and the strange cowardliness on our part, it was as easy as pie for our adversaries to keep it up. I used to say to the Prime Minister when we were in government, "I hate to tell you this, PM, but you lead an army of chocolate soldiers. They melt when the heat is turned up."

So what do I see with my own eyes when I flip on my TV set a few days ago and watch with interest the CPAC coverage of the BC Progressive Conservative picnic on August 16? You are asked the question, "Hugh Segal is known, I guess, in the later years of his political life before he became a commentator and author, as being the chief of staff for Brian Mulroney. Do you think there will be any problem with him being in the shadow of Brian Mulroney, if you perceive that to be a problem?"

And you responded: "The thing is, when you work for people you take on the job, you do what you're told and you, you know you give what advice you can . . . But basically I don't care who anybody has worked for. It's like you . . . I would never pass judgement on you because of anything that you've done in the past in regards to having worked for some particular organization. The fact is that when the prime minister calls on you to serve you serve if you're capable and so inclined . . . I think that's what really happened in that case."

I will not repeat my immediate response to an empty room which caused my husband to call out from another room, "Who are you yelling at?" I'll leave it to your imagination. What a limp-wristed, lily-livered response—you looked and sounded rather like you were ashamed of Brian Mulroney, a sort of "I'm alright Jack—he was the problem." Rather than responding by answering a question with the retort—"Yes, he was Brian Mulroney's chief of staff—you have a problem with that? What actions of the Mulroney government of which we were all proud to be part of do you wish to discuss?"

But no, Gerry. You gave the same timid response that Hugh has given. "He called, I served," sort of like the devil made me do it. Give me a break! And this is supposed to demonstrate leadership? We will never ever succeed if we allow this to continue to happen. Surely we have learned that lesson. Remember, Kim Campbell and those around her employed these tactics and look where it got us. It also cost us in the 1997 campaign as well, as we had people running away from their association with Brian Mulroney and our government.

Last year, on September 24, 1997, Jean Charest admitted the error of this to our caucus when he said, "We made a grave, grave, grave mistake in not defending Brian Mulroney and our government." He is right of course. Too bad some weren't listening.

I've gone on longer than intended but this kind of talk annoys the hell out of me. It always has and always will.

Yours sincerely,

Marjory

cc: Rt. Hon. Brian Mulroney, PC, CC

St. Germain said he was livid, and tried to get the matter raised in caucus. And the "only guy who stood up for me was [Tory senator] Michael Meighen. He said, 'I agree with Gerry.' LeBreton just sat there."

Joe Clark, by far the biggest name seeking to replace Charest, won the party's leadership on a commitment to never sell out the party to Reform. Clark was the reddest of Red Tories, viewing Reformers as angry, intolerant and close-minded. After winning the leadership he referred to Reform as "narrow" and to the party's "taint" as if it was a rotting piece of fish, overlooking the fact that 2.5 million Canadians who voted for the party might take offence at that characterization. This attitude, and Clark's image as an indecisive man dating back to his first term as Tory leader, drove St. Germain crazy. It was the beginning of the end for a man many viewed as integral to the party. In 1999 St. Germain remembers attending a caucus meeting where Greg Thompson, an affable Tory MP from New Brunswick, was making his case on the caucus's position on gay marriage. The exchange between Clark and Thompson was noisy, bitter and at one point looked like it might get violent. "He looked like he was going to go after Joe."

At the same caucus meeting St. Germain brought up an argument he'd been making for more than a decade—that the Tories had to figure out a way to accommodate Reform and its followers, rather than treat the movement as a virus that needed to be flushed out of the Canadian political system. "Joe said he wouldn't make a deal with the devil. I said, 'Joe, they are all our people!' I walked out. I'll never forget that. That's when I realized that this guy wasn't going to listen to us, he was going to continue to run the show like he did in '79 and '80. The difference with Joe Clark is that he would go straight for the jugular, whereas a guy like Mulroney would come back around and have a conversation and draw out somebody like Greg. At least the guy would have felt that he had been listened to."

11

∞

Unite the Right

St. Germain wasn't the only gloomy right-of-centre politician in Canada at that time. The 1997–2003 period was arguably the darkest period in the history of Canada's conservative movement. The old federal Progressive Conservative Party had a long history of backstabbing-filled internal feuds. After the 1997 election PC Party members were frustrated that the campaign had run out of steam in the final weeks, and were deeply resentful over Reform's use of the no-more-leaders-from-Quebec attack ad. There was also the second-guessing of their leader's tactics, and whether he was different enough in nature and ideology from the Liberals they wanted to boot from office. When Charest walked away a few months later, things hardly looked brighter. Joe Clark left no one with the view that he was anything more than a caretaker whose role was only to save the furniture. Reform's troops, meanwhile, could see the writing on the wall. They were led by a charismatic, wise and visionary man in Preston Manning, but he couldn't speak a sentence in French that wasn't written down in front of him, and his folksy western twang played well in rural and some suburban parts of the country but made him come across as alien and unsophisticated in urban Canada.

The nastiness between the two fraternal political entities was deeply personal. Both Charest and then Clark portrayed Manning as essentially un-Canadian because the Reform leader was declaring there should be no more submission to what was perceived as black-mail from Quebec. PCs at the grassroots level were also bitter about the nature of the Reform movement. "It's the religious agenda and the social conservative agenda," David March, a Vancouver-based Tory activist, told the *Vancouver Sun* in late October 1998. "I'm not only the Tory press secretary for this province. I also happen to be a gay single male. And their agenda is not gay-friendly. I've also done an educational stint in Quebec, and their agenda is vehemently, I believe, anti-Canadian. I mean, extreme doesn't cover it."

Reformers, meanwhile, bitterly resented the extremist label during the post-election period. In early December of 1997, when tired MPs were looking forward to their Christmas break, the tensions boiled over in the House. BC Reformer Darrel Stinson was giving a speech when he heard Charest mutter the word "racist." It wasn't the first time Stinson was taunted. Earlier that year he heard the same smear across the aisle from Ontario Liberal MP John Cannis. Dropping all pretence of parliamentary decorum, Stinson cut loose, challenging Cannis to "step outside" to settle the matter. Glaring across the aisle and aiming his thick index finger at Cannis like it was a Glock, he shouted, "Do you have the fortitude or the gonads to stand up and come across here and say that to me, you son of a bitch?" So when Charest made the same accusation during the post-election hangover it was like putting a match to a cloud of gas fumes. Turning to the Tory leader Stinson taunted him as a "fat little chubby little sucker" and made it clear he'd like nothing more than to settle this once and for all in mano-a-mano style. Charest, like Cannis, wisely demurred.

This was an interesting time in the media too. The Southam news-paper chain had been taken over by perhaps the most colourful and opinionated character to emerge from Canada's business class, Conrad

Black. He created the *National Post*, a right-of-centre national newspaper to rival the *Globe and Mail*, which became a forum for those who wanted to end Chrétien's grip on power by uniting Canada's two right-of-centre parties. Manning tried to get out in front of this effort. In 1998 he created the "United Alternative" movement, which was aimed at uniting Canada's conservatives. It seemed logical as a concept, but there were two problems.

First, Manning left little doubt he wanted to lead this new entity. Clark, meanwhile, essentially said he would resist any union with his dying breath. For many journalists on Parliament Hill this soon became a tiring story. It seemed obvious, as illustrated by the Stinson–Charest showdown, that many of these people disliked and disrespected each other more than any other political adversaries. Prominent PCs were saying that if a union ever happened they'd rather vote for the Liberals, especially with popular Liberal finance minister Paul Martin—a hero to many Canadians for finally balancing the budget—about to replace Chrétien.

Manning tried to push the movement further by organizing a United Alternative gathering for February 1999. Soon after that initiative began, the *Vancouver Sun* started getting calls from St. Germain's BC associates suggesting the senator was so disillusioned with Clark's leadership that he was considering attending. St. Germain's participation would be a huge coup for the unite-the-right forces, because while the event had substantial backing from the Ontario and Alberta provincial Tory parties, the old federal PCs had been bitter opponents of Manning's movement from day one, and were determined to sabotage it. Getting a former Mulroney-era minister, party president, prominent fundraiser and senator was viewed as a potential trophy.

But St. Germain, far more cautious after the impetuous mistakes of his youth, took baby steps. He told the *Vancouver Sun* in a front-page story in late October 1998 that he was seriously considering attending the UA gathering. Alberta premier Ralph Klein had already severely wounded Clark's credibility, saying that even with an Albertan like Clark at the helm the PCs barely had a pulse in western Canada. St.

Germain added weight to that argument. "I don't take issue with him [Klein] when he says that we have a severe challenge in western Canada in re-attracting the support that we did have," said St. Germain. "I don't think it's impossible . . . but it would make it a lot simpler if we could find a solution to bring the people back to us who have left us in the West." A few days later he dismissed Clark's claims that he could win a war of attrition against Manning once he took over the leadership of the Tories in mid-November 1998. Finally, in December it was officially announced that St. Germain would be leading a delegation of prominent BC federal Tories heading to Manning's United Alternative gathering in February.

The group joining the unite-the-right "bandwagon," according to a gleeful-sounding news release, included businessman Mike Burns, who at the time was a board member of the PC Canada Fund, and former BC Hydro chairman Chester Johnson. Vancouver lawyer Lyall Knott, a prominent Tory, expressed continued skepticism of the unite-the-right effort but acknowledged the St. Germain move gave him and other Tories pause. "There's a lot of concern and skepticism. Tories are not Reformers," Knott said, before adding, "The credibility of that group certainly will have an impact. Those are leaders of the community." St. Germain, Burns and the rest of the delegation joined some 1,500 delegates, the majority Reformers but with a healthy dose of provincial PCs, who arrived in Ottawa in February 1999 to consider ways to join forces to defeat the Liberals.

The Ontario PC Party, far more right-wing than its federal counterpart, was well represented with ministers such as Tony Clement and John Baird, both of whom would go on to serve in Stephen Harper's cabinet. So was the Alberta PC Party, as both Klein and treasurer Stockwell Day also spoke. Delegates and party members voted to create a new party, but the idea wasn't going far with Clark refusing to go along. Former Mulroney-era minister John Crosbie, a guest speaker, added to the acrimony by criticizing the Reform movement and drawing boos from the crowd. Brian Mulroney, still bitter about the damage Reform had inflicted on his party and especially on his legacy, was working behind the scenes to keep his loyalists in line: "I was determined there would be no action taken whatsoever as long as Preston Manning was leader of the party or involved in it."

Countering forces were also making it difficult for the effort to succeed, as there was a group of hard-core Reformers led by traditionalists like Myron Thompson and Darrel Stinson who were resisting the effort to merge the party into a new entity. The group was called GUARD, or "Grassroots United Against Reform's Demise." Despite such efforts, the United Alternative delegates voted in favour of a motion calling for the winding down of Reform and the creation of a new entity with a different brand name. But it was a messy affair, and great suspicion was raised over the convention format, which seemed geared toward promoting Manning as the obvious leader of a new party. That suspicion was confirmed when delegates received a brochure after the gathering that included five flattering photographs of the Reform leader, smaller photos of other potential leadership rivals such as Klein, and only a single sentence acknowledging the presence of Stockwell Day, a charismatic and functionally bilingual populist and fiscal conservative seen by many as Manning's principal challenger.

That move proved to be too clever by half, as it temporarily cost the United Alternative movement St. Germain's support. A few days after the brochure arrived in mailboxes he distanced himself from the effort. "If these guys think they can promote Preston Manning and at the same time try to make the world believe you're starting something new, their cause is totally hopeless," he told the *Vancouver Sun*. St. Germain ended up criticizing both the Manning- and Clark-led parties for failing to come up with a solution to indefinite Liberal rule: "It's sad because there is no opposition [to the Liberals] in the country." The upshot was that there would be no unity before the coming election, which ended up taking place in the autumn of 2000. But St. Germain was prophetic in saying that the move would ultimately open the door, telling the *Sun*, "I can't see starting a new party affecting anything other than maybe bringing in a new leader to replace Manning, and that will open the door to a dialogue with my party."

A few months later, in May 2000, St. Germain dropped a bombshell. He quit the Tory caucus to sit as an independent and publicly endorsed Stockwell Day, who would go on the following month to defeat Manning and become leader of the newly created Canadian Alliance Party. The hardest part of St. Germain's decision was explaining it to the man who had been indispensable in him becoming an MP, minister, party president and senator. Mulroney "was really upset. He said this guy [Day] will never make it. I said, 'Well, he might not, but we've got to try to unite the parties.'" Mulroney recounted the tense discussion he had with his old friend:

> I told him how upset I was by this. I told him I had put him in the Senate because I thought he would be a loyalist who would defend our legacy until the bitter end. We did not have at the time a large number of seats in the House of Commons. But we were coming back. For a number of years there had only been the two of them there, Jean Charest and Elsie Wayne, with the Reform Party savaging us every day, along with the Liberals and the NDP. There was nobody to defend us. So I had made certain that the people that I put in the Senate were loyalists and they would do that. So I was not happy with this, and I made it abundantly clear to him. But he went off and did his own thing.

St. Germain's entry into the Alliance caucus couldn't be just negotiated by Day's people. The Canadian Alliance had many MPs who had contempt for unelected senators and especially those appointed by Mulroney, the man whose style of governing inspired them to get involved in politics. So there had to be a vote in caucus, with St. Germain present. "Some of them were nervous. It had to be unanimous. I said, "If it's not unanimous then I'm out.'" St. Germain had an added message to the MPs—despite Mulroney's anger with him for abandoning the sinking Tory ship, St. Germain wasn't ever going to renounce his support for, and admiration of, the former prime minister. "I said, 'Obviously some of you exist today as MPs because of the mistakes that were made in the previous administration. In spite of the fact that I have come over, my loyalties and my allegiances to Mulroney will never diminish.' I thought that this was the test. When they voted, they voted 100 percent. 'Anybody against?' Not a soul. And so I was part of their caucus."

St. Germain said his decision led to some brutal criticism from long-time Tories, including sitting senators and former MPs, who called him a "Benedict Arnold" and a "Brutus":

> Somebody had to move, and I had a lot invested in this thing. I've got no problems with the Liberals being in power for a while, but I want to make damn certain they are kept to account. Somebody has to lead. Mulroney was really, really upset with me. I wasn't that worried about Stock winning or losing. Logically I wanted to see him win, but I knew in the long run this was a step that could possibly bring us together. Mulroney treated Margaret and me superbly. But he couldn't see what I could see. I knew the West, I knew Quebec, and I had a fair idea of Ontario and the Atlantic Provinces. I spent time with [New Brunswick premier Richard] Hatfield and [Nova Scotia's] John Buchanan. As president I covered the whole country, and I had an idea of what could take place and what people were telling me. People have a tendency when I sit down with them, they tell me what they think, they trust me. I knew the Reformers, I used to play golf with some of them. These people weren't the enemy as I saw them, they were conservatives. They were disenchanted, just like family members.

St. Germain's dramatic move was a significant blow for Clark's PCs. "St. Germain's defection added important ammunition to Stockwell Day's contention that Joe Clark and the Tory party were a spent force," Bob Plamondon wrote in *Full Circle: Death and Resurrection in Canadian Conservative Politics*. Day's Canadian Alliance won sixty-six seats in the 2000 election, and took a remarkable 46 percent of the vote in St. Germain's home province of BC. But unfortunately for

Canada's conservative movement, Day didn't shine as a campaigner and wasn't able to drive a stake through the heart of the PCs. Clark managed to win a seat in Calgary Centre, which is as left-wing a riding as you can find in southern Alberta, and took eleven more seats to hang on by a thread to official party status. But the Tory seats were primarily in Atlantic Canada, cementing the party's status as a regional rump relying largely on the only part of Canada where party loyalties were still passed down through the generations.

Chrétien, meanwhile, once again benefited from the vote split to win a third straight majority. The split in Ontario vote was fatal, as the Alliance won just two seats with 23.6 percent of the vote, and Clark's PCs none with 14.4 percent of the vote. That 38-percent total was identical to the combined Reform–PC vote in 1997, and slightly above the 1993 total of 35 percent. The 2000 election was disappointing enough, as it looked like the Liberals would rule indefinitely, especially with them about to replace Jean Chrétien with finance minister Paul Martin. In fact, Martin's cocky backroom supporters were so confident of winning power that they felt they had the luxury to wage a nasty internal campaign to oust prominent Chrétien supporters from key party positions, in hopes of forcing Chrétien out. One of Parliament Hill's most thoughtful political essayists, the *Toronto Star*'s Susan Delacourt, produced a book on Martin's ascent to power called *Juggernaut*. While the book was focused on his long campaign to win the party leadership, many felt it an apt metaphor for the party under his leadership for years to come. Nothing seemed more certain than another Liberal majority, especially when the Canadian Alliance started imploding as Manning loyalists revolted against Day's erratic leadership.

St. Germain started to pull back from the action. "I think I was trying to wipe it out of my mind. It was pretty sad," St. Germain recalled. While an admirer of Day's—"I think he would have been a good prime minister"—he was uncomfortable with the new generation of harder-edged, more uncompromising right-wingers around the leader: people like future Harper cabinet minister Jason Kenney and Ezra Levant, Day's media spokesman, who would go on to become an outspoken and controversial TV personality. "They were not bad people. They just weren't my kind of people. I sort of went into a bit of hibernation. I wanted to wait and see how everything would settle out." St. Germain's archived documents show that he was part of a search team to help select a senior staffer in Day's office. The team's recommended candidate ended up not being the one hired, perhaps because Day tended to listen to his closest political advisers and especially his son Logan. "I just don't think he surrounded himself with the right people," St. Germain said. "You're only as strong as your people, because this is a team game, it's not an individual sport. You've got to have a good team."

St. Germain made a rather ambitious attempt to be named official opposition leader in the Senate after the election, as he was the only member of the party that was official opposition in the House. When that predictably failed, he settled into a frustrating existence in the early 2000s. The conservative movement was still flailing, with two parties dividing the right-of-centre vote. He had sacrificed family time for years in order to help his political leaders, and now he was caught out in the cold. Once known as a die-hard Tory loyalist, he was viewed as a turncoat by LeBreton and many other Tory senators. Mulroney, whom he considered a close friend, wasn't speaking to him. There were nasty barbs when he rose to speak in the Senate, and his critics leaked stories to the media about him not pulling his weight. St. Germain had always revelled in the company of his political pals and now he lived an isolated life. It was one of the low points of his political career.

"I was really under pressure from the former PC guys. They just treated me very badly, let's put it like that." Two in particular were Noël Kinsella, a former university professor from New Brunswick who later served as Senate speaker, and the late John Lynch-Staunton, a Quebec senator. St. Germain's critics knew they could get under the skin of the "chicken farmer" who resented "downtowners" and intellectual elites. St. Germain could see what they were up to:

Kinsella, I couldn't stand him, he'd take the odd run at me. One day I got up, we were talking about some legal issue, and he said, 'Is this canon law or civil law?' I said I will defer to the academic because I was busy out working, making a living for my family, so I'm not going to get into a debate over canon law or civil law. And Lynch-Staunton was pretty nasty toward me. All these guys had their guns out for me once I went over to the Alliance, but [after the merger in 2003] they all went over and brown-nosed and kissed up to Harper, once he got in, to get favoured positions. It was sickening. LeBreton and Kinsella and all of them, they called Harper everything under the sun in caucus, and yet when it came to Harper being the leader of the party after the unification you'd swear to God that Harper had gone through a transformation.

The breakthrough that led to the former Harper critics hopping on the bandwagon was rooted in Stockwell Day's decision, after suffering a debilitating caucus revolt, to announce in 2001 he'd step aside but then enter the race to win back the leadership of his party. The gambit to win a fresh mandate in 2002 failed when Stephen Harper returned from self-imposed exile to win the leadership. Despite his admiration for Day and his attempt to convince Harper to run for the PCs against Clark in 1998, St. Germain decided to support Dr. Grant Hill, an Alberta MP who was advocating unity with the Tories. St. Germain still admired Harper, who wisely did not advocate a merger because he knew how suspicious his party's hard-core grassroots were to any deal with the Clark-led Tories. Clark, meanwhile, stepped aside from his caretaker role for Peter MacKay, a youthful rugby-playing Nova Scotian who won the PC leadership in June 2003 on a vow to never negotiate a merger with the Canadian Alliance. St. Germain, disillusioned with events at the time, wasn't seeing much hope as he watched the parties elect two new leaders who appeared to be anti-merger.

But soon after Peter MacKay won the Progressive Conservative leadership, behind-the-scenes talks began to unite the parties. MacKay's written pledge not to go in that direction quickly dissolved as leaders for both parties realized that without unity, they faced obliteration in the face of the upcoming Liberal leadership convention in November 2003, which Paul Martin was sure to win. Seizing on a historic opportunity, Harper named three "emissaries" to try to negotiate a truce and unity pact. One was former Alberta MLA and MP Ray Speaker, a folksy rancher with an ever-present smile. He was a long-time Preston Manning associate who would be seen as a defender of Manning's populist, grassroots focus. The other was Ottawa-area MP Scott Reid, a bilingual, highly educated and outspoken member of the conservative movement's libertarian wing. Except for his criticism of official bilingualism, he was the kind of person who didn't look out of place at a Tory gathering. With two of the party's three bedrock provinces represented, Harper needed a British Columbian, and that could be no one other than St. Germain. While he was persona non grata in the Senate, Harper recognized the value of a man who had countless friends and allies on both sides of the fence. Harper, who in the mid-1980s worked briefly on Parliament Hill for Calgary Tory MP Jim Hawkes, told St. Germain he recognized the clout he wielded in Ottawa. "Harper said to me, 'You were viewed as Mulroney's guy. You were viewed as one of the guys who could really get things done.'"

There was talk that Don Mazankowski, the former "minister of everything" and deputy prime minister, would be one of MacKay's emissaries. The tough-talking, no-nonsense former Alberta car dealer was admired by western Canadians in spite of his close association with Mulroney. One day Gerry and Margaret St. Germain, in Winnipeg to meet with a local First Nations leader, were at the airport when they bumped into Mazankowski. "And I said to Maz, 'Are you going to be one of the negotiators on this?' He says, 'Oh no, this is a dead end. There's no way this is ever going to develop into anything.'" Then St. Germain pulled his ace card. He had been having regular telephone conversations with Harper, and one involved the name of a future party. Harper told St. Germain he was fine naming the new party the Conservative Party of Canada. "So when I ran into Maz, I said to him, 'Maz, you should take this on. You're one of the few guys

Some were surprised when Gerry St. Germain wasn't appointed to cabinet in 2006 despite playing an important role in the creation of the Conservative Party of Canada. But St. Germain kept in close contact with the prime minister, meeting with him regularly to push issues important to Canada's First Nations, including education and self-government. JASON AND DEB RANSOM

that everybody trusts. And it will be named the Conservative Party of Canada.'"

"Those bastards will never agree to that."

"Guaranteed. I guarantee you."

"Well, if they'll do that, I may consider it."

Mazankowski later shared his recollection of that key conversation with Bob Plamondon, author of *Blue Thunder: The Truth about Conservatives from Macdonald to Harper.* "I wasn't thinking merger until I heard the Alliance was ready to name it the Conservative Party of Canada," Mazankowski told Plamondon. "If it had been the Conservative Alliance or the Conservative Reform Party I don't think I would have been there." Mazankowski would join former Ontario premier Bill Davis and Newfoundland MP Loyola Hearn as the Three Wise Men on the PC side. Mazankowski and Speaker were the key negotiators, St. Germain said, and the haggling was not over policy.

Harper, as Plamondon noted in his book, had no problem with the Tory platform, which spoke to traditional small-c conservative values about small government, low taxes and a tough law-and-order agenda. The real struggle was over the rules to determine the new leadership, as both parties sought a format that favoured their side. Acting as another go-between to Mulroney was Belinda Stronach, the daughter of billionaire auto-parts manufacturer Frank Stronach. The PC side eventually prevailed, with the leadership to be decided using a format preferred by MacKay.

It didn't matter, as Harper easily won the leadership over chief rivals Stronach and former Ontario cabinet minister Tony Clement. St. Germain went to work for Harper on a volunteer basis, helping the Albertan build his BC political base. "I talked to my people in British Columbia, the guys in the Okanagan that I knew, and up in Prince George. And I made it known that I had already tried to solicit Harper to run for leader [of the PCs in 1998]. So I knew him. I could see he was someone who gave us a chance." Harper had his weaknesses: he was devoid of the kind of charisma and warmth one normally expects from a politician. He had also taken some hard-line views that alienated many Canadians, and seemed to view it as a sign of valour to have an acrimonious relationship with the media. But he was also a brilliant strategist who had a clear idea of what kind of coalition he wanted to build, and his reasonable French and downtown Toronto appearance made him more acceptable than Manning or Day to the Ontario Tory establishment. The bottom line was that the parties finally merged under a competent and presentable leader, and that spelled trouble for the Liberals.

St. Germain would quickly get credit for his role first as a trendsetter, in being the biggest federal Tory name to defy Mulroney's wishes and jump to the Alliance, and later for acting as a peacemaker and negotiator during merger talks. During his speech at St. Germain's final summer barbecue at his South Surrey ranch in August 2012, Harper honoured his host before an estimated 2,500 attendees: "Gerry was, of course, one of the first to play a role—a big role—in bringing us all together." Finally united, the new Conservative Party entered the 2004 election full of hope. Despite earlier talk about a Paul Martin "juggernaut," the former finance minister wasn't able to import his popularity to the Prime Minister's Office.

One problem was the legacy of the Liberal sponsorship scandal, involving a post-1995 referendum scheme by Jean Chrétien's government to blanket Quebec with pro-Canada propaganda. Some of the flood of taxpayers' money ended up in the hands of Liberal supporters who did little or nothing to earn it. Martin called an independent inquiry to look into the matter, and instead of the inquiry helping to distance him from the scandal, he watched the Liberal brand erode. So Harper went into the 2004 campaign with a clear chance to unseat the Liberals. But it was not to be. Some campaign blunders by the

St. Germain greets Stephen Harper after introducing him at one of St. Germain's annual summer barbecues at his Surrey, BC, ranch. At the 2012 barbecue Harper credited St. Germain for playing "a big role" in the 2003 merger between the old Progressive Conservative Party of Canada and the Canadian Alliance Party. JASON AND DEB RANSOM

Conservatives—and a wave of Liberal ads attempting to portray Harper as "scary"—resulted in a Liberal minority under Martin in 2004.

St. Germain chipped in during both the 2004 and 2006 campaigns, staying in regular contact with Harper and joining him when the Conservative leader met with people like BC premier Gordon Campbell or Vancouver mayor Sam Sullivan. When it became increasingly clear that Harper was poised to oust Paul Martin from 24 Sussex Drive in 2006, St. Germain also began thinking about transition to government. "In 2006, just before the election and during the election period, I went over to Victoria with Harper to meet Gordon Campbell," St. Germain recalled. On the flight St. Germain and Harper discussed cabinet candidates and indirectly touched on the question of what role St. Germain might play in a new Conservative government. At the time there was some speculation that St. Germain would be the logical choice as government leader in the Senate, which was an automatic cabinet spot. St. Germain had

St. Germain, who played a key role in helping Harper construct a political base in BC, was disappointed over the way Harper dealt with him after the 2006 election. But St. Germain was pleased that the new prime minister accepted the top item on his wish-list as a reward for that work—to take him to Washington, DC, for the new PM's first visit to the White House. JASON AND DEB RANSOM

the experience in the Senate, and had shown leadership in previous roles as a Mulroney cabinet minister and party president, and was bilingual—crucial for Harper given his hope of expanding the party's small base in Quebec.

There were counter-arguments as well. Harper, even if he won, had to consolidate the merger and make sure the PC wing didn't feel excluded. The Senate was a bastion of old-guard Tories from the Mulroney era, and to appoint St. Germain—the former party president who bolted to the enemy—wouldn't have played well with many of them. "We never discussed government leader but a lot of people presumed I would get that," St. Germain recalled. He said he told Harper he didn't expect a reward for his work, but wanted one special favour. He asked that he be invited to come along to meet then president George W. Bush when Harper made his first trip to the White House. St. Germain was an admirer of the much-criticized "Dubya," once delivering a speech in the Senate criticizing Canada's 2003

St. Germain meets George W. Bush at the White House, and later gets the president to sign a speech St. Germain delivered in the Senate in 2003 praising the US-led invasion of Iraq. St. Germain, always deeply reliant on staff during his own career, acknowledges the invasion turned out poorly but blames Bush's advisers for flawed post-occupation policies. "You're only as strong as your best adviser." JASON AND DEB RANSOM

decision to not participate in Bush's invasion of Iraq. St. Germain would frame a copy of that speech with Bush's scribbled words of gratitude.

St. Germain said he was in regular telephone contact with Harper heading into the January 23, 2006, election, letting his leader know what was happening on the ground in BC and providing advice on the possible transition to power. The day after Harper won, Bob Ransford got a call from Sam Sullivan, the Vancouver mayor aligned with the Conservatives who had some progressive views on issues like Vancouver's supervised heroin injection site, which the Harper Conservatives adamantly opposed. Sullivan told Ransford that he wanted to discuss with St. Germain the city's priorities under the new government. St. Germain phoned Harper to see what he should do, and Harper replied, "Yeah, meet with him and see what he wants." So Ransford and the Vancouver mayor went to St. Germain's house to discuss key municipal needs. But after the Campbell and Sullivan meetings the calls from Harper stopped coming. Then, on February 6, 2006, Harper named his cabinet. St. Germain was hoping he'd finally make his way back in—a move that would be of great gratification for a man who took years to get over his 1988 election loss. With his strong relationship with Premier Gordon Campbell, he felt he would have been a strong political minister for Harper. But when the cabinet was named, St. Germain was left to watch on television.

It was a remarkable day at Rideau Hall for the swearing-in ceremony. As the soon-to-be ministers showed up in limousines, journalists naturally watched with great interest to determine who was in and who was out. Seeing Peter MacKay arrive was a no-brainer, given his role in uniting the parties. Harper's former Reform colleagues like Chuck Strahl were also a given. Then it was almost as if everyone's heart paused. Eyes squinted and blinked. Were the journalists imagining things or was that David Emerson, who had been a senior cabinet minister under Liberal prime minister Paul Martin, exiting a limo and heading into Government House?

Emerson was a former industry executive and star candidate

recruited by Martin to run for the Liberals in the 2004 election. He had been parachuted into the left-wing BC riding of Vancouver Kingsway. Residents there had voted Conservative only once since the riding was created in 1952, and that was during the historic John Diefenbaker sweep of 1958. On election night in 2006 a defiant Emerson, trying to find a silver lining in his party's defeat and his expulsion to opposition benches, declared that he would be Harper's "worst enemy" in the House of Commons. Yet here was Emerson, an economist and the former chief executive of the forestry giant Canfor, arriving at Rideau Hall to be sworn in as Harper's new minister of international trade.

Ransford was already upset that St. Germain didn't get the call the day before. But it sent him overboard that someone who'd spent the last several years trying to destroy Harper's political career was chosen over his guy. For St. Germain it wasn't the Emerson appointment that got under his skin. Nothing could have prepared him for Harper's decision to name Marjory LeBreton to his cabinet as government leader in the Senate. Not only had he feuded with her since the 1980s, but the nasty letter from 1998 was still fresh. LeBreton was also one of the most severe critics of St. Germain's decision to leave the PC caucus, and she had been a go-to person when the media were looking for someone critical of Harper. Even months before Harper and MacKay launched negotiations to merge, LeBreton was one of those expressing glee in June 2003 when MacKay won the PC leadership based on a promise to not negotiate with the Alliance. A year earlier she stated that there was "nothing to be gained by somehow or other pursuing this phony merger," since the PCs were the best vehicle to defeat the Liberals. Yet here she was, bestowed by Harper with her highest achievement in politics.

"I felt terrible," St. Germain recalled. "You know what upset me the most? I was [prior to the cabinet announcement] in Palm Springs and the phone was ringing. And then I was in Winnipeg, and it was ringing. And it was Harper both times, and he was talking to me about a litany of things. And then all of a sudden he had asked me to meet the mayor and the premier about their priorities with the new government, and then the communications just dropped right off." Asked if he felt betrayed by Harper, St. Germain shook his head. "It wasn't a betrayal, it was just a sheer disappointment that he didn't take the time to call me and say what he was doing, because he had been asking for advice on so many things."

St. Germain reckons some of the people around Harper convinced him to go with LeBreton. He said he turned down Harper's offer of one of two posts: national caucus chairman or Senate whip. As he sat at his home office in Langley during a December 2015 interview, he looked forlornly at a letter from BC's lieutenant governor at the time, Garde Gardom, who had jumped the gun to congratulate him on his appointment as government leader in the Senate: "I thought that I deserved at least a phone call. A phone call would have done it. And I'll tell you, honestly, I might have been disappointed, but not as much as I was. What really, really hit me, right to the core, was that he didn't just give me a call and say, 'Ger, I've had to change plans. I'm putting her in.' I would have said, 'Life's about choices, you've made the choice. God bless you. Carry on.' And that would have been it."

Looking back, he could see there were compatibility issues between him and Harper. "I am so different from him. When you're in the air force you're sleeping with thirty guys in a room, and you walk in the room and everyone's giving you a bad time and hassling you, you learn about survival. And I don't think he was ever exposed to anything like that. It looks as if he went to Upper Canada College. I think he liked me but he just really never was sure. He trusted me, but I think he always maybe thought that I couldn't . . ." St. Germain paused and recalled a speech he delivered at an event in Ottawa in 2008 to mark the Harper government's formal apology on behalf of Canada over the residential school tragedy. "I was dressed in my Metis jacket and I got up, spoke French, and he came to me and said, 'I didn't think you had that in you.'" Harper clearly meant it as a compliment, but it was something Mulroney wouldn't have said in a million years.

St. Germain didn't let the snub sever his relationship with Harper. The new prime minister kept his promise and took Gerry to

Stephen Harper shakes St. Germain's hand prior to the 2007 Speech from the Throne that was read by Governor General Michaëlle Jean, leading the procession to Harper's left. Slightly behind Harper and to his left is a smiling Marjory LeBreton. Despite the smiles St. Germain would resent Harper's choice of LeBreton, his long-time nemesis, as the new Conservative government's Senate leader. JASON AND DEB RANSOM

Washington, where he sat across from the Bushes at dinner. "I think he felt badly about it. He took me to Washington on his first trip. The thing is, I had done so much. I had to just park my ego and my pride and just back up and do something else." There was even a rapprochement with Emerson, who visited him at the Surrey ranch while at the height of the national furor in 2006 over Emerson's floor-crossing, which resulted in protests and extended media coverage for months. "Oh, he was hurt. They were attacking him. He was getting the treatment that I received when I went to the Alliance, when people called me Brutus and Benedict Arnold."

But a moment of levity lightened their meeting. "He was there asking me how he should handle the situation. And while he was sitting there, he was looking out the window and I had my back turned to him. And he said, 'Look at that!' There were two eagles locked together in a tumble. They were coming down and he says to me, 'Isn't that something?' They crashed to the ground, broke up and flew away. And I said, 'Oh, we put that show on for all you guys from downtown.'" St. Germain may have been fond of ending difficult conversations with a wisecrack to lighten the mood, but there is little doubt he nursed wounds from Harper's decision for years afterward. Yet he also recognized that Harper had likely done him a big favour.

12

∞

The Senate and First Nations

The sting of Harper's snub went deep, yet it might have been the most fortunate turn of Gerry St. Germain's career. For most of his sixty-nine years up until that point he'd been obsessively focused on rising above his humble background. That focus meant he missed huge chunks of time with his family, including key events like birthdays and graduations. In business he gained wealth, and in politics he became a go-to player for any Conservative leader wanting support in British Columbia. But what would his legacy have been had he been appointed to cabinet, where under Harper few if any ministers had an opportunity to shine? Freed from his obsessive political ambition and the constraints of party politics, he was able to dive into the deep end of aboriginal issues. "When he didn't get into cabinet, that began the era of his semi-independence," recalled Jack Austin, a BC corporate lawyer who retired from the Senate in 2007.

Austin would develop an interesting perspective on St. Germain. Both men were confidants of prime ministers, served terms chairing the Committee on Aboriginal Peoples and acted as primary liaisons between the BC and national governments. They are cordial with each other even though they not only come from different parties but also different wings of their parties—St. Germain is a social and fiscal conservative, and Austin is a Liberal who is an ardent supporter of an activist government. During their tenures in the Senate they were both adversaries and allies on various First Nations issues. In 2000 Austin played the lead role in passing Liberal legislation to implement BC's first modern land claims and self-government treaty, involving the Nisga'a on the northwest coast near the Alaska border. St. Germain, at the time a member of the Progressive Conservative caucus, took the lead in opposing the deal, which involved the transfer of two thousand square kilometres of land and $190 million over fifteen years. The treaty, reached between the Nisga'a, the federal Liberals and the BC NDP government, polarized the province. Both the Reform Party and Gordon Campbell's provincial Liberals, then in opposition, fiercely opposed the treaty in the federal and BC legislatures.

St. Germain, maintaining that he supported the BC treaty process that was launched by the Mulroney government in 1992, said he opposed this particular deal because neighbouring First Nations, the Gitxsan and the Gitanyow, argued that some of the land going to the Nisga'a was on their traditional territories. But St. Germain, a long-time supporter of the anti-NDP coalition parties in BC, whether Social Credit or Liberal, noted that the BC public was also divided. Speaking in the Senate chamber on April 4, 2000, with visiting Nisga'a leaders including Chief Joe Gosnell in the public gallery, he said, "I believe that fewer than 50 percent of British Columbians really understand the deal and want it. That is a major concern, and it must be a concern to all of us. They do not understand partly because this deal is so complex. As well, British Columbians are doubtful that this agreement will bring the finality and certainty that is intended." St. Germain would argue that his politics were not trumping his principles, pointing to his defence of the neighbouring First Nations. But Austin, in a 2016 interview, remembers seeing St. Germain at airports and expressing bafflement. "For six months he worked to find every argument to undermine and destroy the agreement, which I always found odd. I'd say, 'What the hell are you doing, Gerry? You of all people on the other side of the aisle understand the condition of aboriginal communities in BC.'"

But the Nisga'a deal of course passed, thanks to a federal Liberal majority in both houses of Parliament. After provincial Liberal leader Gordon Campbell became premier in 2001, his party reversed itself and embraced treaty-making in order to bring certainty to the province's resource sector. St. Germain went on to work closely with Austin when the Liberals were in power in the 2000s to bring in other legislation being pushed by First Nations. One instance in early February 2005, when Austin was Martin's government leader in the Senate and a member of the Liberal cabinet, symbolized St. Germain's growing non-partisan commitment to First Nations issues. A group of elders from the Tlicho First Nation had flown five thousand kilometres from their lands in the North Slave area of the Northwest Territories to see their historic land claim and self-government treaty pass in the Senate. The Tlicho, known until 2002 as the Dogrib, had like the Nisga'a been fighting for a proper treaty since early in the twentieth century. Negotiations for the 2005 agreement began in the late 1970s, so many of the original leaders of those talks were elderly or had passed away. This was going to be only the second modern treaty in Canadian history, following the Nisga'a deal, that would "explicitly extend Section 35 constitutional protection to self-government rights as well as to land rights," according to an October 29, 2004, Library of Parliament study of the legislation being enacted.

Liberal senator Nick Sibbeston, then chairman of the Standing Senate Committee on Aboriginal Peoples, rose that day to say that he wished he could move immediately to third reading of the bill, then added, "but I would not be so presumptuous." He therefore moved that the bill be read and passed for the third and final time at the next sitting of the Senate, a full five days later. Sibbeston's motion was technically non-debatable, as Senate speaker Dan Hays noted, but St. Germain had concocted a plan. Frustrated that the Tlicho elders would have to spend five days holed up in their Ottawa hotel, he rose to his feet: "Honourable senators, I seek the floor." After Hays sought and obtained permission from Sibbeston to allow St. Germain to speak his piece, St. Germain explained, "Honourable senators, I respect Senator Sibbeston's comment, but I do recognize that this is an exceptionally special circumstance and would ask that we proceed to third reading forthwith. In this instance there are extenuating circumstances that go far beyond the parliamentary system. Present in our gallery are numerous elders who, for years, have been anticipating the passage of this legislation."

St. Germain knew he needed unanimous consent to pass the legislation immediately, and the members of the governing Liberals in the Senate—who sponsored the bill, after all—weren't going to be the problem. The BC senator had worked behind the scenes with his own Tory colleagues to make sure there were no dissenters. As a surprised Sibbeston looked on, Austin rose to his feet to respond favourably. "I thank him for the statement he has just made," Austin said in a nod to his BC counterpart and nemesis in the Nisga'a debate. "This side is most eager to see the bill passed today. This demonstrates a level of concord and cooperation that is admirable and speaks well of this chamber. It particularly speaks to the Tlicho people and the work they have done, their presence here and the importance of the passage of this bill to their future." The bill passed, with "hear, hears" and desk-thumping all around, and St. Germain and Austin joined others in looking up as the smiling Tlicho elders sat back in their chairs to recognize their decades of work had finally been realized.

In 2006, after the Conservatives took power, St. Germain turned the Senate committee into a welcoming place for aboriginal leaders who felt shunned by the Harper government, according to Austin. "He saw he was coming close to retirement and I think the real Gerry St. Germain, the one not checked by political ambition, emerged," he said, opining that the Harper snub was "the seminal point in his career." St. Germain had asked for and naturally—given the outstanding debt Harper still owed to the senator—obtained the chairmanship of the Committee on Aboriginal Peoples after the 2006 election, and went to work. Rather than strategizing with colleagues in his own party, he decided to make a key ally in Sibbeston, the former Liberal chairman of the committee. St. Germain wasn't naive. He knew Canadians didn't pay a lot of attention to the Senate and its committee reports, and in turn governments didn't bother much with them either. But if a bipartisan committee could produce strong reports on key issues it might actually have some influence on government policy. "We sat down and I said, 'Nick, we've gotta make a difference, somehow.'"

It was an interesting choice as an ally. Sibbeston, six years younger than St. Germain, had had a far tougher childhood. A lawyer and former premier of the Northwest Territories, he was born in the Dene community of Fort Simpson, with no father present and an alcoholic mother. At age five the frightened boy was put on a barge and sent down the Mackenzie River to Fort Providence, to attend the first of a succession of residential schools. While he would grow up to become a lawyer, premier and finally a senator, Sibbeston had to run a gauntlet of abuse to get there. "Those six years in residential school were the most traumatic period of my life," Sibbeston wrote in his autobiography *You Will Wear a White Shirt: From the Northern Bush to the Halls of Power.* "I experienced loneliness, sadness, abandonment, helplessness, insecurity and many psychological and physical hurts. I was constantly teased because I was fairer than the rest of the boys. I was sexually assaulted by a bigger boy. I was treated cruelly by the nuns." The experience left deep and lasting scars. He struggled with depression as an adult, drank excessively, had extra-marital liaisons, and by his own account parented his six children poorly. But his wife Karen stuck with him and thanks to her, his Roman Catholic faith, counselling and Alcoholics Anonymous, Sibbeston emerged as a survivor.

St. Germain and Sibbeston, the committee's deputy chairman, travelled around the country with fellow senators over the next half-dozen years, often staying in cheap motels in remote communities while producing a series of comprehensive reports on economic development, specific land claims, education, water quality, band elections and, just before St. Germain's 2012 retirement, the lack of progress by the federal and BC governments in striking treaties on the west coast more than two decades after the costly process began. Sometimes the reports ended up gathering dust, thanks in part to the Harper government's ambivalent and sometimes acrimonious relationship with First Nations. But the specific land claims report in 2006 was essentially adopted as government policy and the 2011 report on education is believed by many to have strongly influenced the Harper government's bid to reform the system—though its $1.9 billion plan fell apart in 2014 due to divisions within the Assembly of First Nations. Former Alberta premier Jim Prentice, who was Harper's first aboriginal affairs minister following the 2006 election, said St. Germain played a crucial role in the new government's initiatives to help First Nations.

Prentice, who had worked as a member of the Land Claims Commission of Canada, was widely respected by First Nations leaders who were otherwise deeply suspicious of the Harper government. Harper was of course a policy architect for the Reform Party, which enjoyed an electoral breakthrough in 1993 based in part on its vehement opposition to the recognition of inherent aboriginal rights to land and resources, and especially in BC to the salmon fishery. For the life of the Reform Party, from 1993 to 2000, its MPs led an aggressive opposition to aboriginal rights legislation in House of Commons. Some Reform members regularly criticized "race-based" rights, arguing that the federal government was setting up a system of apartheid.

Harper's long-time intellectual collaborator and policy adviser, University of Calgary political scientist Tom Flanagan, was especially reviled for writing the 2000 book *First Nations? Second Thoughts*. The book questioned the "orthodoxy" that residence in North America for thousands of years prior to European colonization entitled aboriginal Canadians to special rights, like immunity from taxation while living on reserves. Flanagan infuriated many by arguing that colonization was in fact legitimate and justified, provocatively noting that "European civilization was several thousand years more advanced than the aboriginal cultures of North America." Another Conservative who aroused suspicion was John Cummins, an outspoken backbench MP from the BC Lower Mainland who helped create the BC Fisheries Survival Coalition prior to becoming a Reform MP in 1993. That group was singularly opposed to the government-sanctioned aboriginal fisheries that had been introduced by the Mulroney government in the early 1990s.

And the final person of concern was Harper himself. One of the new prime minister's first acts was to tear up the $5.1 billion Kelowna Accord, a deal between Ottawa, the provinces and aboriginal groups to ramp up federal spending in areas like education and on-reserve infrastructure. "I had a couple of tough jobs," said Prentice, pointing to his initial assignment as aboriginal affairs minister followed by Harper's decision in 2008 to make him minister of the environment, another area where the prime minister had little credibility. The more difficult of the two, according to Prentice, was aboriginal affairs. "The historic legacy of the Reform side of our party with aboriginal people was very difficult. There was a general perception that some of the members of our party were opposed to First Nations interests." Prentice strongly supported St. Germain's appointment as chairman of the Standing Senate Committee on Aboriginal Peoples. "Gerry and I both knew what needed to be done, and he was immensely helpful at working together."

One of St. Germain's key reports, as part of that behind-the-scenes collaboration, was the May 2007 submission to Parliament titled *Safe Drinking Water for First Nations*. It concluded that "First Nations people in this country have a right to expect, as do all Canadians, that their drinking water is safe." Another was a March 2007 report titled *Sharing Canada's Prosperity—A Hand Up, Not a Handout*, proposing measures—including improved education and training—to stimulate economic activity in aboriginal communities. Both reports, Prentice said, helped build caucus support for a 2008 budget that included $330 million over two years to improve access to safe drinking water, and a further $140 million over the same period to be split evenly between economic development and education. These efforts, according to

Prentice, also helped him lay the groundwork for the historic 2008 apology by Harper to residential school survivors, which was accompanied by a compensation package expected to total in excess of $5 billion. Prentice also saw something in his friend that he and others had never noticed during his time as an MP, cabinet minister and party president. "Throughout that time I saw him become more emotive about his First Nations background. I'd never actually seen that until then."

When St. Germain wasn't holding hearings or working with staff to develop reports he was using his contacts and political clout to help aboriginal leaders meet key political players, including Harper, when they were visiting Ottawa. "He has just been a wonderful champion," said Sophie Pierre, the former head of the BC Treaty Commission and a frequent critic of the Harper government's inaction. Another one of St. Germain's admirers would be Jody Wilson-Raybould, who in November 2015 was named by Prime Minister Justin Trudeau to be Canada's first aboriginal justice minister. When St. Germain and his aide Stephen Stewart were scrambling to put together self-government legislation prior to his 2012 retirement, they obtained help from Wilson-Raybould, then BC regional chief of the Assembly of First Nations, and Tim Raybould, her husband and a specialist on self-government issues. A few days after it was tabled, Wilson-Raybould issued a news release praising the initiative and thanking St. Germain, the sponsor of Bill S-212, "for his dedication and commitment to First Nations peoples." She went on:

> I am extremely pleased that as one of his final acts in the upper chamber, Senator St. Germain has seen fit to introduce this significant bill that will generate much-needed dialogue and debate around the importance of reconciliation and for First Nations to be recognized as self-governing based on our inherent right of self-government and as required by the United Nations Declaration on the Rights of Indigenous Peoples. We are under no illusion that the government of Canada will actually support

Bill S-212. It is not a government-sponsored bill. No doubt there will also be opposition from some First Nations. Nevertheless, Bill S-212 is a step in the right direction and regardless of whether or not . . . it ultimately becomes law in this or a future Parliament, it stands out today as an alternative to the federal government's current neo-colonial legislative agenda for our peoples, that seeks to tinker around the edges of the Indian Act and design our post–Indian Act governance for us.

According to his wife and friends, during those last half-dozen years on the committee St. Germain began to lose some of his sharper edges. One factor was the reduction of stress when he stopped being deeply involved in party work, while another was the birth of their first great-grandchild, Tanner. Gerry and Margaret, despite their advanced years, essentially adopted and raised Tanner after their granddaughter, then a teenager, gave birth. When Tanner returned to his mother at age nine, Gerry and Margaret remained adoring and doting great-grandparents for the boy they nicknamed "Sweet Pea."

Another factor was the development of close and trusting friendships with fellow committee members, in particular opposition senators and especially Sibbeston. Once hyper-partisan, St. Germain would see first-hand the impact of residential school abuse on a human soul. "We were in Whitehorse one day and he says, 'Gerry, I feel bad. I've gotta go to church. Will you come with me?' I said 'Sure.' We went to the Catholic church and knelt down

St. Germain with his great-grandson Tanner, whom he and Margaret nicknamed "Sweetpea." As Tanner's mother was a teenager, Gerry and Margaret raised Tanner for the first nine years of his life. Margaret said Tanner's presence in her husband's life softened his harder edges. GSG PERSONAL COLLECTION

and we prayed together. You could see he needed that. And then when he would lose control in committee every now and then, all I had to say was, 'Nick, c'mon,' and he'd respond. And these are the things that really mean a lot. There were people in my caucus I was close to as well, but I seemed to establish a real bond with the other side, simply because I said, 'Lookit, if you want something or need something, you're as entitled as I am. Just because we're in government doesn't mean anything.' And that's what I evolved into toward the end."

St. Germain's evolution didn't come close to happening overnight. While his pals used to call him "Red Man" and "Cochise," he didn't always embrace his heritage. During one political speech in 1988 to a BC First Nation he spoke of the aboriginal blood "coursing through my veins." His political aide at the time, Sandy Macdougall, included the speech in a political brochure. He remembers St. Germain being horrified when he saw it. "What if my mother sees that?" the MP told his staffer. While he did speak once in January 1985 about his Metis heritage (regarding one of more than a dozen motions calling for Riel's treason conviction to be repealed), he didn't mention his background in his maiden speech in the House of Commons in 1983, nor in his first speech in the Senate in 1994.

During the 1990s St. Germain developed a close friendship with another senator. Chief Walter Twinn was the long-time chief of the tiny Sawridge First Nation, located about 250 kilometres north of Edmonton in the community of Slave Lake. Twinn, appointed to the Senate by Brian Mulroney in 1990, called St. Germain "Metis" and St. Germain in turn called Twinn "Chief." Twinn had been one of Canada's most entrepreneurial aboriginal leaders. During more than thirty years as chief, Twinn used oil revenues from wells drilled on Sawridge land to create a business empire that in the 1990s was said to be worth $250 million. It was made up of considerable real estate holdings in Alberta, including the Sawridge Inn and Conference Centre inside Jasper National Park and similar hotel–conference centre operations in Edmonton, Fort McMurray and Peace River. The band also owned a plant on Annacis Island in BC's Lower

Mainland that produced bottled fresh water under the brand name Spirit Water.

In October 1997 St. Germain and Twinn were kibitzing during one of Twinn's many visits to the west coast. "And he says, 'Let's go out to dinner, Metis.' I said, 'Chief, I don't want to go out to dinner because you won't let me pay.' He said, 'Don't worry about it, I've got lots of money. We're making money.' But he says, 'I'm in trouble on the water plant, I can't make it work. I'm fighting Coca-Cola and Pepsi and they're blowing me out of the water.' It was a Wednesday night and he slaps me on the back and says, 'So Metis, you're going to look after my people for me?' I replied, 'What the hell? Where are you going?' He said, 'Ah, you never know what I'm going to go do.'" That weekend Twinn attended a ceremonial sweat lodge, and during the fourth session he dropped dead of a heart attack at age sixty-three.

St. Germain spoke at the funeral, pointing to the remarkable contrast between the band's corporate jets in the background and the blanket-covered horse-drawn cart that carried Twinn's cherrywood casket from the band's Slave Lake headquarters to the cemetery. After the funeral Twinn's widow Catherine made a beeline to St. Germain. "She sort of grabbed onto me because she knew I was a business guy, and I had told the band what had happened" during his final chat with her husband before the heart attack. For the next eight years St. Germain was in regular contact with Catherine Twinn, who has three university degrees including a master's degree in law from the London School of Economics. The bottled water company was losing millions, the hotels were not being managed well, and the small community was divided over how to run the company. "There was a real Mexican standoff amongst the band members. They couldn't get along." St. Germain said he advised the band to cut its losses on the Spirit Water venture, which at one point was served on British Airways flights. "I said, 'Shut it down. Get rid of it. Right away. Keep the building but get rid of the business.'"

During the 2005–2006 period St. Germain was contacted by a Toronto-based accountant working with the band, who advised him the Sawridge Group was "in real trouble." St. Germain replied that the band needed an independent board of directors. "Will you go on it?" the accountant asked. "No, I don't want to go on any boards. I hate bloody boards." But the accountant and the band trustees, including Walter Twinn's widow, pushed him because they needed an aboriginal person. "And I said, 'I'll do it for a year.' Get them back on their feet." St. Germain joined the board in 2006, a new chief executive officer was hired, the Spirit Water business was shuttered and the company's financial performance rebounded. Catherine Twinn said the turn-around from a near-crisis situation was a result of St. Germain:

> Gerry was willing to come in and help. I think it was a tipping point for other outsiders to do the same, because prior to that I had approached outsiders to help and no one wanted to get involved. They'd say, "We don't need an Indian shitshow. What am I stepping into, a gong show?" So Gerry had the courage and the strength to take it on. And I think the fact he was willing to, and he was a very credible person, this encouraged others to consider it and then be persuaded to do it.

As the only aboriginal on the board, St. Germain made it easier for the other directors to take firm stands to improve performance. "I feel that Gerry's been the heart, soul and glue for that board because the others are non-Native, and most non-Native people don't want to say or do anything for fear of being wrong or crossing a boundary," Twinn said. "That fear creates a lot of paralysis, and good people do nothing when otherwise they probably would do something. So I can't describe to you how important it is to have Gerry there dissolving all those fears that prevent people from being good human beings."

While 2006 marked a turning point, St. Germain's reputation for solid work and advocacy regarding aboriginal issues had been building for years. One of those who encountered him in the early 2000s was Harold Calla, later the executive chairman of the First Nations Financial Management Board. Calla was part of a generation of impressive and

One of St. Germain's proudest moments was being recognized for his lifetime contribution to First Nations causes at the 2012 National Aboriginal Achievement Awards gala in Vancouver. Events like this give him peace as he struggles to this day with guilt over spending so much time thousands of kilometres away from Margaret, their daughters Michele and Suzanne, their son Jay, and their grandchildren and great-grandchild. PHOTO COURTESY INDSPIRE, FORMERLY THE NATIONAL ABORIGINAL ACHIEVEMENT AWARD FOUNDATION

progressive First Nations leaders who grew up with a determination to follow through on Supreme Court of Canada rulings dating back to the 1970s that got the ball rolling on rights recognition. A certified general accountant and member of the Squamish First Nation, he became a board member and audit committee chairman with Fortis BC, a major electric power and gas distribution firm. He was also a board member of the Canada Mortgage and Housing Corporation, Partnerships BC and the Nicola Valley Institute of Technology. He worked for years to advance the interests of the Squamish First Nation, sitting on the band council and pushing for federal legislation to allow the Squamish people to develop their assets.

His work played a key role in the passage of the First Nations Land Management Act (1999) and three offshoot bills that were all passed in 2005: the First Nations Fiscal Management Act, the First Nations

Commercial and Industrial Development Act, and the First Nations Oil
and Gas and Moneys Management Act. All four allowed bands to opt
out of the Indian Act on a sector-by-sector basis in order to encourage
economic development. The latter three were passed at a time when
the Liberals were ruling under Paul Martin in a minority Parliament.
Calla, noting that the Liberals had dragged their feet on this legislation when they had a majority prior to the 2004 election, needed the
support of Harper's new Conservative Party to enact these laws. So he
travelled regularly in the early 2000s to Ottawa, schlepping around
Parliament Hill trying to lobby key players, who invariably told him,
"You want to move a piece of Indian legislation in Ottawa, you better
go talk to Gerry St. Germain." A year before the Liberals lost their
majority in 2004, the two finally met, and Calla was impressed:

> Gerry, being an astute businessman himself, was pretty quick
> to grasp the nature of the legislative reform we were looking for
> as being something that would promote aboriginal economic
> development, support self-reliance and support the inherent right
> to self-government. He was always straightforward, said it like it
> was, but was someone who believed that the status quo was not
> serving the interests of aboriginal people. He was looking for
> opportunities that would change the status quo.

Even after the bills were passed, Calla and other First Nations
leaders needed help lobbying the government, since taking over and
developing land required significant expenditures from a federal
government that had maintained since the mid-1990s a 2-percent cap
on increases in transfers to First Nations. This policy left little money
for some of the more expensive steps in the process, including proving
the band had ownership of the land, and cleaning up any environmental contamination. As Calla put it:

> So we would go and talk to him about those matters. First Nations
> were continuing to live in poverty, there were not adequate

funding arrangements and the 2-percent funding cap was having a disastrous affect. There were a lot of discussions around First Nations financial mismanagement at the time, much of which in my opinion were related to the funding cap and the desperation of councils to respond to some very real social needs. So Gerry was someone we could go to talk to, and through him we could get invitations to appear before the committee, and have conversations with people on the Hill regarding these matters.

Two aspects of St. Germain's character drove his interest in issues like Calla's. The first was his entrepreneurial background, which gave him a strong preference for business initiatives over social programs to help poor aboriginal communities. The second, Calla recognized, was St. Germain's growing consciousness as a Metis:

I think initially it was his Metis background, but it was also the knowledge of what he was able to achieve as a Metis person by becoming engaged in business. And I think from that he hoped that First Nations, if they became more proactive in the economy, could achieve many of their aspirations without being dependent on government. So that became his motivation—"You're not getting it from government, you might never get it from government, don't wait for government. Develop your own economy where you can and start to take control of your own destiny."

St. Germain's work with Calla continued long after he stopped drawing his Senate salary. He volunteered immediately after his 2012 retirement from the Senate to work with Calla's First Nations Major Projects Coalition, both as a guest speaker and as a liaison with the Harper government to secure $3 million in funding to help the coalition do its work in signing up reserves to unite in negotiations with major companies. The funding was earmarked to hire technical experts in areas such as finance, environmental assessment and government procurement. In the long run St. Germain and Calla planned to push the federal government to provide First Nations with loan guarantees for equity stakes in major projects like natural gas pipelines.

Calla and others who have watched St. Germain address First Nations say he has been a huge inspiration, especially for young band members. One of his techniques is to hold up a pencil to his audience, with his beefy hands at each end, and then snap it in half. Then he takes a handful of pencils in his hands, tries to break them in half, and can't. The single pencil, he tells them, represents the power imbalance inherent in a situation where a single First Nation is approached by a sophisticated corporation trying to win support for a major project. This is particularly the case in the Northern Corridor, between Prince George and the BC coast, where a number of major global energy players have been trying to bring pipelines to proposed liquefied natural gas facilities on the BC coast. "He has been instrumental in bringing a vision to communities in the Northern Corridor on energy that no one else could have, quite frankly," Calla said. "In a very open way he said, 'You have aboriginal rights and title, you are entitled to something. There is a difference between being a stakeholder and a rights holder. The federal government needs to step up to the plate, they need to support you.'"

Another BC aboriginal leader who has worked with St. Germain is Theresa Tait-Day of Hazelton, a hereditary chief with the Wet'suwet'en Nation. She said St. Germain's pencil metaphor in his speeches is more than a gimmick. "It works," said Tait-Day, who described St. Germain as having the stature in First Nations communities as a "knowledge-keeper" as well as an elder. "It's a great model because there are many little bands in our nation, and many chiefs aren't aware of the political arena and the business arena. What Gerry does resonates with people. He is Metis and he grew up poor, like many of us, and he came out of it. He's a great speaker and he gets it."

The person with a bird's eye view on St. Germain's evolution would be Bob Ransford, who was writing speeches for St. Germain to help him get elected in the 1980s, and ended up writing a speech honouring his friend's career when he left the Senate in 2012. Ransford was one of those British Columbians who in the 1990s was steadfastly opposed to any recognition of aboriginal rights. But he transformed along with St. Germain:

> Gerry's approach to the whole aboriginal question has evolved over many years. I think it is important to remember that he barely admitted that he had an aboriginal ancestry when he first entered politics. Pride in his Metis roots only began to emerge—and only as a mere acknowledgement—when he joined the cabinet in 1988. It was only after he became a senator that he started really talking deeply about his aboriginal background and his Metis lineage, and that he started being interested in the issues.
>
> My own position has evolved as I learned more about all of the issues, the history of the questions, and as I debated the issues with Gerry. I was opposed to the Nisga'a Treaty because I then saw treaties that both set up nation-based self-government and granted exclusive use of land as anathema to everything I believed in about equality, individual rights, etc. I then believed it created two classes of Canadians. That was something I found hard to accept.
>
> My views have changed because I have understood the need for reconciliation, and also I've understood how much the entire indigenous culture is tied to the land and to a collectivist stewardship of the land as an underpinning of the spirituality of the indigenous people. Gerry helped me understand that by relating his experiences growing up, and I saw it in the way he reacted when he was around aboriginal people.

13

∞

If Mistakes Were Made

Anyone who thought Gerry St. Germain would spend his retirement years sipping margaritas by his swimming pool on his back deck didn't know him very well. "He can sit still for about a day, and that's it," Margaret would say. During his farewell speech in the Senate chamber he was in fact feeling anxious and frustrated that he wouldn't be able to continue his committee work. That he immediately began an unpaid partnership with Harold Calla to help small aboriginal communities form alliances to negotiate with giant corporations underscored his workaholic nature, to say nothing of his devotion to aboriginal issues. When not doing that work he would regularly drive the three hundred kilometres from the Lower Mainland along the Trans-Canada to the vast ranch he and son Jay bought in 2014.

The Stirling Creek Ranch is located on the outskirts of the tiny community of Hedley, a former gold-mining town of a few hundred people in BC's hot and arid Similkameen Valley. There they took on one of BC's larger commercial ranch operations, with close to one thousand Angus cattle on 450 deeded acres, as well as several thousand acres of Crown land leased from the provincial government.

St. Germain considered the purchase the ultimate fulfillment of his dream, as he viewed the Pemberton property—which he sold in the mid-2000s—as more of a farm than a ranch. An added bonus with the Hedley purchase was that it finally allowed him to spend time with his son. "When Jay was a boy it was always 'Dad and me, Dad and me, Dad and me,' but it never happened," said Margaret. "And now it's happening."

For most Canadians it would seem to be an ideal retirement, thanks to financial security, good health and the fulfillment of living out a lifelong dream by owning and operating a vast ranch, in the wake of a successful career as a policeman, businessman and politician. But then came twin disasters. The first occurred one morning in May 2014, shortly after Jay arrived to accompany his parents to the annual Cloverdale Rodeo and Country Fair in Surrey, where St. Germain always addressed the crowd. Jay was anxious to get going but his father wanted to burn a metre-high pile of branches on the property in front of their house. "Gerry said, 'C'mon, let's do this before it starts raining,'" Margaret recalled. "Jay said, 'Okaaaay, let's go.'" The two big men hopped in a four-by-four and rode down to the field. "And I just had a really funny feeling," Margaret St. Germain recalled. "They went outside and I watched for a bit and I could see them, then I came back in. And then I heard an explosion."

Her husband had poured some gasoline over the pile and assumed that the wind would be at his back, blowing the fumes in the other direction. St. Germain sparked the match and was immediately engulfed in a fireball that blew most of his nylon golf shirt off. What was left of the flaming, melting synthetic material was stuck on his left arm like bubbling, scalding glue, and he had to use his right hand— luckily he was wearing a glove—to frantically push the scorching material off. He staggered with Jay's help to the house. Margaret was horrified by what she saw. "I ran outside and couldn't see anything at first. Then I saw them and Gerry's whole chest and arms and face were burned. The look on him—he was in a state of shock, I know that. There were blisters all over his head, his face, his cheeks, his nose. His eyebrows were burned. Holy mackerel, you just couldn't imagine." His son raced him to the hospital.

St. Germain spent three months recovering, passing most of the summer of 2014 in utter despair, sitting alone in his room watching all-news channels "with a coat over him when it was 100 degrees outside" due to the skin loss, Margaret recalled. "You didn't want to know him then. He was miserable. And there was nothing I could do. He didn't even want me around, really, at that time." St. Germain, calling it one of the "dumbest things I ever did," struggled with depression and ended up going on medication. Six weeks into his recovery he had his former aide, Niilo Edwards, drive him to a nearby hospital to have his wounds checked, hoping he'd made progress. "So I dropped him off, I went to get a coffee, and he finally comes down and gets off the elevator and he's as white as a ghost," Edwards recalled. "He just didn't look well. I said, 'How was it?' He said, 'Terrible. They had to scrape the scab off my arm and start [the healing process] again.' I drove him home and he didn't say a word the whole way, just sat there staring straight ahead. That was not like him at all."

St. Germain said his doctor diagnosed him with post-traumatic stress disorder, and Edwards said that he saw how deeply that impacted his former boss. The tours to BC aboriginal communities with Harold Calla to promote economic development became far more challenging. Edwards, who later joined Calla at the First Nations Financial Management Board, said St. Germain used to be able to deliver his inspirational speeches to First Nations communities without notes. But in the months after the accident he had to be hand-held through public events, sticking nervously to a prepared script when he spoke. "He still isn't 100 percent of what he was before the incident, in terms of his ability to focus and his energy levels," according to Edwards. "It aged him." St. Germain concurs: "I went into a real state of depression. If it hadn't been for my faith and my family I don't know what would have happened."

St. Germain was just beginning to get back to his old self when he was staggered by another body blow. Back when he retired in late 2012, a major political scandal—by Canadian standards—began with revelations about alleged inappropriate travel and living expense claims involving four senators, Conservatives Mike Duffy, Pamela Wallin and Patrick Brazeau, and Liberal Mac Harb. There were Senate suspensions, police investigations and eventually criminal charges of fraud and breach of trust against Duffy, Harb and Brazeau, as well as a criminal investigation of Wallin. It was a public relations disaster for the government because the three Tories were appointees of Stephen Harper, who became prime minister in 2006 on a mandate to either clean up or get rid of the Senate, an institution known as "patronage heaven." It got worse for Harper following revelations that his chief of staff Nigel Wright secretly gave Duffy $90,000 to pay back taxpayers for the cost of housing claims deemed politically, if not legally, inappropriate. In the midst of all this Senator Marjory LeBreton, the government leader in the Senate, announced on June 3, 2013, that the Tory majority in the Senate would pass a motion to call on Auditor General Michael Ferguson to conduct a full audit of every Senate transaction over a two-year period ending March 31, 2013.

So this was suddenly a battle of federal institutions—and it was clearly going to be a mismatch and a public relations bloodbath. LeBreton, now a Harper loyalist, was calling in perhaps the most admired federal entity in the country, the official watchdog on federal spending, to scrutinize Canada's most hated political institution. Former auditor general Sheila Fraser became a folk hero after saying in 2002 that federal officials broke "just about every rule in the book" in the Liberal sponsorship scandal. Ferguson, a former deputy finance minister from New Brunswick, was new on the job and a relative unknown—but his office packed a devastating punch. LeBreton, seeming to portray herself as an outsider by calling the upper chamber a "closed boys' club," vowed to clean the place up. "Canadians deserve to know at all times that their tax dollars are being spent wisely and in accordance with the law," said the woman appointed to the upper chamber back in 1993 after she served as, among other things, Brian Mulroney's director of patronage appointments.

St. Germain said it never crossed his mind when the scandal

started developing that he'd be implicated. For one thing, Ferguson's first audit after being recruited to replace Fraser in November 2011 was of the Senate administration. As part of that audit Ferguson's staff looked at some transactions involving senators, and St. Germain was among those who volunteered to have his office made part of the audit. Strangely, given there had been several previous private sector audits in recent years highly critical of Senate administration, Ferguson was glowing in his praise. "I am pleased to say that we found no major weaknesses in the administration of the Senate," Ferguson said in a statement on June 13, 2012. For years St. Germain assumed, because he never heard any feedback, that his office had "passed" the audit. The author contacted Ferguson's office in early 2016 to ask why his team didn't discover any of the problems later revealed in the 2015 audit. Ghislain Desjardins, the AG office's media relations manager, replied in an April 4, 2016, email that senators' expenses and contracts were "tested" as part of the study, but "We did not audit senators' expenses or the work of their offices, or contracts managed by senators."

By then Gerry and Margaret St. Germain had sold their Surrey ranch in order to live on a relatively smaller property in nearby Langley, while ploughing the rest of the profit from the sale into the Hedley ranch. That had meant a major downsizing, which included figuring out what to do with dozens of boxes of documents, speeches, photographs, daily journals, newspaper clippings and every other scrap collected over three decades in politics. "He had to get rid of the stuff, and he phoned everybody to see what he should do with it," Margaret St. Germain recalled. Library and Archives Canada arrived to take perhaps a dozen boxes full of documents, but that was only a fraction of the material. Finally in mid-September 2013, St. Germain hired a company specializing in shredding, and that process took almost a full day.

A week later St. Germain, who had assumed that Ferguson's probe would not involve retired senators, got a call saying he was going to be audited and had to hand over all his office documents. The timing would haunt St. Germain, especially given the suspicion ever since the Watergate era that any politician shredding documents was obviously up to no good. St. Germain spent the next two years exchanging letters with Ferguson's office, attempting to answer the most detailed of questions on everything from specific long-distance phone calls to the whereabouts of office equipment. He didn't handle it well, failing to consult his lawyer and seeming to believe he would be cut slack because he, heading into his late seventies, was a fumbling senior citizen. He felt that, as one of the upper chamber's hardest workers, he deserved better. "I'm computer illiterate," he kept telling the auditors.

There would be no mercy for old men. In June 2015 Ferguson released the audit, which cost taxpayers just under $24 million. It looked at more than eighty thousand expense transactions involving 116 senators during the two-year period ending March 31, 2013, and found just under $1 million in what appeared to be questionable or inappropriate spending. St. Germain was given an advance copy of the findings and knew he was to be among 30 of the 116 senators who were going to be publicly called out. What he wasn't prepared for was Ferguson's recommendation with regards to nine of the thirty senators, including him. It was found that there was "such a pervasive lack of evidence, or significant contradictory evidence, that we were prevented from reaching an audit opinion about whether the expenses had been incurred for parliamentary business." Then came the bombshell: "The Standing Senate Committee on Internal Economy, Budgets and Administration should immediately refer the nine individual cases," Ferguson wrote, in reference to the all-powerful committee of senators who make the key Senate administrative decisions, "to other authorities, such as the Royal Canadian Mounted Police, for further investigation."

Those last few words left the St. Germain household reeling. Ferguson, merely by mentioning the need to call in the RCMP, was signalling to Canadians that St. Germain and the other eight senators may have intentionally stolen from taxpayers. St. Germain and his wife were driving in his truck when they heard a BC radio broadcast focused on him and the call for the Mounties to protect Canadians from people of his ilk. "We just couldn't believe it," Margaret said. "We pulled over on the side of the road, and then our phones started ringing. There weren't tears, but we were just devastated and held each other's hands and said, 'This can't be happening. It can't be true. Where is this coming from?'" St. Germain was apoplectic. In his response, which was published in the report, he gave what was among the strongest of a number of aggressive reactions offered by the named senators. "The presentation and tone of your general observations insinuate that I misappropriated my office resources in a nefarious manner. I find these apparent accusations to be a defamatory affront to my personal integrity." But to some critics, the not only unapologetic but indignant tone of St. Germain and other senators simply worsened the public perception.

Friends and associates reacted with sadness, anger and especially incredulity over the accusations against St. Germain. Sandy Macdougall was surprised and shocked: "Gerry and I may have disagreed from time to time on political issues, but never once on moral issues . . . I am sure that Gerry is capable of making mistakes, but I simply do not believe that Gerry would deliberately steal anything from the public treasury or anywhere else." Ray Castelli was also flabbergasted: "I was shocked and I just assumed it was bad staff work, because that just didn't strike me as being like Gerry. I mean, I don't think the guy needs the money. There are some people in Ottawa where this is the job of their life, they want to milk it for everything they can. He's not one of those guys."

And Sawridge First Nation chief Roland Twinn, who like his late father Walter had been working for years through the Senate to obtain self-government status for his band, was incredulous when asked about Ferguson's conclusion: "I can't believe anyone would question the integrity of Gerry St. Germain. He's always acted with the upmost honour with us, he's always been up-front and honest." Ferguson's report, he said, was a "scandalous" attack on a man who always welcomed Alberta First Nations leaders arriving in Ottawa to pursue their agendas. "He helped open doors and get us meetings. He was our champion in advancing First Nations governance issues."

Kind testimonials were nice, but did nothing to resolve the audit's allegations that from March 31, 2011, until St. Germain's retirement in late 2012, his office had $67,588 in questionable expenditures, and in many cases didn't have adequate documentation to justify them. By far the biggest category, $43,727, involved the cost of sending staff members to BC to attend a number of events that were, according to Ferguson, "not primarily for parliamentary business." Two were events to promote charities, four were political events, one was Gerry and Margaret St. Germain's fiftieth wedding anniversary, one was his retirement charity roast in Vancouver, and one was an awards gala "where the senator was a recipient." Many were at his Surrey ranch. The anniversary got particular attention in the media coverage after Ferguson's report was released, largely because it sounded so outrageously self-indulgent, but also because two senators named in the report, David Tkachuk and Nancy Greene Raine, attended.

St. Germain was adamant that in every instance, except a family dinner expense that he repaid, there were clear justifications. First, the events in BC constituted "Senate business" and that staff presence was therefore legitimate under the Senate Administrative Rules (or SARS as they came to be known during the Mike Duffy trial). Second, St. Germain always made sure that when his staff travelled to Vancouver they had meetings with people who were using his office to advance issues or obtain help. Related to this second consideration was the need, as St. Germain saw it, for staff to spend time in their boss's home province, to get to know his region and his various contacts, and to work with him on key issues during the summer when the Senate wasn't in session. Senate rules explicitly defined partisan activities as part of "Senate business," and the rules further stated that staff could also participate in those activities. The events themselves, according to St. Germain and his supporters, fit easily under the broad definitions of what Senate business entails.

Two of the four political events were the St. Germains' annual summer barbecues that drew as many as 2,500 people, mostly though not exclusively Conservative supporters, and were headlined by the regular appearance of the party leader, which in 2011–12 was Prime Minister Stephen Harper. Harper's presence brought out the who's who of small-c conservative politics on the west coast, including Members of Parliament and members of the provincial Liberal party who supported the Tories at the federal level. If you were a centre-right politician in BC with any ambition, or someone with an interest in getting federal or provincial government action on a particular file, this was an event not to skip. St. Germain had held these annual barbecues since 1984, and used to cover the entire cost—naturally, roasted chickens were served by the former chicken farmer. But the event became so large that he eventually began charging on a cost-recovery basis. The staffers would also need to be available, according to St. Germain, to gather follow-up information if a citizen approached him seeking help on a particular issue.

As for the wedding anniversary celebration, which was attended by Prime Minister Stephen Harper, St. Germain said the Prime Minister's Office needed a staff person to liaise with for planning purposes. Staffer Niilo Edwards, who maintained that he attended the anniversary while working in the days before and after in St. Germain's home office, would explain his presence at the event:

> I was not asked to do any work in relation to Gerry's fiftieth wedding anniversary concerning the event itself. For me, the event was less a wedding celebration and more of a parliamentary networking event, given the level of attendance. There were a number of dignitaries present from both the provincial and federal governments, many of whom I spent the balance of the evening talking to about work. Gerry's office was effective at getting parliamentary work done because we engaged with others on a regular basis. This event was one of those times.

Two other senators also attended the anniversary gathering. Both David Tkachuk and Nancy Greene Raine expensed their costs to the Senate because they felt it was part of their official duties. "Like funerals, anniversaries are personal for family and often political for politicians," said Tkachuk, the former chairman of the Board of Internal Economy, which sets and interprets rules on senators' spending, in his official defence against Ferguson's allegations of inappropriate spending. "Attendance at this event is permitted under the rules that allow attendance at funerals of parliamentary colleagues and participation in party activities and community events. Senator St. Germain, who lives in my region, was not only a parliamentary colleague of mine, but a political VIP." Nancy Greene Raine, the former Olympic gold medal-winning skier appointed to the Senate in 2009, also attended at an incremental cost to taxpayers of $203. While she defended the expense in her submission to the report, her subsequent explanation in a June 12, 2015, CBC interview did a better job of explaining her rationale:

> **CBC:** Why do you believe that [the anniversary costs] should be paid for?
>
> **Greene Raine:** It was billed as a wedding anniversary but it was basically a tribute to his career. He'd been in politics and in public service for many, many years. He was a mentor to me in the Senate. I would have been conspicuous in my absence. You know there were a lot of public leaders there, including the premier of BC and the prime minister, and mayors and leaders from every level of government, recognizing a long and very excellent career, so I considered it Senate business. If it had been strictly a fiftieth wedding anniversary family event I wouldn't have gone. I wasn't really a family friend.
>
> **CBC:** What benefit did taxpayers see in your attending a party like this?
>
> **Greene Raine:** You know, it's an opportunity to network and to talk to leaders at all levels and it's through events like that that you have a chance to speak informally with people like the premier of BC. And really as a senator you have to be out and about in your area, and in contact with other leaders, and in general with the public, to know what's going on, what are the concerns of people. So that was that kind of an event.

While both Tkachuk and Greene Raine eventually repaid all expenses flagged as questionable, the senators initially refused to pay back the anniversary charges because they felt the event was legitimate.

Ferguson listed a number of other alleged inappropriate expenditures, from the hiring of contractors to the purchase of a few hundred dollars in gifts for visiting First Nations leaders that lacked adequate documentation. The most controversial involved $4,415 in charges for six flights to Edmonton. St. Germain listed those expenses as "parliamentary business," but the audit noted that in every case he attended board meetings of the Sawridge Group of Companies. "We determined that the trips were taken to pursue the private business interests of the senator," the audit stated.

St. Germain argued that he always arranged meetings on Senate matters, usually involving aboriginal leaders, while in Edmonton. Sometimes these meetings were with a First Nations–led group seeking government support for an oil refinery project, though his main work in the area involved collecting input and support for self-government legislation that he was trying to advance in the upper chamber. Despite his defences, one of the Senate rules in place at the time was that senators could only claim trips if the *primary purpose* was Senate business. Any personal business had to be "incidental" to the trip's main purpose. In other words, if a senator flew to Toronto to attend a Senate committee hearing but visited his sister or went off to buy a car before flying back, the flight, hotel and meals related to the hearing were still claimable. But if the senator stayed an extra night to see his sister, the additional costs were not.

While the individuals St. Germain said he met in Edmonton confirmed they saw him there during the 2011–12 period, there was little or no documentation of the exact times and days of those meetings. St. Germain said he typically scribbled his appointments on sheets of paper he carried with him, and that those records ended up in the shredder in 2013. Even if he had been able to confirm the meetings, it was still difficult to make a case that the primary objectives of the six trips were Senate-related meetings with Edmonton contacts.

In most cases, St. Germain's datebook listed only the Sawridge board meetings, suggesting that in fact they were the primary reasons for the trips. It is possible that like others in the Senate, St. Germain and Edwards simply misinterpreted the rules—both men have insisted that a single meeting on Senate business could justify a trip in which private matters were also dealt with.

Former Supreme Court justice Ian Binnie blew that notion out of the water in his March 21, 2016, report on the fourteen senators who decided to seek an arbitrated settlement on how much they owed as a result of the auditor general's report (St. Germain was among those who opted out of that process.) Binnie found that "by far" the most common mistake made by senators was trying to justify a personal trip because some Senate business was done. But Binnie was far less harsh than Ferguson. "I impute no bad motives to any of the senators. They acted in accordance with what they believed to be their entitlement. Our disagreement, where it exists, is as to the content of that entitlement." At a news conference he elaborated, saying ignorance, rather than dishonesty, was behind the bending and breaking of rules. "The attitude was, 'If we knew the rules, we would follow them,'" Binnie said. "I didn't feel for the most part that they were gaming the system."

There were several schools of thought on who should take the blame for the expenses mess, with some commentators supporting the punishment of individual senators alleged to have made inappropriate claims. Sun Media's David Akin, for one, argued in a March 21, 2016, column in favour of suspensions or expulsions of those named in the auditor general's report. However Postmedia's Andrew Coyne, while far from sympathetic to Senator Mike Duffy, portrayed the PEI senator's travails as part of a systemic problem in an April 23, 2016, column: "Duffy's defence, after all, was not so much that he did not break any rules, as that there were no rules to break—or that they were unclear, or that they were not properly explained to him, or when all else failed that everybody else did it. That is more an indictment of the Senate than it is exoneration of him." Others believed that the criminal investigations, as well as the auditor general's report, were part of a political strategy orchestrated by Stephen Harper to smear and demonize the Senate, which he and his base supporters detested, and deflect attention away from Harper's role in the Senate scandal.

Ontario Court justice Charles Vaillancourt made it clear his sympathy was with Duffy and not Harper and his political operatives. The judge said Harper's aides displayed "unacceptable" behaviour during their manoeuvres to limit the damage to the prime minister. "If anyone was under the impression that this organization was a benign group of bureaucrats taking care of the day-to-day tasks associated with the prime minister, they would be mistaken," he wrote. Vaillancourt also blamed the system, rather than Duffy, for any spending issues. "Where a senator in good faith tries to apply bad (inadequate, poorly communicated, criteria-lacking) policy, he/she can't be found criminally responsible if errors were made," he wrote. "Bad policy predictably fosters mistakes." But Binnie didn't accept the premise that unclear rules could provide an excuse. The rules in place during the audit period were "perfectly workable in the hands of a senator who wishes to comply with the obvious purpose of a rule, as well as its literal text." At the same time, as noted above, Binnie didn't conclude there was any intent to defraud the taxpayer. The RCMP, in the wake of the Duffy verdict, concluded that prosecutors were never going to be able to prove criminal intent in the Senate scandal. The fraud and breach of trust charges against Brazeau and Harb were dropped, and the criminal investigation of Wallin was shut down. St. Germain was quietly informed by the Senate in late June of 2016 that the RCMP wouldn't be investigating his case.

With all the air streaming out of the Senate scandal balloon it was left to a former Conservative senator to put the sorry episode in perspective. Hugh Segal, widely admired by Canadian union leaders in 2013 after he led the Senate's repudiation of the Harper government's anti-union legislation, took early retirement from the Senate in 2014 to become Master at Massey College and a senior fellow at the University of Toronto's Munk School of Global Affairs. Segal, the only senator who voted against the suspensions of Duffy, Wallin and Brazeau in 2013, gave voice in his final speech in the upper chamber to those, including

St. Germain, who suspected there was a bigger agenda being played out. He urged senators to "champion the central and indisputable importance of rule of law, due process, [and the] presumption of innocence as cornerstones of our democratic way of life, whatever dark forces elsewhere—sometimes in government, sometimes in opposition, the police or the media—might seek to dictate or impose upon us."

Exactly a year later, and only days after Ferguson's report was released, a Segal essay published in the *Globe and Mail* suggested the scandal crackdown had gone too far, noting that the $24 million audit of eighty thousand expense items found less than $1 million in problematic expenses. He also suggested individual senators shouldn't be carrying the blame. "Beginning in 2012, the Senate began tightening its rules (on three separate occasions) and it continues this week," Segal wrote. "This might be read as admission by the Senate that previous rules were inadequate or too vague or imprecise to be broken or enforced." He concluded, "Show trials, public lynchings, and the destruction of reputations of those who may have made honest mistakes because of unclear Senate rules or differences in interpretation may play to the bloodlust of some. But they do nothing for public probity, respect for taxpayer dollars or the issue of legitimacy of our parliamentary institutions."

In July of 2016, after Duffy was acquitted and authorities shut down all criminal investigations, Segal called on the Senate to apologize for essentially engineering a witch hunt against senators, trying to make them take the fall for institutional and political failures. He also upbraided the RCMP, saying it behaved like a national police force in a "banana republic" by allowing itself to be used by politicians to "destroy the reputations of other politicians" while lacking "objective evidence of criminality." Segal, asked to comment specifically on the St. Germain matter for this book, replied: "I have known Gerry St. Germain for decades. He is a good, decent, honourable and hard-working man. If mistakes were made, they would have been unintentional and reflective of practice in the Senate for decades. That is a historical perspective the auditors did not have, or understand."

Epilogue

Parliament is and has always been populated by a reasonably reflective cross-section of Canadians. There is an over-supply of lawyers, journalists, entrepreneurs and professional politicians—those who entered full-time politics as interns and staffers right out of university with the hopes of getting elected. But there are also physicians and nurses, farmers and labourers, teachers and students, police officers and soldiers, and even the odd bus driver and martial arts instructor. It goes without saying that almost all are, like St. Germain, extraordinarily ambitious extroverts with considerable physical and mental stamina. Most have either academic or street smarts, ideally both. What set the Metis chicken farmer from BC apart that allowed him to slip past so many of his generation to make such an impression on so many people? And what are his life's lessons, not only to the party he helped rebuild but also to young Canadians, especially those from aboriginal communities who grew up with poverty and prejudice?

One of his crucial pieces of advice is to be a sponge, recognizing that no individual has all the answers. Success in life, St. Germain would assert, is easier if youth have an open mind and are willing to seek out mentors. A less receptive child might have resisted the push by his grandmother and uncle to make him fluent in French. He had the option of ignoring Sister Monchamp's appeal to recognize his potential and stay away from the pool halls. When he encountered "the Dutchman" and "Colonel Klink" he didn't just dismiss them as eccentric landlords with heavy accents. He recognized their entrepreneurial skills and leveraged that relationship into a lucrative life in business, which in turn took him into politics. After his 1983 entry into federal politics he quickly figured out what assets were valued by Mulroney—a commitment to bilingualism, a strong work ethic, common sense and humour—and took full advantage. His political antenna, by all accounts superior to that of other Mulroney confidants with many university degrees, was fine-tuned thanks to his willingness to genuinely hear the concerns of grassroots party members.

After his 1993 appointment to the Senate, it took a wise colleague appointed that same year to help him develop a more empathetic approach to issues affecting Canada's indigenous population. St. Germain once held the attitude that the recipe to escape poverty was simply to follow in his footsteps—pick yourself up by the bootstraps, don't obsess about the past, start a business and you're on your way. An exchange with this other Conservative senator, Raynell Andreychuk, changed that view forever. Prior to arriving at the Senate in 1993, Andreychuk was a lawyer and provincial court judge in Regina, then went on to become an associate deputy minister of social services in the Saskatchewan government. One of Canada's best parliamentarians, she got fed up one day after hearing St. Germain talk in the Committee on Aboriginal Peoples about the need for aboriginal people to end their dependence on federal handouts and start a small business.

"You have no idea what these people have gone through," she told him. Andreychuk had seen in her courts the depths of misery and dysfunction caused by colonial policies and the soul-crushing residential school system. Her dressing-down hit St. Germain hard. He took one of his many deep dives into a policy area and developed a greater understanding of why Canada's aboriginal population struggles with poor health and education outcomes, high substance abuse and incarceration rates, and shorter lifespans. Rather than throw up his hands, he dug in his heels and did his part to address these profoundly difficult issues. He remembers sitting with a woman in northern Alberta who shook like a leaf as she recounted the horrific sexual and physical abuse she endured as a child in a residential school. Many of these victims were denied the kind of mentorship and support that helped St. Germain. So he stopped judging and started looking for policy options, like self-government and better education, that could break the downward spiral. He became, as so many First Nations leaders stated in interviews for this book, a "champion" for them in Ottawa.

St. Germain wants aboriginal youth to know there's reason to hope, and that a few very simple rules of life could take them a long way. "You've got to learn how to smile sincerely and look people squarely in the eye. And you have to be able to laugh at yourself." Thinking back to his own rash decision to drop out of high school, he said, "If you're going to pursue an education don't waste the opportunity." Above everything is the need to establish and preserve a reputation for trustworthiness: "Integrity and honesty, with yourself and with others, is critical. Without it you're not going anywhere, because people will see through you. Some people are born shysters, con men and women, and eventually they'll fail."

When he speaks to aboriginal youth it's not unusual for them to approach him later to ask how he found success. He thinks back to his own youth. A wide-eyed little boy's visit to a Manitoba cattle ranch, for instance, led to a lifelong dream of owning a cattle ranch. "You've got to dream of what you want to be," he tells them. "If you have no dreams you're rudderless. Dream the dream and then live the dream, and do it with tenacity, perseverance and a deep work ethic." St. Germain also advises youth to recognize that if they do pursue higher education, they shouldn't let their law, politics or business degrees turn them into snobs. "In politics and in many other professions you have to be able to work with every level of society. You can't be pretentious or elitist." He feels that education should be combined with the kind of common-sense rules of life he picked up as a policeman, businessman and politician. "This is what I looked for in a business partner. If you don't have common sense and street smarts it's tough to survive. And you don't get those traits in law school."

St. Germain also counsels aboriginal youth to not be discouraged by criticism and setbacks. He jokes about the "simple chicken farmer" label, but the derision and disrespect was occasionally a force for motivation, not discouragement. Not all his business decisions were winners, and in 1988 he lost his seat despite being anointed BC's top representative in the federal cabinet. St. Germain was taunted and isolated by his former Tory Senate colleagues when he left caucus to help Stockwell Day and try to unite Canada's right-wing movement. In retirement he managed to overcome the burn incident, and being ensnared in the Senate controversy, to continue leading a productive life, travelling the country trying to motivate First Nations communities and especially aboriginal youth. None of these hurdles are comparable to the nightmare faced by the worst victims of the residential schools program. Still, he hopes that his determination and focus might inspire young people who don't see an easy path to success.

As for his party, St. Germain has some advice for Conservatives in the post–Stephen Harper era. He has a unique vantage point as one of the few who worked closely with the only two Tory politicians to win majority governments over the past fifty-eight years. St. Germain has also seen up close how a party can destroy itself by taking important segments of its voter base for granted. An ideal leader, he believes, would combine the greatest strengths of both Mulroney and Harper. During the Mulroney era, St. Germain was frequently fuming over the lack of focus and discipline as cabinet members freelanced, misbehaved and sometimes challenged or disrespected Mulroney's authority. Harper obviously learned from his experience of working briefly in Ottawa for one of Mulroney's MPs. His first government in 2006 pledged only to fulfill its five key campaign commitments. While carefully introducing those policies to Canadians, Harper made clear he would harbour no internal dissent, and was hostile to independent thinking from his caucus.

While Mulroney tried to court the media, and grew frustrated and bitter when many Parliament Hill journalists turned on him, Harper declared war on journalists from day one, seeking to marginalize and weaken the fourth estate just as he looked for ways to weaken potential rivals in his party, the judiciary and the public service. While not an admirer of these specific approaches—like many he was baffled by his leader's antagonism toward the media—St. Germain was impressed with Harper's priority-setting skills and saw in his operation the so-called "discipline of power." His acumen was especially useful when the 2008 global financial crisis struck, when Harper and finance minister Jim Flaherty were responsible for orchestrating Canada's successful response plan to keep the national economy afloat. "I think in 2008–2009 Harper did a tremendous job," St. Germain said. "If you wanted someone to run your company, he's most likely the guy that you would get."

St. Germain said he was generally treated well by Harper, citing his leader's agreement to bring him to Washington for Harper's first White House meeting in 2006 with George W. Bush. But he felt let down by the way Harper handled the 2006 cabinet shuffle, and especially by the 2013 decision by Harper's lieutenant in the Senate, Marjory LeBreton, to bring in the auditor general to target ordinary senators. St. Germain said future leaders should have some of the warmth, charm and especially loyalty that characterized Mulroney's reign. "Mulroney was totally personable and you couldn't help but like him. And he had a great presence. Harper developed a presence as he aged into the job, but never had the people skills that Mulroney had."

Mulroney also let his ministers operate with relative independence. While the old PC Party sometimes paid a price when freelancing ministers got in trouble, Mulroney also got the best from people. "That's why I worked so hard for him, and that's why I think he was such a great PM. He had confidence in people. He didn't care whether you had money or what colour you were or where you were from. If you're good, you're good, and he recognized that. Harper had a tough time trusting people, and if you don't trust people you can't get the best out of them." St. Germain cites Rona Ambrose as a perfect example. When she first entered cabinet in 2006, the Alberta MP appeared shaky and unsure as she operated under Harper's iron grip. But when Ambrose became interim leader in 2016, political observers were pleasantly surprised to see an enormously talented politician emerge to help the wounded Tories rebound from a devastating election loss.

While Mulroney was loyal to a fault to anyone who contributed to the party, Harper's trail is littered with former confidants and supporters—Nigel Wright, Tom Flanagan and Mike Duffy are three of many—who were tossed under the bus when Harper felt his authority was threatened or there was any chance he might be politically damaged. Another problem St. Germain had with Harper's leadership was the austere approach he brought with him from Preston Manning's Reform Party. Reform's social conservative culture appeared to view Ottawa as a place where pure souls went to be corrupted. Many MPs liked to say they were fearful of being "Ottawashed." The many galas, receptions and garden parties of the Brian Mulroney and Pierre Trudeau eras were shunned after 1993, when Jean Chrétien's Liberals took power and were under enormous pressure from Reform to repair Canada's finances.

Symbolism became important. One rookie Reform MP, with cameras rolling in a post–1993 election documentary, proudly walked away from one fancy reception and strolled with his wife to a nearby McDonald's. Chrétien got the message and canapés were replaced by tuna salad and ham sandwiches. The austere approach was even more prevalent when the Conservatives finally took power in 2006 under the ex-Reformer Harper. "You know, when Mulroney was there it was fun to be there, because they made things interesting for the MPs. The mentality of the Reformers was, if you're not living a life of hardship you're not doing it right. Everything became plain-Jane when they arrived. They disbanded all the social evenings after the Throne Speech and all that."

The new atmosphere cast a bit of a pall over Parliament Hill. "You've got people away from home and giving up an awful lot to serve, and sure there's a lot to gain but there's a lot to lose. Look at the divorce level. So you've gotta make it interesting. Mulroney made it fun and interesting to be there, and so did [Pierre] Trudeau." St. Germain also preferred Mulroney's broad approach to politics: "Mulroney understood Canada's history, the compromises that were made along the way, and he understood we're not an easy country to govern." Harper viewed public institutions and the economy through the lens of a university political science or economics classroom. Mulroney, he added, was an "open-minded, big-picture leader" who tried to find the middle ground, while Harper was an "ideologue" who tried to impose results in any public policy dispute.

There's a strong feeling among some Mulroney loyalists that Harper had few significant, durable accomplishments, despite being in power for almost a decade. Mulroney has never had that problem, as free trade, tax reform and the anti-apartheid battle were initiatives that will almost certainly endure for generations. The "sweet spot," according to St. Germain, is to find a leader with Mulroney's courage, foresight and charisma to make important policy shifts, yet has some of the Harper discipline needed to keep the political party— the vehicle needed to gain power—intact.

A final bit of St. Germain's advice to fellow Tories is to set goals that go beyond personal wealth or trophies. Retired politicians tend to focus, naturally, on accomplishments like the construction of a bridge. They're like notches on a belt. St. Germain's most satisfying legacy was appropriately described at the dinner held in October 2012 to mark his retirement. It was a few weeks after St. Germain received a National Aboriginal Achievement Award at a Vancouver gala, honouring his lifetime contribution to advancing causes important to Canada's indigenous peoples. At St. Germain's insistence the retirement dinner at the Four Seasons Hotel was a charity event, raising money for the Zajac Ranch, a facility in St. Germain's former riding that provides camps for children and young adults with chronic, life-threatening and/or debilitating conditions. The dinner ended up being a raucous affair, a roast with a lot of politicians focusing more on crafting wisecracks and boosting their own egos than on honouring a public servant. That task was left to the most obscure name on the list of speakers that evening, St. Germain's long-time aide and friend Bob Ransford.

Ransford brought silence to a boisterous roomful of 350 mostly male attendees with a story that could serve as the appropriate bookend to a remarkable life. He shared an encounter he had with his friend in the early 2000s. The two friends were at St. Germain's 450-acre spread in the fertile Pemberton Valley, about 150 kilometres north of Vancouver. It was a pastoral wilderness setting, with St. Germain and Ransford chatting and enjoying the spectacular views at the ranch. Looking out from the front porch, with bald eagles floating overhead, they could see the Lillooet River, which flows east and south from the Pemberton glacier, just past fields where the two men would spot grizzly or black bears, an occasional pack of wolves, a grazing moose and the odd lynx or bobcat. As Ransford described it:

In his usual restless manner Gerry said, "Let's go for a ride." We jumped in his truck and drove to the other end of the Pemberton Valley, up to the Mount Currie Reserve, home of the Lil'wat people. We drove down a gravel road to an old part of the reserve that Gerry called "Dodge." It was a collection of very old shacks along a short dusty road. Half the shacks were literally built with rough-hewn lumber. They had gaps between the boards and the other half of the shacks were mostly tar paper and plywood boxes. But people lived there. I saw a few small kids running about. I can't tell you what a decrepit, depressing place it really was. We very slowly drove through the settlement. Gerry didn't say much, but I saw the look on his face. I could see in his eyes a determination. It was a deep concern I hadn't seen before. I didn't really understand that concern then, where it came from—how important it was and where it would take him.

St. Germain walks along the top of a fence while loading cattle at his picturesque ranch in this 1983 photo. St. Germain's fitness would regularly impress his younger staffers when they visited the family ranch in the gorgeous Pemberton Valley of BC, about 150 kilometres north of Vancouver. GSG PERSONAL COLLECTION

I only came to understand it a few months ago when I read the report he signed as chair of the Standing Senate Committee on Aboriginal Peoples, on aboriginal education. That's when it dawned on me that the greatest contribution he has made as a servant of the people over thirty years wasn't uniting conservatives. It wasn't setting up the Vancouver International Airport Authority and giving it local control. It wasn't helping secure a commitment to build a gas pipeline to Vancouver Island. It wasn't fighting for a softwood lumber agreement to secure BC jobs. No, his biggest contribution has been a commitment of his humanity to exposing us to the opportunity we have in this great country to be a country of one people—to truly unite our country.

It took Gerry St. Germain, the Stetson-wearing politician who as a child loved the good guys–bad guys Westerns of the 1950s, almost a lifetime to centre on his true calling as a champion of First Nations. But there was some symmetry in his unusual career trajectory. He gradually built up credibility and stature over decades the way a brick-layer lays bricks. He took the skills he learned in the RCAF, police work and police union leadership with him as he pivoted toward his fruitful business relationships. The next step got him to Parliament Hill, and if he hadn't risen up the ladder in that hardball world, his goodwill and big heart would have been no use to the First Nations leaders who relied on his stature to open doors and champion their issues. For these and other reasons St. Germain, according to those who know him, is one senator who didn't deserve the kind of public contempt normally directed at members of the upper chamber. "Gerry," they say, "is one of the good guys."

Acknowledgments

This project began in a pub in Ottawa's ByWard Market in early 2012, when one of "Gerry's Boys"—the legion of former political aides who worked for or alongside Gerry St. Germain during his twenty-nine-year career in Parliament—suggested I write a biography on his former boss. I expressed interest but Byng Giraud's idea didn't get off the ground until the night after the 2015 federal election, when Gerry contacted me to say he was finally ready to sit down and tell his life story.

There are many people besides Byng I must thank. Harold Munro, my editor at the *Vancouver Sun* and the *Province*, was encouraging and supportive. Among those who shared their memories and perspectives were former prime minister Brian Mulroney, former premiers Jean Charest, Jim Prentice and Bill Vander Zalm, and former federal and provincial cabinet ministers John Fraser, Mary Collins, Pat Carney, Frank Oberle and Brian Smith. Others generous with their time included some of Gerry's former colleagues in the Senate: Hugh Segal, Marjory LeBreton, Raynell Andreychuk and David Tkachuk. I am also indebted to a fraternity that is the oil in Canada's political machine—the former political aides who worked for or close to Gerry. They include John Baldwin, Ray Castelli, Niilo Edwards, Doug Eyford, Sandy Macdougall and Bruce Pollock. On First Nations issues Harold Calla and Catherine Twinn were particularly helpful.

I owe a great deal to University of Alberta historian Gerhard Ens, whose expertise on the history of the Metis people and the Manitoba language issue was invaluable, and to Patricia Graham, my former editor at the *Vancouver Sun*, whose judgment has never let me down. Another talented and generous colleague, Vaughn Palmer, read through sections of this book dealing with federal–provincial affairs. I have never met Bob Plamondon, the author of two authoritative books on the history of the Conservative movement. Still, he took the time to read through sections of this book dealing with periods he covered in *Blue Thunder: The Truth about Conservatives from Macdonald to Harper*.

Despite their assistance, I take responsibility for any factual errors that may appear in this book. I should also note that while I interviewed many people to fill in details and add some layers, this is essentially one man's perspective on Gerry St. Germain's career. Others involved in various events in his life and career may remember things differently.

The photographs in this book are from Gerry's personal collection. I want to thank Bill McCarthy and Jason Ransom, respectively the official photographers for Brian Mulroney and Stephen Harper, for giving me permission to share their fine work.

A special thanks goes to Bob Ransford, Gerry's close friend and lifelong sidekick. It was Bob who got this book off the ground, acted as a go-between on delicate matters, and provided me with so much insight that I was tempted at times to put his name next to mine on the cover.

I have to give a word of thanks to the efficient and courteous staff at the Library of Parliament in Ottawa and Library and Archives Canada's Burnaby branch. Canadians are well-served by these invaluable federal institutions and the people who run them. Staff at the Vancouver Police Museum were also of great assistance.

My editor Silas White skillfully trimmed the length of this book without stripping it of its essence, and I salute his talents and patience. Thanks go as well to my copy editor, Pam Robertson. I am also indebted to Harbour Publishing for taking a leap of faith by accepting my book proposal even though I'm a neophyte in the book-writing world. My sister Barbara O'Neil, whom I hired to transcribe interviews, provided helpful advice and strong encouragement during the early stages of writing.

A word of thanks must also go to the subject of this book. Gerry was patient and generous with his time during my visit to BC in December of 2015 to conduct interviews, and was easy to work with during the countless subsequent written and verbal requests for additional details. As Bob Ransford has said, Gerry tends to make any endeavour fun and exciting. He opened up his life to me and I will always be honoured to have his trust and respect. I also must thank Margaret St. Germain for putting up with my daily invasion of her household that week in December. While she is less outgoing than her husband, her anecdotes are just as compelling as Gerry's. Without Margaret this project wouldn't have happened.

My wife, Leslie Scanlon, wasn't just supportive in dealing with my piles of documents, clippings and photos that moved around our house as I shifted my work stations depending on my mood. She and our kids, McKenzie and Will, had to put up with a lot as I dedicated myself to writing this book. Leslie was also a skilled copy editor, providing me with valuable feedback and encouragement. The times the four of us have spent together on holidays, especially when my United Kingdom–based son Devin is with us, are the happiest of my life. It was hard to give up so much family time to complete this project. I will do my best to make up for it. This book is dedicated to them.

Index

BC Chicken Marketing Board, 15,
54–55
Bennett, Bill, 57
Bennett, W.A.C., 54
Binnie, Ian, 219–20
Bouchard, Benoît, 105
Bouchard, Lucien, 73, 132, 135, 163
Brownie's Fried Chicken, 50–52
Burney, Derek, 98, 104
Bush, George W., 10, **185**–86, 190,
226

Calla, Harold, 202–6, 208, 210, 234
Campbell, Gordon, 184, 186, 192–93
Campbell, Kim
  and Gerry St. Germain, 25, 134,
    168
  as member of BC legislative
    assembly, 100
  as Member of Parliament, 121,
    129–31, 137–38
  and Progressive Conservative
    Party leadership, 144–**47**–57,
    159
Carney, Pat
  as cabinet minister, 93, 101–8,
    120–21, 137–38
  and Gerry St. Germain, 25
  as Member of Parliament, 10, 75
  Senate appointment, 134–35, 140

Castelli, Ray
  and Brian Mulroney, 58–59,
    93–94
  and Gerry St. Germain, 62, 80,
    87–88, 125, 214
  political career, 102–4
Charest, Jean
  as Member of Parliament, 79, 84,
    175
  and Progressive Conservative
    Party leadership, 145–**48**–54,
    159–60, 162–64, 168–72
Chrétien, Jean
  as Liberal Party leader, 133, 136–37
  as prime minister of Canada, 148,
    156, 158, 163–64, 172, 177, 183,
    227
Clark, Joe
  as cabinet minister, 86, 89–90,
    92–93, 137
  as Member of Parliament, 126,
    139–40, 144
  as prime minister of Canada, 55,
    74–75
  and Progressive Conservative
    Party leadership, 8, 57–59, 77,
    91, 124, 165, 169–74, 176–79
Committee on Aboriginal Peoples.
  See Standing Senate Committee
  on Aboriginal Peoples

Cowan, James, 11
Crosbie, John, 58, 92–94, 107, 173

Dallaire, Roméo, 15
Day, Stockwell, 173–79
Diefenbaker, John, 77, 135, 166, 187
Domm, Bill, 84
Duffy, Mike, 159, 211, 215, 219–21, 227
Dyck, Lillian, 15

Epp, Jake, 10, 92, 112, 120–21

Fraser, John, 74–75, 85–86, 93, 101, 107, 120
Fraser, Sheila, 211–212
Free Trade Agreement
    controversies, 91–93, 113, 115–16, 125–28
    implementation, 107–8
    and Mulroney, 17, 97–100, 123, 135, 141–42, 228
    support for, 144, 146

Grant, Cuthbert, 19–23
Greene Raine, Nancy, 14, 215–18

Harper, Stephen
    audit report, implication in, 211, 215–16, 220
    and Conservative Party leader-ship, 14, 124, 165, 173, 179–**81**–**83**–**84**–86
    and Gerry St. Germain, relation-ship with, 16–17, 194
    as prime minister of Canada, 11, 149, 186–**89**–91, 196–99, 225–28
    and Reform Party, 162, 165

Indian Act, 16, 199, 204

Jaffer, Mobina, 15–16, 54

Kinsella, Noël, 178–79

LeBreton, Marjory
    and Gerry St. Germain, 14, 131, 133, 136, 138, 166–69
    political career, 73, 178–79, 187–**89**, 211, 226
Lévesque, René, 70

MacEachen, Allan, 55
McKenzie, Dan, 10, 70–71, 83
McKnight, Bill, 10, 112, 120–21
Manning, Preston
    and Brian Mulroney, 141–42, 148–49
    and Gerry St. Germain, 95–96
    Reform Party leadership, 90–91, 126–32, 135, 161–65, 170–75, 177, 180
    and Stephen Harper, 182, 227
Martin, Paul
    as finance minister, 172, 177
    as prime minister of Canada, 15, 149, 180, 183–84, 186–87, 193, 204
Masse, Marcel, 73, 91–93, 134–35
Mazankowski, Don
    and Conservative Party of Canada merger, 180–81
    as deputy prime minister, 72, 81, 101–2, 112, 114, 126
    as Member of Parliament, 10, 120–21, 141
Meech Lake Accord
    controversy, 67, 127, 130–33, 135, 143, 146
    negotiations, 82–83, 96, 99–101
Metis
    and Gerry St. Germain, 11, 15, 17, 19, 23–24, 39–40, 65–66, 72, 188, 200–7
    history, 19–23
    Manitoba Act, 67–68
    See also Riel, Louis

Mulcair, Tom, 12
Mulroney, Brian,
    controversial initiatives, 90–97,
        112–13, 127–35, 141–42, 159,
        197.
    See also Free Trade Agreement:
        and Mulroney; Meech Lake
        Accord
    and Gerry St. Germain,
        62–**63**–64, 72, 78–**87**–90, **93**,
        103–**6**–8, 138, 150, 166–68,
        175–76, 223
    and Progressive Conservative
        Party leadership, 8, 10, 68–78,
        114, 124–27, 136–38, 143–46
Mulroney, Mila, 10, 58, 61–62, **93**,
    138, 143

Nielsen, Erik, **63**, **87**

Oka Crisis, 133–34, 143

Prentice, Jim, 142, 155–56, 196–98
Progressive Conservative Party
    elections, 56, 91, 114, 150–51, 158,
        170
    leadership, 8, 74, 99, 124, 134. See
        also Campbell, Kim; Charest,
        Jean; Clark, Joe; Mulroney,
        Brian
    merger, 14, 162–63, 179–82
    policies, 19, 68, 89, 128, 192

Ransford, Bob
    and Gerry St. Germain, 7–8,
        10–11, 116, 229–30
    political career, 60–63, 76–77, 99,
        102–3, 186–87
Reagan, Nancy, **122**–23
Reagan, Ronald, 10, **122**–23
Reform Party of Canada, 91, 106–7,
    126, 161, 165, 192, 196
    See also under Manning, Preston

Riel, Louis, 19–20, 67–68, 73, 78,
    105, 200
Royal Canadian Air Force, 8, 28–**31**–
    32–34, 40–41, 231
    See also under St. Germain, Gerry

St. Boniface, 23–24, 35
St. Boniface Police Force, 34–40
St. François Xavier, 19, 23–25, 48,
    109
St. Germain, Gerry,
    air force service, 8, 29–**31**–**32**–34,
        40–41, 117, 188, 231
    audit report, implication in,
        210–21
    business years, **41**–42, 49–**50**–**52**–
        55, 65
    childhood, 23–28, 48
    education, 25–**27**–29
    faith, 10, 39, 72, 210
    family, 40, 49, 117–**19**, 199
    First Nations rights advocacy,
        16–17, 199–207. See also
        Standing Senate Committee on
        Aboriginal Peoples, member of
    Harper, relationship with, 16–17,
        194. See also under Harper,
        Stephen
    as Member of Parliament,
        Mission–Port Moody, 8,
        56–**60**–64, 67, 114
    Metis heritage, 11, 15, 17, 19–24,
        29–40, 65–66, 72, 188, 200–7
    Minister of Transport, 105, 110–14
    Mulroney, relationship with,
        62–64, 73–90, 104–109
    police work, St. Boniface Police
        Force, 34–40
    police work, Vancouver Police
        Department, 41–47
    Progressive Conservative Party,
        president of, 125, 129–36,
        146–47, 156, 164, 176

retirement, 11, 15, 194–95, 198, 205, 208–9, 214–15, 225, 228–32

Standing Senate Committee on Aboriginal Peoples, member of, 14–15, 191, 193–94, 197, 223–24, 230

St. Germain, Jay (son), 40, 49, 54, 117–**19**, 122, 133, 208–9

St. Germain, Kathleen (mother), 23–**25**–26

St. Germain, Margaret (wife), 17, 39–41, 46, 49, 58–59, 62, **93**, 117–**19**–**22**–23, 199, 208–10

St. Germain, Michel (father), 23–**24**–**25**–26, 29, 138

St. Germain, Michele (daughter), 40, 49, **119**

St. Germain, Suzanne (daughter), 40, 49, **119**

Sauvé, Jeanne, **64**

Sibbeston, Nick, 193–96, 199

Siddon, Tom, 8, 10, 59, 63, 75–76, 93–94, 102, 120–21

Standing Senate Committee on Aboriginal Peoples, 14–15, 191, 193–94, 197, 223, 230

3M, 41–42, 49–**50**

Tkachuk, David, 14, 215–18, 233

Trudeau, Justin, 47, 198

Trudeau, Pierre Elliott, 10, 55–59, 61, 69–73, 88–89, 95–96, 99, 127, 145, 227–28

Twinn, Walter, 200–2, 215

Vancouver Police Department, 35, 42–48

Vander Zalm, Bill, 99–108, 112, 121, 130, 144

Wayne, Elsie, 148, 160–61, 175

Wilson-Raybould, Jody, 16, 198